THE SECRET IN BUILDING 26

RANDOM HOUSE

NEW YORK

THE SECRET IN BUILDING

26

**THE UNTOLD STORY OF
AMERICA'S ULTRA WAR AGAINST
THE U-BOAT ENIGMA CODES**

Jim DeBrosse
and Colin Burke

Copyright © 2004 by Jim DeBrosse and Colin Burke

Library of Congress Cataloging-in-Publication Data
DeBrosse, Jim.
The secret in Building 26: the untold story of America's Ultra war against
the U-boat Enigma codes / by Jim DeBrosse and Colin Burke.
p. cm.
Includes bibliographical references and index.
ISBN 0-375-50807-4
1. World War, 1939–1945—Cryptography.   2. Enigma cipher system.
3. Cryptography—United States—History—20th century.   4. U.S. Naval Computing
Machine Laboratory—History.   5. Desch, Joseph.   I. Burke, Colin B., 1936–   II. Title.
D810.C88D43 2004   940.54'8673—dc22   2003058494

Printed in the United States of America on acid-free paper
Random House website address: www.atrandom.com
2 4 6 8 9 7 5 3 1
First Edition

Book design by Victoria Wong

For Ira and Charline
—JIM DEBROSSE

To my wife, Rose, who gave me my son, Andy,
my very special gift in life
—COLIN BURKE

Acknowledgments

A NONFICTION BOOK jointly authored by a journalist and an histo- rian would appear to be a natural partnership: both professions dig as deeply as possible into the truth of a story. But while the journalist often validates with telling details and insightful quotes, the historian insists on the bedrock of written documentation and unbiased data. Coauthors Jim DeBrosse, a reporter for the *Dayton Daily News*, and Colin Burke, a leading authority on American intelligence agencies and the emergence of the computer, found theirs an uneasy alliance at times—much like the British and American codebreakers featured in this book. But they hope that, together, they have made accessible a highly arcane but significant piece of modern American history to a wider public.

The collaboration grew out of an eight-part series that DeBrosse wrote for the *Dayton Daily News,* "NCR and World War II: The Un- told Story." Burke was the expert source for the articles. Soon af- ter the series appeared in the paper in spring 2001, Burke called DeBrosse and announced that he had gathered further information on the U.S. Bombe program, including a dramatic espionage attempt.

The two agreed that DeBrosse would research the human side of the story, with as many interviews with survivors and their families as possible, and Burke would supply the historical spine of the book with archival documents—a process he had begun more than a decade before. DeBrosse was responsible for the writing of the text and for creating a narrative; Burke outlined the book's historical themes, established the accuracy of its facts, and helped his coauthor grasp the more daunting technical aspects of the German Enigma machines and their electromechanical foes, the Bombes. Together, the two aimed for a balance—between the claims of the British and the claims of the Americans, between a technical treatise for code-breaking aficionados and a compelling narrative for the uninitiated, between a grand reinterpretation of history and a complacent acceptance of past writings.

Little information was available when, in the late 1980s, Burke began exploring the origins of the modern computer, in which the NCR Bombes played a part. The National Security Agency, the Navy, and the Army had kept the military's 1930s and 1940s computer research under Top Secret and Ultra protections. Histories of the American intelligence agencies released to the National Archives at the time were vague and typically censored. Many surviving participants in America could not talk about their work, and British documents were hopelessly locked away. Even F. H. Hinsley's authoritative series of books on British intelligence in World War II contained little useful information.

Burke's first book, *Information and Secrecy: Vannevar Bush, Ultra and the Other Memex,* had to rely heavily on open primary sources, especially those related to the history of computers and computing, hoping that enough bits of evidence could be gathered and pieced together to yield some answers. He spent years with the Hagley Museum's magnificent and well-managed collection of computer industry documents, with deep gratitude to its helpful staff.

The Hagley's collections provided enough hints to direct Burke's research into primary sources at the Smithsonian Institution, the Massachusetts Institute of Technology, the Rockefeller Archives, Dartmouth College, the U.S. Patent Office, the Library of Congress, the Washington and Suitland branches of the National Archives, the Navy's legal branch, and the Naval Historical Center.

Along the way, many other institutions were contacted for help, including the hundreds of libraries badgered by Burke's home university's interlibrary loan department. Especially tolerant were the archivists and historians at the NCR Archive, the Charles Babbage Institute, the National Security Agency's history office, IBM, and the Eastman Kodak Company. Professor Brian Randall of the University of Newcastle upon Tyne in England also was very gracious.

Although Burke's training as an historian made him skeptical of oral history and after-the-fact reminiscences, several former intelligence officials provided helpful information, including two men who were willing to have their names cited, Waldron S. MacDonald and Joseph Eachus, the latter generously consenting to interviews by both authors. MacDonald and Eachus were considerate and forthright while still protecting the secret aspects of their work.

By the late 1980s, Burke had gathered enough from open sources to persuade the government to release classified documents related to America's codebreaking machines during the 1930s and 1940s. Letters citing the Freedom of Information Act were sent to the National Security Agency, and a few years later, a very large box of documents appeared at Burke's door, which, for convenience, was called the RAM (Rapid Analytical Machines) File.

Unfortunately, the FOIA documents were very heavily censored, with some of the most important facts covered with impenetrable black lines. Burke spent several years trying to turn the unreadable into useful information while also pursuing other leads. He traveled to libraries, historical societies, and government offices in large and small towns in the Midwest and border South. Special thanks must go to the historians who kept the records of the Miami Valley Chatauqua and to Brian Hackett, executive director of the Montgomery County Historical Society in Dayton.

More FOIA requests were sent out to the Department of Justice, the FBI, the Bureau of Prisons, the Selective Service, the CIA, the Army record centers, and the Social Security Administration.

By 1992 Burke felt he had exhausted the primary sources and knew enough to draw some valid conclusions about the Navy's early computer efforts. Soon after the publication of his book, he was contacted by Joseph Desch's daughter, Debbie Desch Anderson. After a decade-long quest of her own to uncover the truth of her father's secret labors during the war, she was organizing a reunion of the Navy WAVES who had worked on the NCR Bombes. Fortunately for all, the reunion in late 1995 came just as the federal government began to relax some of the restrictions on the Bombe project, allowing many participants to grant interviews.

Anderson, who became a friend of both Burke and DeBrosse, first brought them together. She, along with historians at the Montgomery County Historical Society, who are the guardians of the massive, four-million-item NCR Archive, approached DeBrosse in the fall of 2000 about writing a newspaper story on Desch's and NCR's unheralded role in Ultra. Anderson, in turn, recommended Burke as an expert source.

Anderson deserves much credit for bringing the U.S. Bombe project out of the technical history books and into the public eye. Her quest to unravel her father's secret work laid the human foundation for this book and brought credit not only to her father and the other NCR engineers on the Bombe project but to hundreds of Navy WAVES who were never told the purpose of their work.

A year or so after the WAVE reunion, the government decided to release more intelligence agency documents. By 1998 the new RG457 Historic Cryptologic Collection was available at the National Archives. As before, John Taylor lived up to his legend: he was a masterful guide through the series. Then, to the surprise of many historians (and those in the intelligence community), another release soon followed—the RG38 "Crane" materials, which had been held for decades in a secret Navy depository in Crane, Indiana. The Crane collection contained some startling new documents, and Barry Zerby provided much help as he and other NARA archivists struggled to handle a flood of requests.

More surprising than the Crane release was a change in British declassification policies. In the late 1990s, a significant number of documents from the World War II British Ultra projects began to appear at the Public Record Office, outside London. Although difficult to find, there were many significant and, at times, astonishing pieces of evidence.

At the same time, a group of volunteers began to rescue the famed Bletchley Park. They established a museum in the mansion and operational huts and began to publish new information on the Bombes and the other codebreaking machines built in England during the war. Tony Sale and his wife and many others at Bletchley Park provided Burke with tender care on his visits to England as he tried to keep in touch with the new document releases.

Burke also thanks the staffs at the PRO, the National Archives, the Naval Historical Center, NSA's new Cryptologic Museum, NSA's history office, and scholars and researchers Ralph Erskine, Jim Reeds, Frode Weierud, Phil Marks, David Hatch, David Kahn, Robert Hanyok, Rebecca Ratcliff, Edward J. Drea, Lee A. Gladwin, Lou Holland, John Traegesor, Jeffery Wenger, and Henry Schorreck.

Three years ago, DeBrosse began conducting interviews with scores of people involved in the NCR Bombe project and their family members, as well as pilots and sailors who fought in the Battle of the Atlantic. Anderson withstood hours of personal interviews and patiently fielded hundreds of phone calls to clarify details, without complaint and always with the offer of a cold beer for her visitor. The staff of the Montgomery County Historical Society and the NCR Archive never denied a request for help or an unannounced visit. Particularly helpful were Bill West, Brian Hackett, Claudia Watson, Curt Dalton, and Mary Oliver.

Other important sources for DeBrosse were Phil Bochicchio and Gilman McDonald, both of whom know the workings of the NCR Bombes, inside and out, literally; NCR engineers Lou Sandor, Robert Mumma, Don Lowden and Carl Rench, who helped piece together the Bombe project and bring to life the man chiefly responsible for its design, Joe Desch; Peg Fiehtner of the Naval Security Group Command and the volunteer staff of the Wenger Command Display of the Naval Cryptologic Veterans Association, all of whom are dedicated to honoring the proud work of Navy codebreakers; and more than a dozen Navy WAVES who shared their memories of those exciting years, especially Catherine Racz, Evelyn Hodges Vogel, Evelyn Urich Einfeldt, Susan Unger Eskey, and Veronica M. Hulick.

DeBrosse would like to thank the editors at the *Dayton Daily News,* Ron Rollins and John Erickson, who were instrumental in shaping the original series, as well as publisher Brad Tillson for allowing him a six-month leave to write the first draft of the book. DeBrosse also received much encouragement from his colleagues at the paper, especially Mary McCarty, Tom Beyerlein, Steve Bennish, Ken Palen, and Melanie Raley. Kathleen Schamel provided invaluable assistance as a weekend babysitter so that her brother could find time to write the book. Tom DeBrosse, as always, was a bedrock of brotherly advice, and Alvin and Jane Sanoff graciously opened their home, and their hearts, whenever Jim Debrosse needed to conduct research in the Washington, D.C., area.

Finally, the authors express their deep gratitude to literary agent Fran Collin, who never gave up on the idea of placing their book; Random House's Benjamin Dreyer and Timothy Mennel, whose sometimes painful cuts and suggestions made this book a much better read, as well as Dennis Ambrose, who gave it his unflagging attention to detail; and, of course, editor Bob Loomis, whose gentle hand and unerring advice miraculously brought forth a coherent tale.

Contents

Prologue

Building 26—NCR Campus—Dayton, Ohio

THE SECRET IS hidden in plain sight: a nondescript glass-and-panel box of a building standing four stories high, flanked by parking lots and set back far enough from the busy intersection of South Patterson Boulevard and West Stewart Street that few motorists even notice it, much less wonder what might have transpired there some sixty years ago. Inside the now empty structure is another empty building of tan brick and glazed cinder block, a far more interesting art-deco design that has been nearly encapsulated by the newer addition and can now be seen only from the rear.

A granite boulder emblazoned with a small bronze plaque is all that testifies to the building's proud history. It sits along a nearby sidewalk that few people traverse even by day. The plaque reads:

> In 1942, the United States Navy joined with the National Cash Register Company to design and manufacture a series of code-breaking machines. This project was located at the U.S. Naval Computing Machine Laboratory in Building 26, near this site. The machines built here, including the American "Bombes," incorporated advanced electronics and significantly influenced the course of World War II.
>
> October 2001
> Institute of Electrical and Electronics Engineers

Nearly one thousand people worked on the Navy's top secret project in Building 26 between 1942 and 1945. They were sworn never to divulge the nature of their work.

The full story of their struggle, sacrifice, and ultimate triumph has never been told—until now.

March 10, 1943—North Atlantic

ON A MOONLESS night of squalling snow and frothing waves, U.S. Seaman First Class Edward P. Rego kept watch for U-boats from one of the two four-inch gun platforms on the stern of the SS *William C. Gorgas*—unaware, as was most of its crew, that the merchant vessel, part of Allied Convoy HX228, was carrying nine hundred tons of TNT for delivery to Liverpool. Rego, a seventeen-year-old gunner from Massachusetts, was on his first transatlantic crossing. He was also cold and bored. There was so much shifting ocean out there and so little he could see.

But the enemy was closing in for the kill.

Earlier in the day, *U-336* had spotted the sixty-ship convoy and had radioed its location to U-boat Control. By midnight, a wolf pack of six submarines had been assembled and was preparing to strike at close quarters.

The first to fire a spread of torpedoes was *U-221*, whose ambitious young skipper, Kapitänleutnant Hans Trojer, was out to prove himself. A torpedo soon found the 5,400-ton British *Tucurinca*, causing the vessel to explode with such force that "hundreds of steel plates flew like sheets of paper through the air," as Trojer noted afterward in his log. A second hit the 6,600-ton American *Andrea F. Luckenbach* and sent "heavy debris [crashing] against my periscope, which now became difficult to turn. The whole boat re-echoed with bangs and crashes." A third damaged the 7,200-ton American liberty ship *Lawton B. Edwards*.

Rego was far enough away that the explosions sounded like distant thunder, but within the next two hours he had his first taste of death from below. Just before midnight, two torpedoes from *U-444* ripped into the engine room of the 7,200-ton *Gorgas*, instantly killing the crew there but miraculously missing the tons of explosives amidships, in the hold.

The fully loaded ship went dead in the water, and the waves started crashing over its deck. Fearing the *Gorgas* was a sitting target for another torpedo attack, sixteen of the twenty aft-gun crew jumped over the fantail, never to be seen again. But Rego had been grabbed in time by the ship's cook, Manuel Moralis, who urged him to move forward, along the side of the sinking ship, to where the two men were able to don survival suits and launch a lifeboat. Over the next two to three hours, Rego and Moralis pulled other survivors from the thirty-seven-degree waters, until the British escort *Harvester* came to their rescue.

In all, fifty-one survivors of the *Gorgas* were retrieved by the *Harvester*, but their ordeal that day was far from over.

Like sharks trailing the scent of blood, the U-boats pressed their attack against the crippled convoy late into the morning. The *Harvester*, already limping from a ramming incident with *U-444*, was given the coup de grace at 10:00 A.M. with two torpedoes from *U-432*. This time, Rego had no time to reach a lifeboat; Moralis, who had saved him during the first attack, did not survive the second. Rego jumped overboard and began swimming through the icy waves. He soon spotted a life raft, but like a mirage it disappeared and reappeared from his shifting line of sight and seemed never to come nearer, no matter how hard he struggled. After nearly an hour of battling the water, he decided to free himself from his thick rubber survival suit and, with only his own adrenaline to protect him from the cold, at last reached the raft. Four hours later, a British corvette spotted the raft and retrieved Rego and four other survivors—so weakened by the cold that they had to be carried onto the ship. Of the seventy original crew aboard the *Gorgas*, only twelve, including young Rego, had earned the unenviable distinction of surviving two torpedo attacks in nearly the same day.

And so it went during one of the darkest months in the Battle of the Atlantic, when ninety-five merchant ships, hundreds of seamen, and 567,000 tons of Allied shipping went to the bottom of the Atlantic and Arctic oceans. In ten days alone that March, more than forty ships were sunk by U-boats. The battle seemed to be turning in favor of the Nazis, threatening the lifeline between America and England and, ultimately, the outcome of the war. The loss of tonnage wasn't some abstract number to be tallied and forgotten. It meant less fuel, less food, and more deprivation for the British fighting on the home front and fewer armaments and supplies for the Russians driving the Nazis from Kharkov and the Allied troops trying to outfox Rommel in North Africa. Perhaps even more crucial, it meant delaying the all-important buildup to D Day and the liberation of Europe. As a U.S. Navy training manual pointed out at the time:

> If a submarine sinks two 6,000-ton ships and one 3,000-ton tanker, here is a typical account of what we have totally lost: 42 tanks, 8 six-inch howitzers, 88 twenty-five-pound guns, 40 two-pound guns, 24 armored cars, 50 Bren carriers, 5,210 tons of ammunition, 600 rifles, 428 tons of tank supplies, 2,000 tons of stores and 1,000 tanks of gasoline. . . . In order to knock out the same amount of equipment by air bombing (if all this material were on land and normally dispersed) the enemy would have to make three thousand successful bombing sorties.

On March 10, 1943, the same day the *Gorgas* was torpedoed and sunk, the German Navy had switched to a new set of codes for its weather signals, breaking Britain's tenuous hold on reading U-boat messages. Although the weather signals themselves did not reveal the location of the U-boats, the lists of codes and their plain-text translations had provided British codebreakers an important wedge in cracking U-boat radio signals and predicting where the wolf packs would strike next. The codebreaking blackout meant the U-boats could strike with a vengeance—without the Allies listening in. In the thirty-two-million-square-mile expanse of the Atlantic, finding a lone submarine with no clue to its location or course was akin to hunting for a roadside mailbox in all of Texas, without an address.

Of course, the U-boats faced nearly the same challenge in finding the Allied convoys in their long voyages across the Atlantic. But unknown to the Allies, the Germans were reading the convoy ciphers with relative ease from 1941 through nearly all of 1943. With the help of Germany's very competent radio intelligence unit, known as B-Dienst, U-boat Control knew where to align its submarines along convoy routes, waiting for the kill.

Grossadmiral Karl Dönitz, now supreme commander of the German Navy, kept in close radio contact with his skippers, requiring them to report their positions and fuel supplies with every communication. Once a convoy was located, Dönitz gathered the available U-boats into wolf packs to maximize their killing power and their defensive strength. The frequent radio contacts between headquarters and the U-boats gave the Allies ample opportunity to intercept and to home in on the signals with the latest direction-finding equipment. But direction finding was simply that: it could show the Allies what path a U-boat had been following but not its destination. To determine where the subs were going and why—whether to attack, regroup, refuel, or head home—the Allies needed to read the content of the radio messages, and that was a far more daunting challenge. In transmitting its signals, the Kriegsmarine made optimal use of the Nazis' remarkable encryption machine, the Enigma. In simplest terms, the Enigma put German radio messages into an enciphered form of seemingly random letters. An Enigma machine on the receiver's end, set up in exactly the same way, returned the cipher to plain text.

The Germans were confident that their coding system was impenetrable—even if their machines were captured—and they had good reason to be. Theoretically, at least, the number of ciphering possibilities generated by the advanced naval Enigma of 1942 was far greater than the number of all the atoms in the observable universe—an incredible 2.0×10^{145} possible encryption settings compared to a mere 1.0×10^{80} known atoms. After purchasing the rights to the commercial version of the Enigma Cipher Machine in the 1920s, the German military began adding its own bedeviling improvements and innovations and continued to do so throughout most of the war. But what the Germans did not count on was that lapses in their own security and procedures would greatly reduce the number of unknown possibilities and bring their seemingly unconquerable cipher system within the grasp of adversaries who were far more clever than the Germans realized.

First conceived of by Arthur Scherbius in 1922, the Enigma was a marvel of the machine age. Looking much like a portable typewriter with its own wooden carrying case, it scrambled each keystroke of a message through a series of tumbling rotors that turned the result into seemingly random gibberish. When a clerk pressed a letter on its keyboard, the corresponding cipher-text letter lit up on a display panel at the top of the machine and was written down by a second clerk. Once the entire message had been scrambled into cipher text, it was radioed by Morse code from the submarine to headquarters or vice versa.

Pressing down a key advanced the first rotor forward one letter and sent an electric current through the wiring of the naval Enigma's four rotors. All but the last rotor were joined to a ring with a tumbler pin on it that, in turn, advanced the next rotor. So, after the first rotor moved through all twenty-six letters of the alphabet, it would tumble the second rotor and, after the second rotor advanced twenty-six letters, it would tumble the third, much like the mileage numbers on the odometer of a car. As a result, the naval Enigma would never repeat the same position of its scrambling wheels for hundreds of thousands of keystrokes ($26 \times 26 \times 26 \times 26 = 456,976$; however, a complex feature of the Enigma, a double turnover of one of the rotors, reduced the number of positions by some 18,000).

The fourth and final disk, called the *Umkehrwalze*, or reflector, served to reroute the current back through the first three wheels, ensuring that the plain text and the scrambled text were always reciprocal at the same settings. That way, the clerk receiving a ciphered message could set up the machine the same way, then type in the scrambled text and automatically reproduce the original plain text. The German military liked the economy and simplicity of the Enigma's operation: one machine could do both tasks of enciphering and deciphering messages.

The ever-changing wheel positions of the Enigma were only the beginning of a codebreaker's nightmare. Each rotor was wired to scramble the letters in a different way, and all the rotors but the fourth could be ordered differently within the machine, from left to right. The different wirings for the rotors and the different orders for placing each rotor inside the machine created another staggering set of enciphering possibilities—26.0×10^{105}—again, far greater than all the atoms in the known universe. Fortunately for the Allies, the capture of several Enigma wheels and a machine during the early part of the war revealed the wiring inside the rotors and vastly reduced the number of possibilities.

But the hurdles for codebreakers didn't stop there. Each of the four rotors could be set manually to a different starting position, at letter A and on through Z, with the starting letters visible through small windows on the Enigma casing. The total number of possible initial settings for the four rotors was, again, 456,976. Likewise, the tumbler rings on each of the first three rotors, which caused the adjacent rotor to advance, could also be set to different starting positions, multiplying the possibilities by yet another 456,976.

If all that weren't enough to drive codebreakers mad, the Germans added what looked like a tiny telephone switchboard to the front of the machine, on which double-ended wires, called *Steckers* in German, could be plugged into jacks for swapping individual letters, so that A became E, for instance, and vice versa. Anywhere from one to thirteen different letters could be steckered in this way. The stecker board proved to be one of the biggest headaches in breaking the Enigma. With twenty letters steckered to one another and six letters unplugged, the standard practice during the war, the number of plugboard possibilities alone was nearly 533 trillion.

In the blind man's game of finding and sinking enemy vessels at sea, the German Navy realized the importance of making their Enigma operating procedures no less secure than the machine itself. While the German Air Force and Army allowed their cipher clerks to choose at random the starting positions of the rotors—which were then encrypted and sent along with the message to the receiving clerk—the German Navy didn't trust such potentially sloppy methods, and wisely so. The laziness of some Army and Air Force clerks led to repeated and predictable starting positions, such as HIT (the first three letters of Hitler) or, in the case of one love-struck cipher clerk, the frequent use of CIL, which happened to be the first three letters of his girlfriend's name, Cilla. British codebreakers, never short on humor, dubbed that whole class of starting position giveaways "Cillies" or "psillies."

In the German Navy, the Enigma operators were required to select the starting positions from a book containing long lists of randomly generated letter pairs, then to convert those letter pairs to a second set of letter pairs for each starting position of the wheels. These bigrams, or doubly disguised letters, were then sent at the beginning and end of each Enigma message as an indicator for the receiving clerk. The clerk deciphered the indicator from his own codebook and set his Enigma to the same starting position.

In fact, the entire sequence of steps for setting up the advanced U-boat Enigma was dictated by the Kriegsmarine high command. Before sending a U-boat message on a given day, the Enigma operator checked his current list of "keys" from headquarters. Going by the list, he selected three wheels from a box of eight, plus the special fourth rotor from a different store of components offering four choices. He placed all four rotors in the proper order within the machine along with the three tumbler rings, then set the starting positions of the wheels and rings, and, finally, plugged in the steckers to the correct letter sockets.

Breaking into the Enigma was like trying to open a series of locked doors. Each door could have thousands or even trillions upon trillions of possible keys, but only one would open it. And not until all the doors were opened could the message be read. Luckily, some of those doors had been pried open through the capture of Enigma components and operating instructions. From experience, the British knew that the toughest keys to find were the selection of wheels, the wheel order inside the machine, and the steckers. Once those were found, it was relatively simple to find the ring settings and the *Grundstellung*—that is, the starting positions of the wheels. And once the grund for the day was identified, it was easy to read the rest of that day's messages.

From the 1920s, when the German military adopted the Enigma, to the end of World War II, there was a never-ending search for methods and special machines to attack the cipher. By 1943, the Allies were building some of the most complex machines ever devised to try to conquer the Enigma and other Axis code systems.

Since the mid-1970s, much attention has been given to the British successes in cracking the Nazi Enigma and, more recently, to the early Polish breakthrough that laid the groundwork for the British. The Poles called their first decoding machine a "Bombe," perhaps after the brand of ice-cream cones favored by the codebreakers or perhaps because a loose chunk of metal dropped to the floor whenever the machine arrived at a solution. Just before Poland fell to the Nazi blitzkrieg in 1939, the Poles shared their secret success with both the British and the French, but it was the British who capitalized on this remarkable feat. Operating from the top secret Government Code and Cypher School (GCCS) at Bletchley Park, outside of London, British codebreakers refined and further mechanized the device, based on the advanced work of mathematicians Alan Turing and Gordon Welchman. Their machine, which first appeared in 1940, was also dubbed a Bombe (pronounced *bomb*), perhaps as a nod to the contribution of the Poles or, others say, because of its menacing ticking sound.

In the broadest terms, the British Bombe worked like a series of Enigma machines in reverse. Spinning commutator wheels were wired to simulate the rotors on the Enigma, with twenty-six electrical contacts running past twenty-six metal sensing brushes for tracking the possible letter pairings of cipher and plain text. To do their work, the Bombes needed special clues the British called "cribs." A crib was a word or phrase that codebreakers suspected as the underlying plain text matching a stretch of nonsense letters in a message. The codebreakers had to not only surmise the underlying plain text but be able to pinpoint its exact location, letter by letter, within the ciphered message. For example, if the suspected crib was HEIL HITLER and the corresponding Enigma cipher was ZQAT KFBCMJ, the plain-cipher pairings would H-Z, E-Q, I-A, and so on.

Having been fed a crib and told which sets of Enigma wheels to test, the machine crunched through hundreds of thousands of possible wheel and plugboard settings—and, more important, eliminated

those settings that were inconsistent with the design of the Enigma—
until it arrived at a setting that may have generated the matching cipher text. Once the rotor positions and the plugboard settings were
known, it took just a few more simple steps before the scrambled text
could be read by running it through a captured Enigma machine or its
analog.

The British, with the help of information from Poland's codebreakers and the brilliance of its own cryptanalysts at Bletchley
Park, made inroads on a variety of Axis codes and machines, including the Enigma, by 1940. Winston Churchill's pet code name for the
top secret operations at Bletchley Park was "Boniface," now better
known publicly as "Ultra." Although Britain never attained a fully secure grip on any of the German code systems, it had learned to handle with reasonable success the three-wheel Enigma machine by
1941.

But when the German Navy switched to a four-wheel Enigma in
February 1942, the challenge facing the British was overwhelming.
The new fourth wheel still acted as a reflector and was stationary, but
its daunting new feature was that it could now be set to start at any
letter of the alphabet, just like the first three rotors of the machine.
While the German Army and Air Force continued to use three-wheel
machines, the new naval system, called Triton by the Nazis and M4
Shark by the British, added one more door of protection to the U-boat
messages. Shark increased the number of possible wheel orders to be
tested on the Bombes from sixty to more than three hundred. The
hurdle was too much for Britain's twenty-some hard-pressed Bombes,
which had been designed to attack a three-rotor Enigma, and was far
beyond the reach of its codebreakers' hand methods.

From early 1942 until December of that year, when the capture
of new Enigma materials came to their aid, British codebreakers
were almost totally shut out from the U-boat radio traffic. No
wonder that North Atlantic sinkings more than tripled in the last
half of 1942 compared to the last half of 1941—from six hundred
thousand tons to two million tons. Even when codebreakers finally
managed to read U-boat messages again in late 1942, the decoding
took days and sometimes weeks, and the information often came too

late to be of use in tracking down U-boats or shifting convoys away from wolf packs.

To grapple with Shark, the British had begun work on a new high-speed, four-wheel Bombe not long after they learned from messages in late 1941 that the Germans were going to introduce the new Enigma. Progress was slow and, even as late as the spring of 1942, the British felt they had little hope for success against the trillions of new possible wheel orders.

But by this time the British weren't alone in their struggle. After a misguided start on the Enigma problem in late 1940 and a visit by American codebreakers to Bletchley Park in early 1941, the U.S. Navy began work on a top secret program in early 1942 to develop a Bombe of its own. It gathered its own Bletchley Park of bright young engineers and theoreticians, recruited from some of the nation's best colleges.

Under some of the most stringent security measures of the war, the codebreaking machine would be designed and produced in Dayton, Ohio, at the National Cash Register Company, then a world leader in electronics. Only two companies in the United States had the technical capability at that time to produce such a marvel: IBM and Dayton's NCR. The obvious choice for the Navy at that time was NCR, where chairman of the board Colonel Edward A. Deeds had a long working relationship with Vannevar Bush, the famed MIT scientist who had forged an alliance between military and academic researchers through his National Defense Research Committee. Even more propitious, NCR had at its disposal eleven city blocks of mostly idle factories and office buildings and a regional network of skilled labor and parts suppliers, all waiting to be put to work. NCR, unlike IBM, had been ordered by the War Production Board to stop making its chief product, cash registers, to conserve much-needed materials. The project would be entirely self-contained inside NCR's Building 26, so named because it was the twenty-sixth structure to rise on the company's ninety-acre business campus. It was only a coincidence, noted by researchers at the time, that the work in Building 26 would revolve around the seemingly endless possibilities in scrambling the twenty-six letters of the alphabet.

Like the British, the Americans at first put their faith in the rapidly emerging field of computational electronics—precursors to modern computers—as the best and perhaps only hope against the nearly impenetrable possibilities of the Shark Enigma. The initial aim of the four-million-dollar Navy project was lofty: to construct a state-of-the-art electronic decrypting machine fast and smart enough to crack Shark in a matter of hours, not days or weeks. The program at NCR would be equal in priority to the Manhattan Project, aimed at developing the atom bomb, and perhaps second only to it in hastening an end to the war. Because of the wartime shortage of men, the project would recruit some six hundred young women through the Navy's WAVES auxiliary to perform the delicate handwork in assembling the machines. None of the women was to learn the vital nature of their work until fifty years after the war.

Although the official U.S. naval histories have exaggerated the contribution of Ultra and the Bombes in subduing the German U-boat threat, the latest data do show that, by drastically reducing the time needed to decrypt Shark messages, the Bombes helped find and predict U-boat locations in one of every four U-boat sinkings from 1943 until the end of the war. Harder to gauge is the extent to which those pinpoint strikes disrupted the German wolf packs and kept them at bay, but they were certainly an Allied advantage in the Battle of the Atlantic.

But to build its machines, America needed the help of Britain's invaluable experience against the Enigma—help that was rejected by the U.S. Navy's top codebreaker at a critical juncture in the struggle against Shark. That rejection, unknown at the time to the rest of the American intelligence community and unreported for more than fifty years, fueled simmering resentments on both sides of the Atlantic in 1941 and 1942 and reinforced Britain's fear that the Americans couldn't be trusted with Ultra's deepest secrets.

The British never knew how close the Americans came to fulfilling their worst fears when, half a year before D Day, a potential traitor inside Building 26 nearly exposed the Ultra secret to the Germans. With brute justice, the Navy stemmed the crisis and, in the end, the American codebreakers kept the secret for nearly thirty years after the British revealed their own role in Ultra with the publication of F. W. Winterbotham's unauthorized book in 1974.* The eight hundred U.S. Navy men and women who worked on the U.S. Bombe never once opened their mouths, until the U.S. government itself began to declassify and release documents related to the project in the mid-1990s.

Hundreds of Americans involved in Ultra have taken the secret to their graves—and, for the few who bore its greatest burdens of stress, often an early one. The men responsible for designing and building the U.S. Bombe were racing not only against the Germans but against their own endurance.

* Since the publication of Winterbotham's *The Ultra Secret,* the original meaning of the term "Ultra" has become distorted through years of popular misuse. American and British codebreakers in World War II had used "Ultra" only as a label assigned to top-secret decrypts, translations and intelligence reports derived from a high-level enemy code or cipher. "Ultra" was neither a synonym for any one code or cipher product, nor was it a cover name for any cryptologic organization or activity.

THE SECRET IN BUILDING 26

1

Building the Perfect Machine

March 1943—Dayton, Ohio

IN A SECURE meeting room inside NCR's Building 26, while shot-gun-toting Marines stood guard outside, chief engineer Joe Desch grew increasingly impatient as he listened to one staff member after another report on continuing glitches with the two prototypes of the U.S. Bombe, Adam and Eve. After enough bad news, Desch resorted to what was becoming an all-too-familiar motivational technique among his hard-pressed group of seventeen engineers and techni-cians. He jumped out of his seat and onto the meeting-room table and began pounding his fist into his hand with every word he shouted. "No more excuses! We've got to work harder, faster, smarter! Every-body's ass is on the line!"

What Desch couldn't tell his staff, and what had been pointed out to him repeatedly by his own Navy supervisors, was that too many ships were going down, too many men were dying at sea, while the team failed to produce a working codebusting machine that had been promised for delivery to the Navy three months before.

Because of the project's ironclad security, Desch's staff was not permitted to utter even among themselves the words "Enigma" or "Bombe" or the seemingly innocuous name for the top secret opera-tion, "U.S. Naval Computing Machine Laboratory." The project was self-contained within NCR's former night-school building, constructed seven years before on a large, open tract that had once served as the city dump. Behind the building, on a lonely spur of railroad track, sat an empty baggage car with an overdue delivery date to Washington, D.C.—the Navy's not very subtle way of reminding the project's managers that the top brass was impatient for results.

But OP20G, the Navy unit in charge of analyzing and decoding enemy radio communications, may have been asking for the impossible. As late as August 1942, the Americans still had high hopes that an all-electronic decoding machine—at least one hundred times faster than anything built before—would be able to crunch through more than four hundred thousand possible Enigma solutions in the unheard-of time of fifty-five seconds.

From those wildly optimistic expectations, the American team plummeted two months later into a misinformed pessimism. Desch then thought his best possible Bombe might take hours to complete a run of all the Enigma possibilities, not just a few seconds, and that the Navy would need 336 of the sophisticated machines to get the job done. A big part of the problem was that the Americans had still not mastered the information the British were supplying about all the challenges in the Shark system, nor did they know all of Bletchley Park's clever methods in attacking them.

For the Navy and Desch, the race was on, not only against the Germans and the U-boats in the Atlantic but in some ways against the British. The Americans knew that Bletchley Park was working on its own design for a four-wheel Bombe and that their careers, their nation's prestige, and the Navy's investment of millions of dollars and scores of highly skilled personnel were at risk if they failed to arrive first at a working machine.

The designing engineers in both countries were under enormous pressures: they were told that only a perfect machine—one that was fast enough, reliable enough, and could be produced in sufficient numbers quickly enough—would be able to turn the Battle of the Atlantic. What was needed was a high-speed machine that could complete each of its runs without a single mistake. The codebreaking method it embodied could not tolerate even one missed connection, one electrical spike, or a tiny slip of its gearing.

Navy theoreticians had envisioned an all-electronic machine, using thousands of Desch's fast-firing miniature tubes, that would leave the more mechanical British three-wheel design clanking far behind.

In the end, the weight of the Navy's demands—and the nation's—fell most heavily on one man's shoulders: those of thirty-five-year-old Joseph R. Desch, NCR's chief of electrical research.

FROM THE FRONT steps of Building 26, Desch could have looked out across South Patterson Boulevard to the steep, grassy banks of the Great Miami River, in which he had swum and fished as a child, and across the river to his roots in Edgemont, the working-class neighborhood where his German-immigrant mother, Augusta Stoermer Desch, and most of his relatives still lived. Desch's escape route to a new life had been the Stewart Street Bridge, the link from Edgemont to Dayton that crossed Patterson Boulevard just a few yards north of Building 26. As a college student living at home, he had crossed the bridge countless times on his beat-up Henderson motorcycle, traveling to and from classes at the University of Dayton campus, a mile farther east on Stewart Street, until the freezing winter morning he hit a patch of ice on the bridge, spun out of control, and crashed. Though not gravely injured, he never again mounted a motorcycle.

Like the machine he was charged with engineering in late 1942, Desch was complex and temperamental. He was a devout Catholic, a heavy after-hours drinker and a chain-smoker considerate enough to confine his habit to his own office. He loved to use his hands as much as his brain. He delighted in gardening, in chopping wood, and, even in his teen years, in designing and making his own glass-blown gas tubes for his many electronic exploits. He could be brash and irreverent and had a temper that, when triggered, could propel a torrent of harsh invective. But he also had a gentle side that shrank from physical violence—a trait that had kept him from seeing war as anything but "a damned, dirty business."

Although he passed his childhood days like an early twentieth-century Huck Finn, canoeing and camping and fishing along the banks of the Great Miami, he was never interested in hunting like the rest of his young friends. He couldn't bring himself to kill—not even, according to his daughter, Debbie Anderson, the rabbits his father had asked him to raise. "He loved taking care of the rabbits and building the hutch and all, but when it came time to do what he had to do with them, he couldn't do it," she said. "I don't know if he sold them or gave them away, but they ended up with a friend."

Born in 1907, four years after Orville and Wilbur Wright took their first flight and fewer than ten blocks from the bicycle shop where the brothers had built their first airplane, Desch was the only son of his mother and a Dayton wagon maker, Edward Frank Desch. On his days off from school, young Desch often visited his father at his wagon-making shop, which the Great Depression later forced into closure. His father was a quiet, modest man who never raised his voice with his son and two younger daughters. Desch's mother was the disciplinarian as well as the outgoing, social half of the couple, well-known and liked by everyone in the neighborhood, including the Italian family across the street who ran a bootleg winery during Prohibition and often stored their casks in the Desch basement whenever a police raid was imminent.

Desch would have been content to go to the local cooperative high school and, after graduation, enter a skilled trade like his father's. But his mother and his Marianist instructors at Emmanuel Elementary recognized his greater gifts and pushed him toward the preparatory school at the local Catholic college, the University of Dayton. The deciding factor, however, may have been the influence of his lifelong friend Mike Moran, who got Desch a job as an usher at the Victory Theatre when they were both sixteen. Desch's exposure to national touring acts at the Victory, including the Ziegfeld Follies, vaudevillians, and opera companies, opened his eyes to a much wider world.

Thanks to NCR and the vision of its eccentric founder and business pioneer, John H. Patterson, much of the world had come to Dayton in those years. Patterson had bought the rights to one of the first cash-register machines in 1884 and then set about persuading the entire business world it couldn't live without them. His determination to build NCR into a world-class industrial organization, dominant in manufacturing, marketing, and research, drew to Dayton the likes of Edward Deeds and automotive genius Charles F. "Boss" Kettering.

Patterson epitomized the bold thinking and odd quirks of the men whose leadership ushered America into the twentieth century. Growing up on his father's sprawling farm outside of Dayton, Patterson

> was desperately eager to be a businessman, and almost as desperately ignorant of what businessmen did. He decided to follow his own best advice, creating thereby most of the forms of American merchandising—the trained salesman, the sales territory, the quota and the annual convention. . . . There may today be captains of industry who, like John Patterson, take four baths a day, wear underwear made from pool table felt and sleep with their heads hanging off the side of the bed so they may avoid rebreathing their just exhaled breath, but if there are, they keep pretty damn quiet about it.

Patterson also was an extremely visual man, perhaps ahead of his times. He was fanatical about recording every detail of his company's growth and operations. The NCR Archive in Dayton today contains some four million images from around the world, stretching back to the early 1900s.

Ironically, among the images of Dayton's early street life are two pictures of a young, barefoot Joe Desch—one of him shooting craps in an alleyway and another of him shimmying his hand up a baseball bat against another urchin to see whose team would take the field first in an overgrown sandlot. The pictures make clear that Desch had grown up in a rough-and-tumble neighborhood. But true to his mother's dreams, young Desch never neglected his schoolwork. He had been an altar boy and a straight-A student at Emmanuel, yet enough of a troublemaker to have punched and knocked down one of his instructors in a dispute over a math solution. Still, he managed to earn a scholarship from the Marianists to the university's preparatory high school. He went on to work his way through the university and graduate in 1929 with honors in electrical engineering.

His professional career began inauspiciously enough, running the tube-testing laboratory at Dayton Electric. He lost that job in 1933 in the midst of the Great Depression, after General Motors Radio bought out the company and consolidated its operations. Desch became a freelance inventor and engineer, working out of his parents' basement and turning into hardware mostly other people's ideas, some sillier than others, including a washing machine that generated sound waves to pulverize dirt from clothes. Unfortunately, the machine vibrated so much, its buttons kept falling off.

A chance encounter led to another important job. Desch was building a radio for a client in the basement of the client's home when Boss Kettering, the inventor of the automobile ignition system and the dean of American industrial engineers at the time, happened to walk in and observe him. Kettering didn't say a word as Desch worked, but the elder scientist was impressed enough with the young engineer to offer him a job at his Telecom Laboratories, where Desch later helped develop new radio and wire teletype equipment. But Desch lost that job, too, when the entire company was purchased by IBM in 1935.

Desch was officially unemployed, living off his meager savings, when he met and married Dorothy Brockman in the summer of 1935. They went off on their honeymoon, a car tour of the western United States with the obligatory stop at the Grand Canyon, knowing that Desch would have only a part-time teaching job at the university when they returned.

Desch's big break came later that same year when Harry M. Williams, chief of research at Frigidaire, hired Desch as a laboratory foreman. Williams, in turn, was later hired by Colonel Deeds to head the research division at NCR, where Desch followed and was given the task of launching the company's new electrical-research lab. Deeds and Williams gave Desch the freedom and the resources to be a true innovator. The year was 1938, and Desch was just thirty-one.

In the three years before the war, Desch built a national reputation for his work at NCR in designing miniature, fast-firing gas tubes no bigger than a thumbnail. These were the microchips of the 1940s and the basis for electronic calculators of the era. In the late 1930s and early 1940s, Desch and his staff designed and patented the first electronic accounting machine—capable of operating at one million pulses per second, at least one hundred times faster than any device had achieved before. Although it was not programmable and never went into production, the Desch calculator was on a par with the best work at IBM and was an important step toward the modern computer.

It was during this period, too, that Desch earned the admiration of MIT's Vannevar Bush, whom Deeds had retained as a research adviser for NCR. By the time the Navy had come to Desch with the Bombe project in August 1942, he had already contributed heavily to the war effort; unknown to him at the time, his electronic counter would be used in developing the first atom bomb. His inventions for Bush and the National Defense Research Committee included a remote detonator, a superfast "flash" communications system, and an electronic means of screening aircraft known as the IFF (Identity Friend or Foe) system. In a private letter to Desch in December 1942, Bush informed him of the success of one invention, perhaps the remote detonator: "It can now be told, within our own group, that new devices developed through the close collaboration between the services and the NDRC, have recently been used in combat with the enemy and have not been found wanting."

Unlike the Navy's theoretical engineers and mathematicians, who were mostly graduate students and professors at prestigious universities, Desch had earned his engineering and managerial stripes on the factory floor. He had become as savvy about front-office politics as he was knowledgeable about state-of-the-art electronics. Even the Navy's more academic engineers soon came to respect Desch's hard-nosed, practical advice, though they didn't entirely understand his factory milieu. In the late 1930s, when Desch took Dorothy to Cambridge to meet the MIT crowd, she was startled when graduate students at the welcoming cocktail party greeted her husband as "Dr. Desch." Desch made no effort to correct them, realizing that in academic circles it was incomprehensible that a man of his stature would not have a Ph.D.

Desch was self-possessed and self-confident but not cocky—a welterweight of a man with a wry smile, a big laugh, and a strong, Teutonic jaw. "We were a good team. I took care of the details, he took care of the front office," recalled Bob Mumma, Desch's assistant and business manager. "He knew how to talk to those people down there. . . . And we both knew a hell of a lot about electronics." For those who worked for him and with him, his name was always just Joe. But the lack of formality by no means meant that Desch failed to command the respect, and even fear, of his employees. Jack Kern, who worked for Desch on the Bombe project and learned from him the art of handcrafting gas-filled tubes, later remembered a boss who was as personable as he was demanding.

> He and I worked in the tube lab, alone, for many months to get things started [in NCR's electrical research division]. We usually worked in our shirtsleeves, but in the summertime it was in our underwear shirts. We couldn't have the windows open because the gas flames would blow away from our work. . . .
>
> About once a month, first thing on a Monday morning, Joe would have a general meeting in his office and really chew people out. . . . Accolades were rare.
>
> I always said that Joe was the hardest person in the world to work for. I told him this once and he wanted to know why. So I told him that he knew everything about every project that was going on.

Desch read his engineers' daily notebooks and looked "over your shoulder once or twice a day and suggested things," Kern recalled. "He wouldn't say, 'Hey, you're doing it wrong.' That wasn't his way. He would tell you in a nice way that 'you know, there's something else here that might help.' You would listen to his advice, so it was quite a treat to work for him. He was one of a kind."

The Bombe project would prove to be not only the biggest technical challenge of Desch's career but an overwhelming emotional drain. By spring 1943, Desch couldn't help feeling the odds had been stacked against him in his mission. Years after the war, he told a Smithsonian Institution historian that the British had been allowed to look at what he was doing, but the codebreaking pioneers at Bletchley Park had not been forthcoming with many of the details that might have made his job easier. In the summer of 1942, just as Desch began his design work, the British sent over the specifications for the three-wheel Bombes. In September of that year, they delivered blueprints of their more advanced machines in progress. But for reasons that aren't clear, not all of that information filtered down from Navy headquarters to Desch until much later in the year—just several months shy of the U-boat offensive expected by the Allies that spring.

2

Guesswork, Moxie, and Just Plain Luck

JOE DESCH WASN'T the only engineer struggling to design a machine nimble and reliable enough to take on the four-wheel Enigma. Throughout the summer of 1942 and into early 1943, the British were still battling internally over the design of their own four-wheel Bombe. In fact, when the Americans pressed them for blueprints of their latest Bombe in April 1942, none may have existed. By then, C. E. Wynn-Williams, the renowned British scientist who had invented the most advanced electronic radiation counters of the 1930s, was exploring an add-on device for the three-wheel Bombes that would make them fast enough to attack the four-wheel problem.

The Cobra, as his device was called, allowed a high-speed fourth wheel to be added to the existing Bombes and required a bank of vacuum tubes to track spinning-wheel positions lasting less than one-thousandth of a second. A thick black cable of nearly two thousand wires connected the add-on to the three-wheel Bombe; hence the name Cobra. The first Cobra prototype was not tested until April 1942, and then it ran into problems with the metal brushes on its high-speed wheels bouncing and skipping over the electrical contacts. The design was scrapped, and a second prototype was tested in June, again with poor results.

That the British had been able to break into the German naval ciphers at all owed much to good guesswork, moxie, and just plain luck. The Bombes themselves wouldn't work without a steady supply of good cribs, often created by German lapses, laziness, or predictable routines such as standard greetings for commanders. Timely captures of procedural manuals, Enigma wheels, and codebooks had rescued the British from several blackouts as well. So desperate was the need for codebreaking crutches that the British Navy had hatched a strategy of ambushing German weather ships, isolated far out at sea, to capture their Enigma materials.

In the first months of 1942, the British codebreakers were still hoping they might acquire copies of the German Navy's new weather and short-signal codebooks. These contained a kind of shorthand for frequently used terms in U-boat messages, such as those relating to weather observations and U-boat and convoy locations. Aware that the Allies were using new direction-finding equipment to zero in on longer radio transmissions, the Germans kept their U-boat reports as brief as possible. Until Britain could steal the new codebooks and thus gain a flow of cribs, even four-wheel Bombes would have been of little use against Shark. Good cribs were hard to find and remained so throughout the war.

More fundamentally, the Allied codebreakers and their machines were dependent on a variety of inherent weaknesses in the Enigma system—flaws that at any moment the Germans might take steps to correct. OP20G's request for the millions of dollars necessary to start the Dayton project contained an ominous warning to the Navy's top brass: the Bombes might be turned into useless contraptions if the Germans changed their procedures and tweaked the workings of their Enigma machines. Even as OP20G's leader, Joseph Wenger, and the man he put in charge of the Enigma problem, Howard Engstrom, were pressuring Desch to deliver his Bombe, they also worried that the machines might become expensive and very embarrassing cryptodinosaurs.

The Allies got their biggest break from the Germans themselves: their cryptologists suffered from a smug complacency based on the Enigma's staggering number of ciphering possibilities. But if the Enigma suffered from any flaw, it was that it, like the rest of the German military, relied on a consistent, predictable logic that could be turned in favor of its enemies. First of all, the Enigma never enciphered a letter to itself—A could never scramble to A, B could never scramble to B, and so on. What's more, the machine's enciphered letters were always reciprocal to their plain text partners: if X ciphered to Y then Y would always cipher to X at the same setting. Finally, the machine's plugboard allowed only one letter at a time to be steckered to another, so that if A was swapped with B, then B would always be swapped with A.

Before the war, codebreakers had developed a variety of hand methods based on these features to narrow the possibilities and to locate suspected cribs. One attack, called rodding, was used successfully against simpler Enigma machines that had no plugboard. Strips of scrambled alphabets were drawn up to represent the encipherings for each of the possible Enigma wheels and glued to sticks or rods. The columns of scrambled alphabets could then be lined up against the text in the message and slid into different pairings, creating a paper analog for the wiring inside the Enigma machine. Rodding eliminated the many wheels and starting positions that the Enigma did not allow—such as A enciphering to T while T enciphered to X. It was also used to test the validity of a suspected crib: any plain-text letter in a crib that enciphered to itself was again contradictory and called a "crash."*

Knowing that the commercial Enigma had been vulnerable to such attacks, the German military added its letter-swapping plugboard to all its models before the war—a devilish hurdle, but not enough to keep the British from penetrating their system.

THE BREAKTHROUGH INTO the wartime Enigma was achieved not by an experienced codebreaker but by a young Cambridge University mathematician named Alan Turing, recruited by GCCS in 1938. Turing found a way of turning the internal logic of the Enigma machine

---

* If no contradictions were found in a particular wheel combination, the setting was tested on a copy of the Enigma machine by entering the cipher text and seeing if plain text emerged.

itself into an ingenious codebreaking machine, the first British Bombe. Turing sought methods that would withstand tweaking of the Enigma and its code systems. One of his methods, dubbed Banburismus because it used punched sheets of paper made in the nearby town of Banbury, employed a statistical approach—an expansion of an earlier cipher-breaking strategy that the American Army's code guru, William Friedman, had called the Index of Coincidence (IC) method. In essence, the IC was based on laws of probability: to find out if two messages had been encrypted by the same Enigma setup, an analyst slid the text of the two messages over each other to see if there was more than a random percentage of letter matches.

Banburismus and the IC method, developed independently by the British and the Americans, both exploited laws of letter distribution that any good Scrabble player would recognize—that is, every letter and letter combination within a language occurs with a signature regularity. For example, it was known that the letters E, I, and N were among the most frequently appearing letters in German military texts; their replacement letters also would appear more often if enough message text was analyzed. In an IC analysis, a second message had to be shifted one letter at a time over the first message until all the letter positions of the first message were compared to the second. The reason was simple: the starting positions of the enciphering machine's tumbling rotors changed with each keystroke, creating what seems like a random stream of letters. But, eventually, even the most complex ciphering machine completes a cycle and begins again with the same rotor starting positions. So, wherever the alignment between the two messages created more matches than one would expect from a random distribution of letters, both messages were probably produced by the same wheels, wheel settings, and portion of the machine's encryption cycle.

To speed up the process, Banburismus used punched sheets of paper, with the positions of the holes representing different letters of each enciphered message. Two punched sheets of cipher text were aligned, then shifted over each other one letter position at a time. Wherever the holes matched, the letter matches could then be tallied and weighted.

Clever as it was, Banburismus suffered from several drawbacks: it was labor intensive and slow, demanded hundreds of messages for analysis, and was practical only for reducing the number of wheel orders to be tested—and even then only against the three-wheel Enigma machines. As soon as they had enough Bombes in 1943, the British dropped Banburismus.

Much like the British, the Americans, too, began with high hopes that their own IC methods and machines could conquer the Enigma. But they learned that this approach could tell them only the starting positions of the Enigma wheels after the harder parts of the setup were known.

Turing had predicted that Banburismus might not be powerful enough to tackle all the Enigma keys and searched for another method of attack. In mid-1939, after studying the techniques of other British codebreakers and those of the Poles, Turing took a truly brilliant leap that perhaps only a theoretical mathematician could have devised. He realized that the identity of the ciphered letters generated by the Enigma did not matter as much as the patterns of their relationship to the plain-text letters of the crib. Of particular value were those series of letter pairs that formed a "loop," or closed circuit, back to an original letter. Such loops could be simulated and tested in the electrical circuitry of a machine.*

For instance, if a crib text was suspected of having A enciphered to E, followed by E enciphered to D, and finally D enciphered back again to A, that series of letter pairs formed a loop. A loop "test" on a machine could help eliminate vast numbers of wheels and wheel positions that could not have produced such a distinctive pattern.

In another stroke of genius, Turing combined his loop test with a second test that could help conquer the most difficult part of the Enigma, its steckers. He realized there was a basic weakness in the Enigma plugboard: if one letter was steckered to another, that letter and its mate could not be steckered to any others. A could not be steckered to both B and X, for example. And, of course, if A was plugged to B, then B must be plugged to A.

* The British term for loop was "closure."

Turing's idea was to exploit this reciprocal relationship by seeing if a potential Enigma setup produced more than one stecker for any letter. If so, then even if the loop test had been passed, the setup would be ruled out. But if the setup passed both tests, then the correct stecker combination could be identified out of the 533 trillion possible.

Although created with a three-wheel Enigma as its target, Turing's Bombe approach would remain the basis for the war's most potent attack against the Enigma. Even so, the Bombes were neither all-powerful nor fully independent. They were not intended to and could not identify all the components of an Enigma setup. The method was aimed at only two: the combination of wheels used in a machine and the steckers. It did not solve the wheel wirings, and it left the identification of the ring settings and starting positions of the wheels to hand attacks.

The Bombes assumed prior knowledge of the wiring of the Enigma wheels, which already had been captured. And unless there were ways to eliminate possible wheel combinations, the method demanded that all be tested. In the case of the four-wheel naval Enigma, that meant an average twenty-minute Bombe run for each of the 336 possible wheel combinations—or more than four and a half days for a single Bombe to crunch through all the possibilities.

The Bombes also relied on finding cribs that contained loops and other helpful patterns. Only with relatively long and rare combinations of letter relationships would the Turing tests be powerful enough to eliminate most possible wheel combinations and stecker assumptions. Good cribs not only were hard to find but were vulnerable to changes in German procedure.

Finding useful cribs and their precise location within a message was both an art and a science. It required an intimate knowledge not only of German but of Enigma message formats and German military conventions and terminology. Routine messages were a blessing for crib analysts, as was the need to spell out numerals on the Enigma machine's alphabet-only keyboard, often leading to repeated patterns of text such as NULLNULLNULL. Routine weather reports and submarine reports of convoy sightings were sources of predictable content and, hence, cribs. The big break into the Enigma for D Day, for instance, came with the words WETTERVORHERSAGE BISKAYA—in English, "weather forecast Biscay."* As a result, Allied forces were better able to predict where and when German defenses would respond.

TURING'S LOGIC NARROWED the search for the correct Enigma setting from trillions to more manageable millions, bringing a timely solution within the grasp of codebreakers—but only if a machine could be invented that could plow through those remaining possibilities at unheard-of speeds. When Turing first thought of embodying his test in an ultrahigh-speed machine, electronics seemed the rational choice. Bletchley's codebreakers turned for help to H. H. (Doc) Keen at the British Tabulating Machine Company (BTMC), the equivalent of America's IBM. Keen, BTMC's experienced chief engineer, could, like Desch, be counted on to produce tried-and-true technical results. Faced with the challenge of producing a working machine in a short period of time, Keen quickly declared an electronic machine impractical. Bletchley's codebreakers, trusting in Keen's judgment, handed him control of the Turing Bombe project, and he delivered the first machine in March 1940. The result was crude, lacking many later features and designed only for three-wheel Enigma problems—but it ran.

Although it proved too slow and too weak in its cryptanalytic power to provide timely information, it vindicated Turing's design and Keen's technological choices. GCCS decided to use some of its hard-pressed budget on an improved model, which was delivered in August 1940. That second machine—although it, too, lacked many automated features—became the model for the architecture of all the British and American Bombes produced during the war.

---

* Good cribs could be neither too short nor too long. On the one hand, a long crib helped ensure that a plain-cipher match was correct and that only one such match would appear in a message. A crib based on short, repeated terms such as UBOOTE were of much less value. But longer cribs also contained a technical danger. Turing's Bombe method was premised on only the first Enigma wheel moving during encryption. Long cribs might trigger a "turnover" of the other wheels. Turnover could be overcome, but it required extra Bombe time and intensive work by analysts.

Keen had taken on a difficult task with little time for experimentation. His machine had to turn loops and stecker contradictions into electrical flows and do so within the framework of Turing's logic of elimination. The Keen Bombe was what computer scientists now call a parallel/analog machine: it sensed the amounts of electrical current running through the machine and the states of its electrical switches, either closed or open.

The technology was electromechanical, not electronic, which meant the use of motors, gears, and spinning drums as well as typical electrical parts such as relays and resistors. Much of the Keen Bombe came from the standard pool of parts for tabulating machines and telephone systems. The spinning drums, or commutators, designed to simulate the Enigma wheels, had twenty-six electrical contact points, one for each letter of the alphabet. The only proven technology at the time for sensing the current passed on by the spinning disks was the small wire brushes already in use on IBM punched-card equipment. Relays, such as were in use at the time for telephone switching, were added to track the movement of the drums from letter to letter and turn their voltages into useful signals.

To create a machine that could make thousands of connections and decisions every second, without a single error during runs of ten to twenty minutes, Keen often had to push components beyond their limits of speed and reliability. Turing's attack demanded a machine that was "perfect," but, many times, the existing technology refused to cooperate. The metal sensing brushes, for example, had a bad habit of breaking off and causing short circuits. The tumbling action of the middle and slow wheels could easily cause them to miss the voltage sent through the fast wheel. And the relay switches refused to perform fast enough to keep track of the signals from the commutators when they whirled at their highest speeds.

Those stubborn relays are what made cracking the M4 Shark so daunting. In theory, at least, a modified three-wheel Bombe could have attacked the Shark, but with the increase in the number of possible starting positions from 17,500 to 450,000, the standard relays of the first Keen Bombes simply were not up to the task.

Keen and his technicians quickly constructed a simulation of the

Enigma wheel that could be run accurately at high speeds without deteriorating. Each drum contained the input and output contacts needed to change one letter to another, just like an Enigma wheel. Based on a clever idea suggested by Turing, Keen's wheel combined both the forward and backward wiring of an Enigma rotor into a single spinning drum, allowing signals to pass in both directions, greatly increasing Bombe efficiency.*

Keen's ingenuity was limited by the technology of his day, however. He could not build a drum that could be automatically changed to mirror the wiring of each of the many Enigma wheels. He had to construct a separate drum for each wiring—a manufacturing and logistical challenge for Britain's scarce wartime resources. There were six different wheels for the Air Force Enigmas and eight for the naval Enigmas alone. Each of the Enigmas simulated in a Bombe called first for three, then four wheels. A typical run on the early Bombes often meant changing hundreds of different wheels because each possible combination had to be tested separately.

Permanently mounting that many wheels on a Bombe and designing a way to move each wheel automatically to its correct starting position was impractical. Technology limited the Bombes to testing a single wheel combination per run. Keen's design allowed the wheels to be removed manually or reset at each run. Which wheels were selected depended on the analyst's best guess as to which ones the Germans were using. The letter positions of the wheels were dictated by the "menu"— a very specific portion of the crib that included loops and other special patterns formed by pairing the cipher and plain text letters.

Rather than sandwich the three rotors together as in the Enigma itself, Keen fit each commutator flat on the front panel of the Bombe, which made their replacement easier. The wheels were arranged with the fast-moving rotor at the top, the middle next, and the slow wheel

---

* In the Enigma itself, the current flowed in only one direction through the wiring in its wheels. But the Bombe wheels "opened out" the flow of electricity in both directions, tracking twice the number of wheel positions. To accommodate the flow of current back and forth, each wheel had four sets of electrical contacts, or 104 contact points per wheel. The metal brushes of each spinning drum rubbed against the four concentric circles of twenty-six fixed contacts on the machine's panel, each contact representing a letter.

at the bottom. Connections behind the panel joined the three rotors together.

Ironically, the very part of the Enigma machine that the Germans felt made it impenetrable was turned to the Allies' advantage through Turing's genius—its letter-swapping stecker board. Guessing at the stecker for a menu letter improved the efficiency of the Bombe by eliminating even greater numbers of settings. If the Bombe operator guessed the correct stecker and the Bombe was set up with the correct wheels and positions, then the current would zip at nearly the speed of light around the letter loops of the menu and stop without sending current to any other of the twenty-six wires. The flow of current through the correct wheel positions would create what codebreakers called a "hot point" on the Bombe's register board—and only one of them. Sensing this point, the Bombe stopped and indicated that the wheel positions might be a solution.*

Single hot points, however, were rare and inefficient. A bad guess at the stecker often proved more useful to codebreakers. It led the Bombe to conduct more tests of inconsistencies and allowed an instantaneous check for solutions.†

If the guess at the stecker was incorrect but the wheel positions were correct, the current would race through all but one of the twenty-six connections, creating what codebreakers called a "cold point." The register's relays would sense the all-but-one condition and signal the Bombe to stop.‡

---

* A second test was then made on the register, either by hand or automatically, to see if there were any stecker contradictions. If no contradictions were discovered, the wheel positions were noted, as were the steckers indicated by the test board and relays. Together, the positions and steckers were called a "story." With those in hand, a codebreaker would set up an Enigma clone and see if the message deciphered to readable German text. If plain text did emerge, the Bombe run was said to have led to a "Jackpot."

† If the Bombe operator had guessed the wrong stecker, the machine would produce one of two results. First, if the Bombe did not have correct wheels or was not at the correct wheel positions, the current would flow through all the wires on the cable, and the test register would display all hot points. This indicated contradictions in the menu and, thus, no solution.

But the Bombe kept running, advancing the wheels in synchronization through the 17,570 possible wheel positions (for a three-wheel machine) until a "hit" was again sensed.

‡ Again, this stop was only a probability worth looking into. As before, a stecker-consistency check was done, and then the story was used on the Enigma clone to see if a jackpot had been produced.

The Bombe's primary task was to eliminate vast numbers of impossible settings rather than to pinpoint a correct solution. To do that well, it needed menus with enough letters, loops, and special relationships to focus its search on worthwhile solutions. The British soon calculated that a menu with eleven or twelve letters and two or three loops would prevent excessive false stops. Keen thus increased the number of Enigmas in each Bombe bank to twelve, so that the Bombe could test each menu letter and stecker guess simultaneously and speed the way to a solution. Keen tried to make his machines even more efficient by having three sets of banks (twelve Enigmas) in each of his Bombes so they could run more than one wheel order at a time. But that wasn't enough to make the Bombe a full-power elimination machine.

For that, Keen needed another important component, outlined by Turing's colleague Gordon Welchman, called the Diagonal Board. Its power came from the reciprocal nature of the Enigma's plugboard— that is, if A is steckered to B, then B must be steckered to A. The board was so named because its wiring made a diagonal connection between a column of letters, A to Z, and an identical row of letters. The columns and rows were all connected reciprocally to one another, in the same way as the plugboard on an Enigma machine. During a Bombe run, if current was sent to column B row A on the Diagonal Board, the board automatically shunted it back through row A column B and zapped it again through the Bombe's circuitry for more tests. Welchman's revolutionary idea increased the power of the Bombe's loop and stecker-contradiction tests by 60 percent.

Bletchley's 1941 breakthroughs did not create a secure future against the Enigma. In early 1942, when the U-boats began using M4 Shark, Bletchley was locked out of the system until the three-wheel Bombes at last broke into Shark in December, and then only after codebreakers got some unintended help from the Germans, who began using some M4s in the old three-wheel Enigma mode.

Even at that, the powerful cribs needed for the turnaround were secured at the cost of the lives of two brave British sailors who captured the weather-signal codebooks from *U-559* in October 1942. Lieutenant Anthony Fasson and Able Seaman Colin Grazier of the

HMS *Petard* were trying to retrieve the last of the sub's secret materials when the damaged U-boat, without warning, plunged beneath the waves and pulled them to their deaths.

IN THE SUMMER of 1942, the U.S. Navy was just beginning to digest all the information that Bletchley Park had given them on the Enigma and the Bombe, including Welchman's ingenious Diagonal Board. In light of the new information, the theoreticians at OP20G redrew the logic of their machine to draw on the power of the Diagonal Board, Turing's cold-point test, and Keen's two-way flow of current. They then set off to Dayton in August 1942 to have Desch turn their ideas into hardware.

But the Navy researchers did not bring with them to Dayton a finished plan. Desch had much to figure out on his own and many adjustments to make in the fall of 1942 as further information from the British about their Bombes and their methods trickled down from OP20G.

Desch's struggle might have been less hurried, less intense, and less frustrating if he and his Navy superiors had known more about the workings and the successes of the British Bombes prior to the summer of 1942. Whether the British withheld crucial information from their closest ally was, and still is, being debated. But all the arguing would have been moot—and the U.S. Bombe on schedule to prevent the U-boat slaughter in March 1943—if the year before, another Ohioan had not spurned an offer of help from Bletchley Park.

3

Miss Aggie's Big Blunder

August 18, 1941—Washington, D.C.

WALKING WITH A cane and a severe limp from her buckled right leg, Agnes May Driscoll—at age fifty-three one of the Navy's top codebreakers—entered the office of her boss, OP20G director Laurance F. Safford. Waiting there to meet her was the head of Bletchley Park, Commander Alastair G. Denniston. From the moment of their introduction, Driscoll and Denniston must each have been fighting a feeling of distrust—which is why Denniston had traveled to Washington in the first place. After months of misunderstanding and tensions between the British and American codebreaking operations, Denniston was prepared to be more open about what the GCCS had learned in tackling the Enigma—in part because the British feared that the Americans, if left too far out of Ultra's tight circle, might try to build an anti-Enigma device of their own. Denniston wanted the U.S. Navy to leave the Enigma message cracking to the British, who (unlike the Americans, in his view) could be counted on to keep a secret.

The two veteran codebreakers presented a striking contrast as they sat across from each other in Safford's office. Denniston, sixty-three, a diminutive and dapper Scot who often wore a flower in his lapel, was ten years Driscoll's senior but a robust, outgoing man known for his relaxed, conciliatory ways. In fact, his easygoing nature was to later lead to charges that he was a poor manager of people and was a factor in his eventual removal as head of Bletchley Park.

On the other hand, Driscoll, who was crippled and increasingly frail since a car accident four years before, was a conservative dresser, a workaholic, and, although pleasant to others, largely a social recluse. She was also deeply religious, a convert to Christian Science who had declined medical care after the car accident that had broken her jaw and right leg below the knee. As a result, the leg had never healed properly, and it bowed outward from her slight frame at about twenty degrees.

Despite their differences in temperament and appearance, the two were remarkably similar in their backgrounds. Both were children of small-town professionals—Denniston's father had been a doctor in rural Scotland and Driscoll's had been a music professor at a college in Westerville, Ohio. Denniston had taught foreign languages before he was recruited for naval-intelligence work as a German linguist; Driscoll had been a math teacher in Texas before signing up with the women's naval auxiliary during World War I. Both were dedicated to their craft and their countries.

But Denniston, unlike Driscoll, had seen that codebreaking was now moving into a new era, a mathematical one. Even before the Nazi invasion of Poland, he had begun recruiting a new class of codebreaker—young mathematicians such as Alan Turing and Gordon Welchman—who would lead the way toward automation and state-of-the-art electronics to help turn the new methods into practical attacks.

Driscoll, however, still put her faith first in the codebreaker's intuition and the old-fashioned, hard-earned methods of pencil and paper. To Denniston's surprise, she was more than uninterested in Britain's automated attacks against the Enigma. In that critical August 1941 meeting, she declared she did not want or need a Bombe, nor did she ask any questions about the machine or its supporting technique of Banburismus. And, further, she told Denniston she had already devised an Enigma method far better than those in use at GCCS. She then refused his invitation to travel to England, where she would be shown all GCCS had achieved and could tell all about her own attack. Her brush-off of Denniston was to cost the United States dearly, and its effects were compounded when the British commander was soon "promoted" out of GCCS and replaced by leaders less sympathetic to the Americans.

Neither Driscoll nor Safford informed their Navy superiors of Denniston's offer—an oversight that hampered British-American relations for the next four years. Driscoll's blunder never found its way into U.S. Navy records.

Why did Driscoll spurn Denniston's overture? Perhaps it was professional hubris. Perhaps it was the Navy's continuing distrust of England, whose military leaders had so dominated the American venture into World War I. Or perhaps it was a product of too many years of isolation at OP20G as the Navy, understaffed and overwhelmed, tried to hold on to its precious few tricks and secrets. Driscoll and Safford seemed to have been cozily optimistic and dangerously ignorant about the ability of their small and inexperienced crew to conquer the intricacies of the Enigma.

Driscoll's age may have been a factor, too. At fifty-three, she was beyond her peak creativity and increasingly prone, like many of us, to inflexibility. Codebreakers, like mathematicians, tend to produce their most innovative work early in their careers. At the same time, OP20G's restricted budgets prior to the war had made it difficult to bring young, bright, and well-trained people into its fold—people who could stimulate new ideas and new methods, the way Agnes Driscoll had been able to do decades before.

Driscoll may not have been on the cutting edge in 1941, but she had reason to trust her own professional judgments. Prior to the war, she had often been the first to break into the latest and toughest codes and cipher systems confronting the Navy. In the 1920s and 1930s, she had trained the first generation of Navy officers and civilian cryptanalysts inside the sprawling Main Navy Building on Constitution Avenue in Washington, including Safford, who became her commanding officer and biggest advocate. Safford had been not only one of Driscoll's star students but the first regular Navy officer to commit his career to cryptology. Both he and Driscoll were from the old school of codebreaking, and neither had taken the lead in OP20G's sometimes disappointing ventures into statistical, automated cryptanalysis. Together, however, they shared an unwavering commitment to the Navy's, and the nation's, vital stake in cryptanalysis and were quick to defend its boundaries and its secrets, even against the British.

HISTORIANS KNOW MUCH about Driscoll's many career accomplishments but frustratingly little about her personal background. For professional reasons, Driscoll jealously guarded her private life, shunning the spotlight and even refusing, except on rare occasions, to be photographed. From the record alone, however, it is clear that she was as pioneering in her career path as she was remarkable in her abilities.

She was born Agnes May Meyer in 1889 in Geneseo, Illinois, the second daughter and third child of a music-professor father and a mother who reared eight children. Despite the large family to support, her parents made sure that Agnes received a thorough education. She graduated from high school and went on to college, an unusual privilege at the time for men or women.

From 1907 to 1909, she attended Otterbein College—a small Methodist institution in Westerville, Ohio, where her father then taught music theory. Founded by the United Brethren in Christ, Otterbein was among the first colleges to welcome students from nonelite backgrounds and among the first in America to encourage female students to take all types of courses, including those in the sciences.

Meyer finished her undergraduate degree in 1911 at Ohio State University, not far from Westerville, in Columbus. There, her main subjects of study were mathematics, physics, music, and languages. After college, she wasted no time striking out on her own, venturing west to Amarillo, Texas, where she served first as a music director of a small military academy and later as head of the mathematics department at Amarillo High School, a position of considerable status at the time.

America's entry into world war in 1917 changed forever the safe course of Meyer's professional life. No doubt driven by both her adventurousness and her patriotism, she was one of the first to answer the call when a shortage of labor, and some intense political prodding, induced the Navy to open its doors to women. She and her sister enlisted in the brand-new women's Naval Reserve, known as the Yeomanettes, in June 1918. Meyer was given the highest ranking attainable for a woman at the time, chief yeoman (F), partly because she had a working knowledge of stenography but as much because of her education and her age, which was nearly thirty. Even the Navy at the time couldn't ignore her many other skills—including proficiency in German, French, Latin, and Japanese, as well as in statistics, math, physics, and engineering.

After the war, she was discharged from the reserve and rehired as a steno clerk for the Office of the Director of Naval Communications. But given her skills for codebreaking, the Navy soon sent her off for special training in 1920 with George Fabyan, the wealthy and eccentric textile magnate who had founded his own school of codebreaking at Riverbank Laboratories, near Chicago.

Meyer so impressed Fabyan with her abilities that he offered to pay her expenses and match her Navy salary in order to keep her working at Riverbank until the Navy wanted her back. Nevertheless, after her training ended Meyer returned to the Navy, where she helped develop an enciphering machine called the CM. Congress later awarded her a large cash sum in lieu of patent rights for her invention.

In 1921, Meyer ran across a challenge she could not resist. Edward Hugh Hebern, the inventor of one of the first cipher machines to use rotors, placed an ad in a maritime magazine touting his device as "unbreakable." Meyer solved the sample message in the ad and sent it off to Hebern, who must have been both humbled and dazzled to have a woman prove him so wrong. In February 1923, Hebern did the sensible and politically astute thing by hiring her as his technical adviser and liaison with the Navy. Even though she remained a Navy employee, Meyer worked for a company that was trying to sell its products to the Navy—a touchy ethical issue today but not so uncommon then.

In the spring of 1924, with Hebern's company in financial straits, Meyer decided to return to the Navy and continue her work in cryptanalysis. There were no doubt personal reasons as well. In August of that year, at age thirty-five, she wed Washington lawyer and fellow Illinois native Michael Bernard Driscoll.

Driscoll began her codebreaking duties for the Navy in earnest in the early 1920s, not long after the Office of Naval Intelligence had secretly financed a series of break-ins at the Japanese consulate in New York City whose scope and daring make the Nixon-era burglary at the Watergate Hotel look like child's play. The entire Japanese fleet codebook was photographed, page by page, during repeated undercover operations never detected by the Japanese, and then translated over the next four years. The result was called the Red Book—two thick volumes of encoded word groups bound in red material.

Codes and ciphers are two different methods of disguising messages. Codes substitute words, letter groups, or numbers for other words or letter groups, usually copied from a list or book. Ciphers are generally harder to crack because they are not simple substitutions: they replace plain-text letters with other letters or numbers according to a specific procedure, known as a "key." Ciphers were increasingly generated by machines as World War II approached, but codes continued to be dispensed in books.

A good example of a code system, the Red Book contained a numerical value for every word or syllable likely to be used in a Japanese naval message. But those simple substitutions, easy prey for a crack team of codebreakers, were further disguised by a cipher. Before sending a message over the radio, a Japanese code clerk needed a second book filled with page after page of random numbers. Starting from the top of the page and working down, the clerk added (in some systems subtracted) a different random number, or "additive," to each of the code groups. The addition was done digit by digit, without carrying the sum, to keep each code group to five letters. Buried somewhere inside the message was an indicator telling the receiving clerk what page in the additive book had been used to encipher the basic code. The clerk turned to that page and stripped off the additives before looking up the meaning of each code group.*

In 1925, the immense job of turning the Red Book into a useful codebusting tool fell to Agnes Driscoll. She devised craftsmanlike ways of stripping off the additives and of identifying the meaning of underlying code groups that had not been easily translated. Even though most of the code-group meanings were known by then, this was no small feat: the two volumes contained some one hundred thousand code groups, with as many as three groups assigned to each word.

Driscoll got a raise and a promotion for her breakthrough, which at last gave the Navy a chance to tap into the secret messages of its chief antagonist in the Pacific. Although handicapped by a lack of people and resources during the 1920s and 1930s, the Navy's codebreakers were able to process some important Japanese messages, revealing details about their naval maneuvers, fuel supplies, and advances in aviation. But OP20G's weak hold was always under threat: the Japanese had the smart habit of changing their code systems just before any major shift in their strategy.

By the spring of 1930, when the Japanese Navy began conducting fleet maneuvers in the Pacific aimed against its envisioned enemy, the United States, they introduced a new cipher system. But they still turned to their Red Book for the underlying code groups. Driscoll showed her stuff again and got the first break into the new system. The results shocked the Navy: they discovered that Japanese naval intelligence had been able to obtain a very accurate picture of the Navy's own latest war plan, dubbed Orange. The revelation convinced the Navy's codebreakers that they had to persuade the government to invest in radio intelligence.

---

* In *Battle of Wits*, Stephen Budiansky cites this possible example from the Red Book:

  Plain message: FROM KAGA ESTIMATED TIME OF ARRIVAL 2130
  Plain text: From Uppercase Kaga stop ETA 2130 stop Follows
  Code text: 21936 48322 01905 38832 87039 11520 38832
  Additive: 02923 41338 00989 15861 28959 23693 18229
  Enciphered message: 23859 89650 01884 43693 05988 34113 46051

Driscoll's reward this time was something she had not asked for or even felt she needed: an IBM tabulating machine to help relieve some of the drudgery of her clerical labors. "Miss Aggie," as she was called by colleagues, was none too excited about mechanized approaches to her labors, having relied for more than ten years on little more than pencil and cross-section paper. But Driscoll soon found the unwanted tabulator a necessity when Japan dramatically altered its main naval code. She had been the first to notice in the fall of 1931 that the Japanese had at last dumped the Red Book for a new code and cipher system. This time, without the benefit of burglary and secretly photographed pages of codes, Driscoll and her team would have to crack both code and cipher. It was tedious, mind-numbing work, but the new machine helped keep track of the nearly eighty-five thousand code groups and changing cipher keys as each Japanese message was intercepted and processed.

Others at OP20G may have taken the lead in making use of the tabulators, but Driscoll's analytical acumen and doggedness eventually broke the code. Thanks to her work, the Americans learned in 1936 that Japan's newly refitted battleship, the *Nagato,* had reached speeds of more than twenty-six knots, a significant leap over its projected twenty-four knots. As a result, the Navy quickly redesigned the newest American battleships to eclipse the Japanese by reaching twenty-eight knots. Laurance Safford ventured that this coup alone "paid for our peacetime RI [radio intelligence] a thousand times over."

Driscoll continued on her roll of breakthroughs. In the mid-1930s, she led the Navy's attack against a new automatic enciphering machine for Japan's naval attachés, the M-1. Cracking it was a major accomplishment that gave her and her team the confidence to tackle more sophisticated mechanical ciphers, including the Enigma.

Like many cryptanalysts, Driscoll paid a personal price for her successes. The stress of grappling with the Japanese codes led to periodic bouts of weight loss, and often she returned to her family in Westerville and the slower pace of life there to regain her stamina.

Still, there was nothing frail about Driscoll's dealings with her male counterparts in the Navy. Those men who tried to patronize

"Madame X," as her colleagues sometimes called her, seldom did a second time, according to several Navy veterans who knew her after the war. They recounted a famous confrontation between Driscoll and a gung-ho Navy lieutenant who had dared to question her application to renew her security clearance after the war. The young officer barged into her office, approached her in an overbearing manner, and said, "Ma'am, in this section where you are required to list five references, you have listed the names of five admirals. You are supposed to list the names of people who know you well."

Driscoll looked up at the young man with a squint in her eye and said, "Sonny, I knew all of them when they were ensigns and lieutenants, and if you don't straighten up, I'm going to tell them to never promote you."

In his book, *And I Was There,* Admiral Edwin T. Layton wrote that Driscoll

> was sensitive to her role as a woman in a man's world. Because of this she kept to herself as much as possible and none of us was invited to socialize with her and her lawyer husband. While she could be warm and friendly, she usually affected an air of intense detachment, which was heightened by her tailored clothes and shunning of makeup. It was surprising to hear Miss Aggie curse, which she frequently did—as fluently as any sailor whom I have ever heard.

Driscoll had many contacts among Washington's tightly knit cryptanalytic circles, in all branches of the military, including Elizebeth Friedman, the Coast Guard's chief codebreaker and wife of the famous Army cryptanalyst William Friedman. Driscoll may have been party to the exchanges between the Army and Navy in the 1930s that, some in OP20G claim, eventually helped William Friedman and his colleagues use statistical techniques, as well as cribs, to conquer Japan's most secure diplomatic cipher machine, known as "Purple," in late 1940.

After piling success upon success, Driscoll's private life took a sudden, tragic turn in October 1937 when she was seriously injured in an auto accident. Two other passengers were killed. She took nearly a year to recover fully from her badly broken leg and jaw. When she finally returned to full-time duty in September 1938, she needed a cane to walk and, by some accounts, had grown even more reticent and withdrawn.

Regardless, within two years, she was leading the Navy's attack on JN-25, the newest Japanese naval-operations code. She and her team were able to make some inroads, but by late 1940 only a fraction of JN-25 was readable, even though Driscoll and her group had solved the logic of the system. The remaining grunt work was turned over to a new team of relatively inexperienced reserve officers who arrived in Washington as the Navy quietly prepared for war. As the team labored slowly and tediously to reconstruct the new codebook, the Japanese introduced a new, fifty-thousand-group list of additives on August 1, 1941, forcing the codebreakers to start their arduous task all over again.

In the meantime, Driscoll had been reassigned to what the Navy apparently felt was a more pressing matter: the German U-boat codes and ciphers.

THE EXACT WHEN, who, and why of the Navy's decision to divert its most experienced codebreaker from the critical Japanese problem—a year before Pearl Harbor—are unknown. But surely the growing involvement of the American Navy in the Atlantic and the fears that England, under Nazi siege by air, might be invaded must have been factors in redirecting Driscoll and her team, as well as much of America's radio-intercept equipment, to the Atlantic.

Because the Americans couldn't read the German messages, they concentrated much of their effort on radio-direction finding and traffic analysis—that is, studying the number, origins, and types of radio transmissions rather than the content of the messages themselves to guess at enemy activities. OP20G had begun intercepting and logging German naval communications as early as 1938 and was gaining at least some knowledge into the nature of the U-boat communications network.

Driscoll decided to attack the German systems with a labor-intensive approach, despite the Navy's scarcity of experienced people. She started with former Navy radioman Milton Gaschk and at least two women. In late 1940, she added to her team four young Navy officers, led by a new Annapolis graduate, Robert Weeks. Those four officers, Gaschk, and one of the new civilian employees, Eunice Rice, were assigned a near impossible task: define the inner workings of the mystery machine that was generating the German naval messages without a copy of the machine or any of its decrypted messages. She asked the young group to perform "pure" cryptanalysis against a foe they couldn't even identify.

Driscoll provided them with copies of 113 intercepted messages, and that was it, except their own ingenuity. The team put the messages through a variety of analyses, ranging from the statistical Index of Coincidence techniques of William Friedman to the use of cribs. Amazingly, they came close to understanding how the naval Enigma worked but could not define enough of the machine's parameters to allow decryption to begin. They were able to report that the machine, one they had never seen, generated a cipher that corresponded letter for letter to the plain text, used all twenty-six letters of the alphabet, never enciphered a letter to itself, and used X and Y as special characters, such as punctuation. They also spotted that the machine had two basic and changeable components: one that generated encrypted letters and another that was some sort of means to link thirteen pairs of letters together (the plugboard). The group's findings were a code-breaking tour de force, but they had to admit they still did not fully understand the workings of the machine.

That the Navy would expend its top talent on a blind attack on the Enigma raises some interesting questions about the motivations of its decision makers. Safford, who may have played a key role in Driscoll's reassignment, was to make it clear over the next two years that he feared America's dependence on Britain for tackling the Atlantic problem, especially as more of the Navy's own men and ships entered harm's way. On the other hand, Driscoll's reassignment orders might just as well have come directly from the White House, where President Roosevelt was determined to give the European war the highest priority. There are no documents to support either theory.

Certainly, as bombs rained on London during the Battle of Britain, its leaders were pressing the United States for more supplies and technical aid; by the summer of 1940, Britain was asking to exchange cryptanalytic as well as scientific secrets. Roosevelt and his advisers, including William Donovan, who would become his chief spy, were receptive and began putting the pressure on Army and Navy signals-intelligence divisions to come up with plans for collaborating with the British.

The sharing of intelligence is fraught with risks even between the closest of allies, and, as the two countries moved by necessity toward partnership, both employed ruses and smoke screens to hide their intentions.

While it's hard to imagine today, with the Internet, satellite TV, and scores of daily transatlantic flights, the communication and cultural barriers between the British and the Americans ran deep sixty years ago. Most citizens of either country had seen the other only in movies, where stereotypes were reinforced: class-conscious, snobby Brits talked down their noses, and uncultured, boorish Yanks couldn't keep a secret.

But while the Americans sometimes gave the British ample justification for their distrust, the British presumed that their colonial offspring were naïve, undisciplined, and childlike. The British Army's Captain Geoffrey Stevens, Bletchley's liaison to the U.S. Army's code-breaking unit in Washington, sent a letter to Bletchley in September 1942 with a scathing report on the Army operations that included this observation:

> Sometimes I think they are just a lot of kids playing at 'Office.' You must have noticed yourself how very many childish qualities the American male has: his taste in women, motor-cars, and drink, his demonstrative patriotism, his bullying assertion of his Rights, his complete pig-selfishness in public manners and his incredible friendliness and generosity when he likes

you—Hell! Anyone would think I didn't like them. But perhaps
it is as well I'm fond of children.

The British sometimes affectionately teased the Americans about
their stereotyped traits, including their heavy reliance on machinery.
Joe Eachus, the first American codebreaker to work at Bletchley Park,
recalled what a British officer had had to say when he found Eachus
trying to assist a clerk whose skirt had been caught in the wheel
mechanism of a Bombe and was being twisted and pulled from her
waist: "Don't you Yanks ever do anything by hand?" The American
military, and especially the Navy, had its own caricatures of the
British and, like younger brothers out to prove themselves, were sensitive to any signs of being treated as a junior partner.

When Driscoll's group began its work on the Enigma in late 1940,
U.S. Army and Navy codebreakers were feuding over how much information to reveal to the British. Both services were willing to exchange radio intercepts, but Friedman's Army codebreakers, who
dealt mainly with diplomatic systems rather than military ones, were
more willing to share their successes and failures. The Navy, on the
other hand, was more concerned about its dependence on Britain and
may have still been smarting from the domineering treatment it received from the Royal Navy during World War I, when the British
tried to dictate U.S. naval standards down to the types of weapons
and ammunition they should use. Safford and his boss, Leigh Noyes,
the director of naval communications, stubbornly refused to reveal
any of the Navy's cryptanalytic conquests, including one the Army
later considered its own, the then imminent break into Japan's Purple
enciphering machine. After all, in a world still hungry for empire,
Britain had always been among the Navy's list of potential enemies at
sea.

In November, a final top-level promise was made in Washington
to send American codebreakers on an exchange mission to England.
Friedman's Army group quickly devised a complete "gift list" for the
British, including copies of the Purple machine, then under construction at Navy facilities using Navy funds. The Army felt it had

every reason to expect full reciprocity from the British, but to be on the careful side they drew up a detailed list of what they wanted in the exchange.

The head of naval intelligence, Rear Admiral Walter S. Anderson, informed the British that both he and the Army demanded an unambiguous answer to what British codebreakers had meant by a "pretty free exchange" of secrets in their latest offer. He insisted that unless there was a guarantee of a complete exchange on Italian, German, Japanese, and Russian systems, the Army and Navy might withdraw. Even if the guarantee was made, he said, the Navy was not going to send any of its codebreakers on the exchange trip—on the excuse that it had none available.

Meanwhile, the British were grappling with their own reservations about the Americans: "We are entitled to recall that America sent over at the end of the last war the now notorious Colonel Yardley for purposes of cooperation. He went so far as to publish the story of his cooperation in book form." Indeed, Herbert O. Yardley—ladies' man, high roller, and head of America's codebreaking effort during World War I—had penned a memoir in 1931, *The American Black Chamber,* that became a bestseller. In it, he detailed his successes against enemy codes; later, he supplied the background for a Hollywood spy film.

Thus, the British codebreakers were not planning to reveal all, especially about the Enigma. If an American expert did arrive at Bletchley, "steps will be taken to steer him away from our most secret subjects," an internal memo read. But to avoid alienating America's leaders, the British sent an ambiguous response to the proposed exchange.

It worked. The top echelons of the Army and Navy told their codebreakers the British were to be trusted, the Americans were to share all their secret machines, and both Army and Navy were to send representatives. By mid-December, with the planned trip to England just weeks away, OP20G had to race to catch up with the well-prepared Army team. Laurance Safford, however, remained convinced that the Navy had little to learn from Bletchley Park, and his last-minute selection of rather junior people reflected that attitude. In contrast, the Army quickly promoted its two top civilian code-breakers to high military rank to try to ensure that they would be respected by the British.*

In February 1941, two young Navy communications officers selected for the exchange with Bletchley Park—Robert Weeks and Ensign Prescott Currier—boarded Britain's new, showpiece battleship, the *King George V,* for what would become a stay of several weeks in England. The final leg of their trip, from the Orkney Islands to the Thames, proved to be an adventure when German planes attacked their British destroyer, but with little effect. Lieutenant Weeks, from his work in trying to identify the German cipher machine, should have known what information Driscoll sorely needed. Currier was far less experienced. He had been a noncommissioned officer and then a civilian employee at OP20G before being recalled to active duty in December 1940.

Neither Currier nor Weeks was mathematically trained, and neither considered himself a polished cryptanalyst. Originally, Robert B. Ely, a Navy reserve officer with the background to grasp the intricacies of the British method, had been assigned to the exchange, but Weeks took his place at the last minute.

Likewise, William Friedman did not make the trip, claiming "illness" as a cover for what his subordinates knew was a nervous breakdown suffered just after New Year's Day. Instead of going to Bletchley, he checked into Walter Reed Hospital. Friedman was replaced by an electrical engineer, Leo Rosen, who had recently joined the Army's codebreaking team as a civilian employee. The head of the Army's mission, Abe Sinkov, was one of the young civilians Friedman had hired when he created the Army's cryptologic branch in 1931. But neither Sinkov nor Rosen had significant experience with German

---

* As the men tapped to represent the Navy prepared for their departure in late January, Safford fumed, perhaps hoping that Driscoll's recent reassignment would—as she strongly hinted—lead to a major discovery that America could keep to itself. Independent U.S. power over the German naval-code systems might persuade American policy makers that the nation had little need for further "exchanges" with the British.

military systems. In fact, none of the Army's codebreakers had spent much time on even the earliest Enigma machines.

The Americans weren't the only ones nervous about the visit. Barbara Abernethy, Alastair Denniston's personal assistant, remembered her excitement and her fears when the commander told her to prepare for the arrival of Bletchley's first American visitors and to serve them sherry in his office: "So at twelve o'clock the bell rang and I went in and I somehow managed to pour glasses of sherry for these poor Americans, who I kept looking at. I'd never seen Americans before, except in the movies. 'What were they doing here?' we said to ourselves."

With the United States still not officially at war and with opposition at home from isolationists, the American visitors to Bletchley wore civilian clothes to hide their mission. They were housed just a few miles from Bletchley in the mansion of Lord Cadman, president of the Anglo-Persian Oil Company. A stenographer was made available to the team, and food rationing was suspended for their hearty meals. Two large cars with drivers—one for the Army, one for the Navy—were provided for their travels, perhaps because the British had made separate promises to the two branches. The generosity was all the more notable considering the privations the codebreakers faced at Bletchley: a pencil sharpener was rare, paper scarce, copying equipment only to be dreamed of. Their working quarters, called huts, were near-primitive, sectional-built wooden structures made of Canadian pine and covered in either shiplap boarding or asbestos sheets.

The four American codebreakers brought with them nearly one ton of documents and machinery. Among the items delivered to the British was America's crowning intelligence achievement at that time: two working copies of Purple, the Japanese diplomatic service's cipher machine. The Americans handed the British two copies of nearly every item, including Japanese consular codes, JN-25, and Japanese naval attaché ciphers. The double copies were a generous offering in the days when highly secret material had to be reproduced by hand.

In return, the Americans were given a tour of Bletchley's decrypting room and shown the techniques and machines the British were using against Germany's Enigma system, including the only device capable of quickly penetrating the Enigma: the Bombe.

The Americans never knew how close they had come to leaving Bletchley without having seen its prime treasures. Permission to show them Britain's Enigma capabilities had been withheld until literally the last days of their scheduled stay. In seeking that permission, Bletchley's leaders argued that England would probably have to depend on American help in the future, especially for Japanese problems, and that the Americans would be bitter if they learned of the Bombe and its methods after their aid had been secured. Brigadier Stuart Menzies, the head of British intelligence who was then known only as "C," passed the request to Prime Minister Churchill on February 26. Churchill gave his approval the next day, less than a week before the Americans were scheduled to leave.

But their access wasn't complete: the visitors were to be shown only the new technology, not the operational "results" of British codebreaking.

On March 3, 1941, the Navy men visited Hut 3, where Alan Turing was refining his attacks on the naval Enigma. Turing described to the Navy men his method of Banburismus, the formidable challenges of the naval Enigma, and various German transmission systems. Although critics later complained the Americans were not given enough information, what Currier and Weeks were told and shown at Bletchley Park was significant—if disappointing.

The machinery and methods that two of the Americans finally did see in Hut 3 were skimpy—the later hustle and bustle and technical sophistication of the 1944 and 1945 Bletchley Park that came to dominate its postwar public image was still a long way off. The Americans in 1941 saw four, maybe six Bombes at most, and what they saw was rather crude. The first models that printed their results did not arrive at Bletchley until the end of March, after the Americans had left.

The first electromechanical Bombe, with its sets of noisily whirling commutators, had begun its work at Bletchley less than a year before. Its first break into Enigma had required a full week of runs.

In that early Bombe, the commutators continued to spin for some time after a hit. When the machine at last stopped, its operators had to feel the relay switches in its circuits to discover which were warm and which were cold in order to identify the hit positions of the commutators. Then the machine had to be cranked back to where it had made the hit before it could restart its search.*

Turing no doubt told Currier and Weeks of his complex way of turning cribs into menus. But he no doubt told them as well that, to be effective, the Bombes required long, rare cribs containing loops and other telling patterns between the cipher and plain text.

The Bombe attack relied, to some extent, on old-fashioned cryptological craftsmanship, not to mention the theft of enemy documents. But such captures, which allowed the naval system to be read for much of the remainder of 1941, did not come until after the Americans had left Bletchley.

We do not know exactly how much of Bletchley's technical history and frustrations were revealed to the visiting Americans. But if there had been a frank discussion, Weeks and Currier may have brought back a less-than-optimistic picture of the Bombe and Turing's methods. The British had found that the Enigma was not going to yield to any simple or inexpensive solutions.

The Navy's team did not leave empty-handed, however: Weeks and Currier received a paper analog of a naval Enigma machine, which used strips of encoded paper rather than wheels for scrambling the plain text. They also were told the wiring of the machine's eight code wheels and were assured that when enough copies of real Enigmas became available, the American Navy would receive one. In addition, Turing promised them much more would be exchanged in the

---

* That original 1940 machine was even less efficient at testing for the setting of the Enigma's steckers. Soon after, the British upgraded the Bombe by including an automated stecker test when the Bombe stopped. The addition was called a Machine Gun because of its staccato sound as it searched the stop data. The new Standard Bombe, as it came to be called, was put to work on Air Force, not naval, problems because too little was known about U-boat communications to make the Bombes useful. But even the Standard Bombe was slow. The speed of its thirty-some spinning commutators had to be restrained because the electrical relays that sensed a hit were sticky and slow.

future, including information about German errors in using the Enigma systems.*

Although all four Americans had learned enough from their visit to prevent them from thinking that the British had reneged on their agreement, Sinkov and Rosen had found a brighter scenario at Bletchley: they had learned of Britain's longtime success against the Axis diplomatic and Air Force ciphers and of more recent breaks into the German Army Enigma networks. Currier concluded they had been "shown everything" and that the exchange had been open and equal.

Nevertheless, Bletchley's gifts to the Americans had come with some severe restrictions because the British felt the Ultra intelligence was crucial to their country's survival. What the two teams saw and learned at Bletchley Park was to be held top secret, never written down, and conveyed by word only to their immediate superiors who themselves were expected to keep the secrets. The knowledge was never to be put to use before GCCS was contacted or, by implication, without its permission. The four Americans willingly signed iron-bound oaths of secrecy before their departure in the first week of March 1941. By contrast, what the Americans gave to the British was offered without restrictions.

The Americans also revealed to the British, in broad terms, their plans to build revolutionary codebreaking machines, including electronic ones. Rosen, the technological expert among the Americans, may have engaged in a bit of puffery, leading the British to expect far more advanced machines and more of them when they visited the United States later in the year. There was at least one omission as well: the Navy team seems to have kept the British unaware of Driscoll's German naval project.

Even so, the British, too, felt the exchange had been worthwhile. After all, they had gotten their hands on a Purple machine and had felt reassured that, based on the demeanor of Currier and Weeks, their secrets would be safe with OP20G. On the day the Americans

---

* Besides the Enigma aids, Weeks also carried away a large packet filled with documents concerning the Russian, Vichy, and Italian codes, German merchant-marine ciphers, bare bones documents on German naval systems, and, perhaps, some old Enigma keys to allow OP20G to practice Enigma decryption.

were first shown the Bombe, Denniston wrote to "C" that "complete cooperation on every problem is now possible and we are drafting plans for its continuity when they return to the USA." All that was needed now were secure telegraphic and courier links between the liaison officers.*

But trouble came almost the instant the four Americans left. British intelligence quickly informed GCCS that one of the men on the Army's team had talked about his work so much on the British ship from London to the Royal Navy anchorage, in the Orkney Islands, that its officers knew what his visit had been about.†

In the next few months, there were further incidents that made the British regret opening Bletchley's doors. GCCS received a letter in plain language from the American Army asking for a Bombe. The British view of the American State Department as an intelligence sieve was reaffirmed when a long newspaper article appeared in Britain describing the American plans to launch a new intelligence covert operation in England. The June 24, 1941, London *Daily Express* reported from New York that William "Wild Bill" Donovan "has a new hush-hush mission—to supervise the United States Secret Service and ally it with the British Secret Service. . . . The American 'Mr. X,' as he is known privately, will report directly to the President."

But America's aid was too valuable and its Navy too involved in the Atlantic to be cast aside. Bletchley Park had no choice but to fulfill its promises. It sent a list of Enigma settings requested by OP20G to Washington in late May and early June 1941, as well as a copy of the bigram tables, which were vital to determining the indicators for setting up the machines.

---

* The relationship was still far from candid. The American visitors remained unaware that the British, so gracious in accepting their gifts, thought little of most of what they had been given, with the exception of Purple. And out of fear of providing the Americans with a bargaining chip, the British did not reveal their admiration for IBM, which they saw as a possible manufacturer of English-designed and English-controlled codebreaking technology.

† The British were guilty of their own leaks. During his visit, Currier had been "stopped by a roadblock in a small village, when the local constable saw two men in civilian clothes, obviously not British, riding in a War Department staff car." The constable "reacted quickly and asked if we would 'mind getting out and accompanying him to the police station.' This infuriated our diminutive Scottish driver who jumped out and confronted the policeman: 'Ye can nae do this, they're Americans on a secret mission.' "

Sharing Enigma research with the Americans was worrisome enough for the British. Sharing Ultra secrets seemed unthinkable. Even after the U.S. Navy had begun escorting merchant ships across the Atlantic in 1941 and its vessels were being hunted by German subs in an undeclared war, British leaders resisted the idea of sharing U-boat locations with the Americans. Britain had its own very stringent rules for using Ultra in its naval operations: if the information could not be covered up with a phony source, such as an airplane sighting, it could not be used at all. "C" wrote to Churchill in June 1941 with his fears about supplying Ultra information from U-boat intercepts.

> I find myself unable to devise any safe means of wrapping up the information in a manner which would not imperil this source. . . . [I]t [is] well-nigh impossible that the information could have been secured by an agent, and however much we insist that it came from a highly-placed source, I greatly doubt the enemy being for a moment deceived, should there be any indiscretion in the U.S.A. That this might occur cannot be ruled out, as the Americans are not in any sense as security minded as one would wish.

IN MID-1941, Agnes Driscoll and Laurance Safford were still convinced that they had found a way to break into the Enigma without the aid of a machine—by generating a huge paper catalog of the plain-cipher letter combinations it produced. Catalog attacks were a mainstay of codebreakers in the West because they were logical and obvious, even if labor intensive.*

---

* There were several types of catalogs, but all were limited in usefulness because they depended on prior knowledge of the inner workings of the encoding machines they attacked. The most typical catalog was a complete list of a machine's possible encryptions for a common word such as "Eins" ("one," in German). An analyst looked through the list to see what settings had produced his "Eins" crib. A more complex and statistical approach was to encrypt a common letter, such as I, at all settings of a known machine. Then an analyst tallied the frequencies of encrypted letters and compared that distribution to those in the catalog.

Driscoll's anti-Enigma catalog used another variation, the encryption of letter pairs. Unfortunately, catalogs ran to millions of entries. Driscoll's catalog for finding just the starting positions of the Enigma wheels filled a room twenty-four by thirty feet.

What Driscoll and Safford either didn't realize or resisted, despite the information brought back from England by Currier and Weeks five months earlier, was that they were dealing with a whole new breed of the Enigma that demanded a much more powerful attack and the aid of advanced machines. Driscoll's approach could get only a small part of the solution for the steckered three-wheel Enigma—that is, the starting positions of the code wheels—and only after the much tougher keys to the wheel order, steckers, and ring settings had been found.

It was Driscoll's dogged attachment to her catalog attack that proved her undoing. Indeed, Driscoll and her colleagues at OP20G were ignorant of their own ignorance about the challenges of the Enigma. Driscoll launched her effort assuming that the best German systems and enciphering machines would be little more complex than earlier commercial Enigmas. Driscoll's mistaken image of a simple electric code-wheel machine and her realization that the Navy could not steal or capture a machine or its supporting documents led her to a historic commitment: the American attack, she decided, would be based on approaches that needed little knowledge of German operational procedures and that would be as free as possible of a dependency on German procedural errors.

Typical of her work habits, "Miss Aggie" left no record of her anti-Enigma methods. And there are few references to her projects in late 1940 and 1941 in the histories and technical documents written by her associates. But it is clear that her goal, like Safford's, was to make the American attack independent of the British and of everything but intercepted messages. Just as important, the attack had to be "economical," since she and Safford did not anticipate the Navy providing them with expensive equipment or a large staff. Indeed, in the last months of 1940 and the first quarter of 1941, OP20G did not have the machinery or even a fraction of the personnel needed for a successful catalog attack against the Enigma. The only path left for her was a tried-and-true approach—and a dead end.

IN AUGUST 1941, five months after the American visit to Bletchley, Denniston traveled to America to cement relations with the codebreakers there, leading to his historic encounter with Driscoll. Denniston's aims in Washington were not only to smooth over the conflicts so far but to coordinate, appease, and control the Americans. His first step was to persuade Friedman at the Army's Signal Intelligence Service (SIS) that England had no Bombe to spare for them. But he also had to prevent Friedman from turning to IBM to build one of his own. His goal was to persuade Friedman that SIS had no need to venture beyond its research role in grappling with German Army and Air Force codes. England would tell SIS everything they needed to know about methods and would supply them with timely information as soon as the American Army had any real involvement in Europe. In a last-gasp tactic, Denniston was prepared to invite SIS to send some of its mathematicians to Bletchley so that they could feel they were part of the system and save face. But Denniston hoped that offer would not be necessary; the British continued to have deep fears about American security.

On the positive side, Denniston urged Friedman's group to concentrate its energies and, he thought, its vast technological resources on Japanese systems. But he was surprised and disappointed after he toured SIS headquarters to find it had few tabulators and none of the more advanced machines that Rosen had alluded to.

Still, Denniston got full compliance from the SIS. He came to consider SIS "our friends" who wanted to learn from—and be subordinate to—Bletchley's codebreakers. Denniston concluded that Friedman was the real force in American cryptanalysis, and the two became close friends. Friedman may have sealed the friendship by sending Denniston, an avid golfer, a package of golf balls, which were in short supply in England during the war. Denniston sent a heartfelt thank-you note, adding, "Believe me, no one loses a ball here these days. It may add an hour or so to the round, but *balls must be found!*"

DENNISTON FOUND QUITE a different reception at the Navy's OP20G headquarters, where he met with the leaders of the naval communications section. Denniston agreed to furnish more information on French and Italian systems, and he established procedures for secure communications with England. But a few days later, during an intense meeting with Safford, he probably admitted that the American Navy deserved more help with the German Enigma because its ships and sailors were virtually at war in the Atlantic. Even so, Denniston continued to press for affirmation of what he believed the Americans had promised: to do nothing more than research on European naval systems.

Always the gentleman, Denniston held his tongue when he learned that Currier and Weeks had given information about Bletchley's work to others at OP20G besides Safford, violating their handwritten agreement. For when Denniston met with Agnes Meyer Driscoll, it was clear that she had been privy to those secrets. She was probably using Britain's knowledge of the Enigma's wheel wiring by then, and she seemed informed of the Bombes and even Banburismus, he concluded.

But his biggest shock no doubt came when Driscoll told him that the American Navy didn't want a Bombe, didn't want to use it, and thought little of the other methods against Enigma that Turing had revealed.

Driscoll declared she had found a far better approach than the British—a special catalog method. With a bit more work, she said, it could become operational. It was, she claimed, much simpler, demanded less material than the Bletchley attacks, and would be better able to withstand changes in the Enigma systems. It would need only a few daily messages and very short, commonly worded cribs—not the hard-to-find ones the Bombe required. No revolutionary machinery would be needed. And her attack would be more effective in dealing with the problem of Enigma wheel turnovers after only a few letters were encrypted.

She showed Denniston, who by this point must have been appalled, a sample solution based on an eight-letter crib. She believed that, even with fewer than two dozen people using her soon-to-be completed catalog, messages could be solved within a few days. Those claims probably seemed outlandish to Denniston, given Britain's need for hundreds of people and very expensive machines to penetrate any Enigma system.

Denniston remained composed—a British gentleman to the

last—even though he must have felt insulted. And although his goal to keep the naval Enigma under British control was not endangered by Driscoll's method, he seemed threatened by her attitude. He was unable to dissuade Driscoll from pursuing her catalog attack.*

Regardless of how much detail he may have supplied, Denniston stressed that most catalog methods, when faced with a complex machine like the naval Enigma, could not solve enough of the machine's settings to work on their own. And he no doubt emphasized that the Bombe—despite its reliance on hard-to-find cribs, expensive methods such as Banburismus, and the exploitation of German procedural errors—was so far the only machine to have penetrated the Enigma on a timely basis.

But when he offered to provide more information about the Bombes and Turing's methods, Driscoll wasn't interested. He might have been willing to supply OP20G with a Bombe when one became available, but if so, Driscoll certainly wasn't requesting one.

"Miss Aggie" did bend a little. She admitted that she was somewhat "stumped" in her quest to fully understand the Enigma. (Denniston might have suppressed a smile at this point.) She had been unable to build a fully working Enigma from the paper analog and the other documents Currier and Weeks had brought from England. She voiced frustration over the double turnover of one of the Enigma code wheels, and she demanded clarification on how it and a number of other Enigma features worked.

Denniston also had to bend. He promised to send responses to all her questions and asked her to compose a list for him. He also promised to forward relevant codebooks and a working naval Enigma machine when one was available.

But when he invited Driscoll to come to England and to learn firsthand about British methods, as well as to inform Bletchley about hers, she turned him down cold. A visit was out of the question, she

---

* He may even have revealed that England had finally made the breakthroughs that were allowing relatively constant reading of the German naval systems. At the very least, he must have explained to her that Bletchley had explored the same letter-pair catalog approach years before as a full Enigma attack—and failed—before deciding to use it only as an aid to the Bombes and Banburismus.

said, because of her health. Yet she did not suggest that any of her crew take her place, nor did she invite a British expert to Washington to work directly with her.

The meeting seems to have concluded with Driscoll reaffirming her faith in her approach. She promised to inform Bletchley Park of the details of her superior method and, indeed, did send off her list of questions to Denniston. The list was very specific and did not reflect what Leigh Noyes later insisted was true: that OP20G had expected the British to supply everything about the Enigma, without specific requests.

Driscoll's list of questions only further reflected her hubris. It did not include anything about the Bombe and or any of the other British attacks. She was just after enough details about the Enigma and the German naval systems to allow her to advance her own attack. So, with a tiny staff of four, Driscoll pressed on with her catalog approach to Enigma.*

Driscoll's work continued to have Safford's full support. In late 1941, he approved her requests for more resources, although she had admitted that one of her attacks had failed. By the end of the year, her team had more than tripled, to fourteen people. Letter pairs were generated and punched on tabulator cards, using precious machine time and manpower, while Driscoll, thinking she needed an actual Enigma machine, awaited her copy from the British.

In mid-December 1941, Driscoll finally sent the British some information on her special method, with only cursory answers to the few questions Denniston had posed four months before. Driscoll again declared her faith in her approach, but GCCS concluded that it had "apparently failed." For one thing, it could not, as she had claimed, overcome the problem of turnover—that is, the tumbling of the Enigma's wheels before enough letters had been enciphered to identify the wheel being used. And as Turing pointed out to her in a letter in October 1941, her method would take seventy-two thousand

---

* She did not leave a helpful and detailed record of her special 1941 attack. She kept her crew at work on the catalog even after Turing sent her a long memo in October 1941 full of understated criticism of what he understood her method to be, along with a not-too-guarded demand for the details of her approach she had promised in August.

hours—more than eight years—to find a solution. Given Driscoll's obstinacy, Bletchley Park began to have second thoughts about providing more technical information.

As luck would have it, an apparent mix-up in the mail delivery between OP20G and Bletchley Park soon brought the simmering distrust and jealousies between the two agencies flaring to the surface. Denniston's early October dispatch—a bag of materials containing detailed answers to all but one of Driscoll's questions—never reached OP20G, the Navy claimed. It didn't take long for Safford, who feared the British were breaking their promises, to push Leigh Noyes into firing off a series of complaints to the British. Through November and December 1941, angry memos and accusations flew across the Atlantic. Noyes didn't mince his words: Britain had broken its promise to OP20G; America had no use for the Bombe; and if GCCS cooperated, Driscoll could have her method working on real problems.*

On December 5, Denniston telegraphed Captain Edward Hastings, the liaison for British intelligence in Washington: "I still cannot understand what Noyes wants and am disappointed at my apparent failure as far as the Navy Department is concerned. . . . About October 1st I sent out material, answers to Mrs. Driscoll's queries, technical details and a covering letter to Safford. Only one parcel has been acknowledged and there has been no reply to the questions in my letter. This may be one cause of this misunderstanding."

More puzzling still is why neither Driscoll nor Safford launched a search for the materials. Safford had received Denniston's cover letter, listing the contents of what had been sent to OP20G and asking for answers to three questions about Driscoll's method. She never responded.

---

* Denniston and his colleagues declared they had fulfilled all the agreements and were not holding back vital information. They fired back with accusations of their own: Driscoll had not responded as quickly as she had promised; she wasn't fully sharing her secrets; and the Americans had waited a month before telling them that Denniston's information on the Enigma had not been received.

On November 27, 1941, British captain Edward Hastings wrote Denniston from Washington, "There is grave unrest and dissatisfaction in free exchange of special intelligence. . . . Noyes is in a mood to withhold further information unless he receives full reciprocal information on European work."

Noyes, who was unaware of the complexities of the mail mix-up, continued to fire off angry memos to the British, some of them clearly threatening. The U.S. Navy, he said, had never agreed to confine itself to Enigma research. It had always intended to be "operational"— that is, intercepting and decoding messages on its own. He told Hastings that all the Navy wanted from the British was the information on the Enigma and the codebooks and Enigma machine that Safford and Driscoll had requested.

Then, belying later histories of GCCS and OP20G relations, Noyes apologized to the British, twice. On December 10 and again on the twelfth, he declared that British explanations and actions since his outbursts had satisfied him and "everyone" at OP20G. The missing package, of course, was found. On December 13, Bletchley received a cryptic yet pointed message from someone in the U.S. Navy Department: "Luke Chapter 15, v 9: And she found it. She calleth together her friends and neighbours saying: Rejoice with me for I have found the piece which we lost."

Noyes's repentance did not mean all was well between the two crypto agencies, nor that Driscoll had abandoned her stubborn cause. Tensions continued as the Navy once again requested a copy of the Enigma machine. And the Americans and the British drifted even further apart in early 1942 as both OP20G and GCCS dealt with their own internal shake-ups.

That changed in mid-1942, however, when the bureaucratic upheaval settled and new leadership under Joseph Wenger took control at OP20G, in part because President Roosevelt insisted on forging closer ties with the British. The Americans admitted to themselves that Driscoll's catalog would not find all the Enigma settings needed to read messages. Her technique eventually found an important niche in OP20G's codebreaking operations, but it proved useful only after the harder work had been done by the Bombes.

DRISCOLL'S REFUSAL OF British help was one of the biggest Allied intelligence mistakes of World War II—second perhaps only to the British refusal to believe for several years, until mid-1943, that the

Germans were reading their convoy Cypher Number 3, which Safford had repeatedly criticized as a "third-rate communications system" endangering Allied ships in the Atlantic. And yet Driscoll cannot carry the blame alone: the roots of the error were deep in the soil of America's intelligence history.

With its attention before the war focused on the threat from Japan, the United States had been late in realizing the importance of the European theater and even tardier in recognizing the importance of attacking the German encryption machines.

But if "Miss Aggie" had possessed a more open attitude and perhaps a little less self-confidence, the outcome of Denniston's visit could have been quite different, and the Americans could have saved at least six months in the search for their own Bombe—six months that would have been crucial in turning the Battle of the Atlantic in the Allies' favor sooner.

Denniston left Washington for England in August 1941 with deep concerns about OP20G and its leadership. He concluded that Driscoll was America's version of Bletchley's Dillwyn Knox, the crusty old English codebreaker (and Greek scholar by training) who had no use for technology or mathematicians.

At least some of the Navy's radio-intelligence officers would have agreed with Denniston. Long before they could gain control of OP20G, Joseph Wenger and his mentor, Admiral Stanford Caldwell Hooper, had been trying to move the Navy into a new era of automated codebreaking and advanced mathematical approaches. On the day Driscoll turned down Britain's experience with its Bombes, the new guard was poised to drag American cryptanalysis into the electronic age.

4

Toward an American Bletchley Park

November 3, 1941—Washington, D.C.

THE MEETING AT OP20G that day must have begun uneasily, perhaps even more so than Alastair Denniston's encounter with Agnes Driscoll two and a half months before. The group of three young engineering graduate students, recruited from MIT, came to offer their expertise to Driscoll, the Navy's top cryptanalyst, and her supervisor at OP20G, Laurance Safford. The MIT students, viewed by the Navy as prestigious academics, didn't object when Safford introduced each of them as "doctor" or "professor." And Driscoll, who had spurned Denniston's earlier offer of help, likely had a more open mind after months of grappling in the dark with the Enigma.

Here was a face-to-face encounter between two generations of codebreakers. The emerging engineering and math experts who placed their faith in automation and electronics were reaching out to the old guard, who believed there was no viable substitute for brainpower, the traditional techniques of pencil and paper, and a good dose of luck. While Driscoll and Safford knew and sometimes even used the newer statistical techniques, such as the Index of Coincidence, their years of experience taught them that cracking a code or cipher usually depended on the lightning strike of human intuition or some unpredictable entry into the system—the theft or capture of machines and instruction books, for example, or an enemy slipup, such as transmitting the same message in plain and cipher texts.

The MIT students spent the day at OP20G's offices on Constitution Avenue delivering the same message to anyone who would listen: tell us what you need to do your jobs better and faster, and we can build the machines to help you. (Driscoll and Safford must have wondered if the hands reaching out to help weren't also intent on dislodging them.) The new guard and its sponsors—most notably Stanford Hooper and Joseph Wenger—believed that the demands of cryptanalysis had changed forever. The latest wave of electromechanical ciphering devices, such as the Enigma, were forcing codebreakers to become mathematicians, statisticians, and engineers—not just linguists with a bent for puzzle solving. Without machines of their own, they believed that cryptanalysts would have to perform seemingly impossible feats of calculation to penetrate the new machine-enciphered messages. The only hope, the new guard felt, lay in the potential of high-speed calculators and the emerging use of photoelectric sensors and microfilm to detect patterns of text.

The three MIT students—John Howard, Lawrence Steinhardt, and John Coombs, all in their twenties—went on to form a key part of OP20G's new M section, a math research group established in 1942 that eventually included eighteen mostly engineering and math types who were given a broad mandate to do scientific research for OP20G. Much like the young British mathematicians who were then working wonders at Bletchley Park, the new guard at OP20G had been trained at MIT and other prestigious universities in the country. It included Yale graduates Howard Engstrom, Marshall Hall, and James Wakelin; Harvard graduates Willard Quine and Andrew Gleason; Columbia's James Pendergrass; and Princeton's Donald Menzel. Although East Coast schools dominated the roster, the group also included Al Clifford from Cal Tech, and graduates garnered from some of the top midwestern universities, including Michigan (Charles B. Tompkins), Illinois (Louis Tordella), and Northwestern (Howard Campaigne).

. . .

HOOPER, WENGER, AND even Safford had done all they could to recruit such men in the 1930s. They had scoured the university
ROTCs, set up faculty scouts in math departments, and persuaded as
many college men as possible to take OP20G's cryptologic course by
mail. At least six of the eighteen recruits had entered the Navy
through ROTC and reserve training or by taking the correspondence
courses.

Though criticized by the British for being largely inexperienced in
codebreaking, the men in the M section had backgrounds that in
many ways mirrored that of Bletchley's driving force, Alan Turing:
they were young, creative, and fascinated by numbers. The youngest
of M's college recruits was twenty-year-old Gleason; the old-timer of
the bunch was its leader, thirty-nine-year-old Captain Howard T. Engstrom.

Engstrom had the perfect credentials for leading M, although it
hadn't been an easy climb for the first-generation Bostonian. Born of
a Swedish-immigrant fisherman and a Finnish nanny, Engstrom was
only ten when his father died. His mother took in laundry in order to
keep her talented boy in high school. According to his daughter, Engstrom never forgot his sense of shame as he transported home his
teachers' dirty clothes from school each afternoon and brought them
back clean the next morning.

Engstrom climbed into the top academic echelons through hard
work and smarts. He was only twenty when in 1922 he earned his undergraduate degree in chemical engineering from Northeastern University, the old YMCA college intended to educate boys from poorer
families. He spent several years at Western Electric, acquiring a practical background in communications. After getting his master's degree from the University of Maine in 1925, he was accepted at Yale,
where he earned his doctorate in mathematics, and then at Cal Tech,
where he was one of the National Research Council Fellows.

Fluent in at least four languages, including German, Engstrom
was admitted to the most prestigious mathematical center in the

world, Göttingen, where he found himself among the great figures of twentieth-century mathematics and physics, spending his days in lectures and cutting-edge tutorials and his nights in *Ratskellers* and *Biergartens*. He had returned to Yale as a junior mathematics professor when he joined the Naval Reserve and began taking OP20G's correspondence course.

Another of the more senior members of the new guard—and one of the few with a Navy background—was thirty-four-year-old Robert Beelville Ely III. Ely had found his way into the Ivy League by way of ability as much as wealth. His father, Robert E. Ely II, was a successful dye merchant who had sent his son to prep school, Penn Charter in Philadelphia, and then off to Princeton. There Ely had taken honors in mathematics while compiling a record of extracurricular achievements worthy of fictional Ivy League hero Frank Merriwell. Athletic, handsome, and well-spoken, Ely was on the crew and debating teams all four years at Princeton and was twice named class orator.

Perhaps because of his strength as a speaker, he turned from math after his undergraduate years to the study of law, and after taking his law degree from the University of Pennsylvania he founded an organization to serve young up-and-comers like himself: the Philadelphia Junior Bar Association. Ely entered the Naval Reserve in 1933 by way of the supply corps but soon grew discontented with such mundane matters as writing procurement contracts. He, too, signed up for OP20G's correspondence course and qualified for a transfer there, where his abilities in math landed him in the M section.

Not present at that November 3 meeting but certainly there in spirit was Joseph Wenger, who had been assigned to the Office of Naval Communications in July 1941, after a tour of sea duty. Perhaps more than anyone else in Navy communications intelligence at the time, Wenger was determined to crystallize OP20G around the new scientific types. He and Stanford Hooper had to fight a near constant battle from the early 1930s through the 1950s to gain the support they needed to bring naval communications into the electronic age.

Hooper had been the first to create a Navy section in advanced code and signal research in the 1930s. He soon entrusted it to

Wenger, then a thirty-year-old Annapolis graduate and one of Agnes Driscoll's first students at OP20G. Wenger also had practical experience as a seagoing communications officer, having served on the cruisers *Pittsburgh* and *Milwaukee*. He became the driving force behind what by the late 1940s would become the world's most technically advanced codebreaking agency.

Born in 1901 in the bayou country of Patterson, Louisiana, Wenger had the mind of a scientist but the soul of an artist, according to his son, Jeffrey. When Joseph Wenger was four, his father—a Swiss immigrant with a doctorate in philosophy—moved the family to Washington, D.C., to take a job as an economic analyst with the State Department. It was in those early years in Washington, as well as the summers on his mother's family plantation in Louisiana, that Wenger developed his talent for painting and sketching. But by the time he was seventeen, Wenger's more practical side took over: he realized that art would be a risky way to make a living and opted instead to apply to the U.S. Naval Academy, where he could get a free college education. Even at Annapolis, Wenger appeared to suffer second thoughts about his career choice: a haunting 1922 self-portrait in academy uniform shows a wary, serious young man with penetrating brown eyes.

Quiet and reserved, Wenger frowned on smoking, never swore or lost his temper, and never took a drink until he suffered a nervous breakdown in the fall of 1943, following the worst of OP20G's wartime struggle, and only then occasionally imbibed in alcohol per his doctor's orders. To a man, those who worked in the Navy with Wenger during and after the war say they never saw him laugh or joke. "He was all business—a very dedicated man—and he had his mind on his work," said George M. Robb, who worked under Wenger at the Naval Security Annex in Washington after the war. Joe Eachus, a member of the M section, concurred that Wenger appeared to be utterly humorless but that his grasp of codebreaking techniques and the latest communications technologies "made everybody he commanded respect him."

Those who met Wenger rarely forgot him. He was six feet tall and exceedingly thin, with hawklike, studious features, which explains why his nicknames at Annapolis included "Skinny" and "Buzzard." Stomach problems that plagued him most of his adult life later gave him a frail, hollow-cheeked appearance that made him seem taller than he actually was.

Following graduation from Annapolis in 1923, Wenger began his Navy career in the Bureau of Ordnance but by 1929 had found his way into communications intelligence and the tutelage of both Agnes Driscoll and Hooper, who became his lifelong mentor. Wenger was hospitalized for his stomach problem in 1934, but by 1935 he had bounced back and was made head of OP20G's new research desk, called Y. The new section, also created at Hooper's urging, was devoted to the application of science to cryptanalysis. But Wenger was soon rotated out to sea again, from 1938 to 1941, and the Y section languished without him, leaving OP20G's commander, Laurance Safford, to do it all. The Navy's rotation policy, which dictated a tour at sea every few years for its officers, was a source of practical experience for men like Wenger, but it was clearly a hindrance to advanced research and other Navy programs that demanded specialized personnel.

The chain of influence from Hooper to Wenger and, later, to Engstrom ultimately led back to one of the most respected and controversial scientific figures in America at the time, MIT's Vannevar Bush. Bush was not only one of the nation's outstanding academic engineers but one of the most powerful scientist-politicians in the nation's history—a mover and shaker in the rise of government-driven Big Science before and after World War II. Bush believed in close ties between the military and research engineers, as long as the engineers were given enough money and freedom from bureaucracy to accomplish their best work. As the first man to conceive the idea of a desktop personal computer (though he was far from designing a successful working one), Bush launched a decades-long quest to build an information machine that would aid both scientists and codebreakers.

In 1931, Bush and his students at MIT achieved national and international fame by building the world's largest and most powerful calculating machine—a room full of gears and rods and shafts and motors that took mechanical analog computing to its limits but looked as though it were inspired by Rube Goldberg. Bush called it a differential analyzer, but the popular press was quick to dub the sprawling device a "giant brain." Although international visitors flocked to MIT and clones of the analyzer were built in Europe and America—including one by General Electric and another at the U.S. Army's Aberdeen Proving Ground—the invention didn't bring in the flood of money that Bush had expected for MIT.

The analyzer also overshadowed other projects at MIT, ones with far greater potential for the future of calculation because they were based on electronics and photoelectricity—technologies that promised to deliver results at close to the speed of light. To support his students and to continue his research, Bush began a search for ways to raise funds. Over the years, he refined his grantsmanship skills to a high art, wedding the hottest technologies of the time to the desires of funding agencies. To provide resources and jobs for his "boys" at MIT, he also developed a network of contacts among the executives of the nation's leading companies, including NCR.

Bush's connection to the Navy went back to World War I, when he was recruited to its New London, Connecticut, research laboratory to work on new devices for detecting German U-boats. (Hooper, too, had worked on the U-boat problem during World War I, but there is no evidence the two men ever met.) Bush never forgot his experience in New London, nor the fact that the Navy ignored most of his research group's advice. As a result, he developed an intense dislike of bureaucracies.

In 1935, as Hooper and Wenger scoured the country looking for technical advice on how to update Navy communications and intelligence gathering, one of their first stops was MIT, where Bush was now regarded as perhaps the top academic engineer in the nation. Bush, Wenger, and Hooper joined forces at a time when their interests seemed in perfect harmony. Bush needed funding, Wenger needed technical assistance, and Hooper needed someone of Bush's reputation to pry open the Navy coffers.

Hooper and Wenger described to Bush the latest cryptanalytic methods and challenges. Bush already knew the limitations of electromechanical tabulating, and he had begun to think of less cumbersome alternatives. Tabulating machines of the day used stacks of cards with holes punched in them to represent numbers or letters. Tabulators pulled individual cards past a reading station, where electrified metal brushes "sensed" the holes in the cards by making contact and generating electrical pulses. The pulses were then tallied by counters. While small banks of relays were later added to the tabulators to make them more efficient at counting, the mechanics of moving and stacking cards always limited the speeds of the machines.

On little more than a gentlemen's agreement in 1935, Bush began to draft a plan for the Navy, with the promise that he would be paid ten thousand dollars in consulting fees—four times what a senior engineer hoped to earn at NCR in the late 1930s. Bush dashed off his report and submitted it in the first weeks of 1936. In it, he sketched the general outlines of a series of high-speed, optical-electronic devices that would be hundreds of times more powerful than IBM's tabulators. How Bush had arrived at his plan so quickly was no mystery: he and his colleagues at MIT had begun thinking of ways to exploit the combination of electronics, optics, and film well before 1935.

Bush had long been convinced that the technology was in place for developing marvelous new machines that could instantly calculate numbers, store and retrieve business records, or count letter frequencies in codes. A photoelectric sensor combined with digital circuitry could search long spools of microfilm for specific words or patterns. As an easily reproducible and compact storage medium, microfilm already had captured the scientific imaginations of the day. At the 1925 International Congress of Photography, Emanuel Goldberg, a Russian-born inventor and industrialist, dazzled the scientific community with a grainless microfilm that could store the entire text of the Bible fifty times over on one square inch of film. But the problem for Bush, and those who followed him on his technological quest, was finding a workable way to search and tally the "hits" in such minuscule print.

That was still the primary technical challenge in 1936 when Bush recommended that the Navy design and develop what became known in the intelligence community as rapid analytical machines (RAMs). But Wenger and Hooper, for all their enthusiasm for the project, ran headlong into a Navy bureaucracy that didn't cotton to "college professors" who asked exorbitant fees for fancy, abstract ideas.

Although Hooper did eventually land a Navy contract for MIT in 1936, Bush turned his attention to other projects and another source of funding—the nation's corporations. Again, timing and chance shaped the history of the U.S. Bombe project: just as Bush was beginning his search for more donors, an old and influential friend of MIT returned as the operating head of NCR—Colonel Edward A. Deeds. The friendship between Bush, Deeds, and Charles "Boss" Kettering, the engineer who had come to replace Edison and Ford as the guru of American industrial science, was to link the futures of NCR, MIT, and the Ultra secret.

Deeds and Kettering were both hardworking farmboys from central Ohio who had seen education as a way to escape life behind the plow. A graduate of Denison University, Deeds began his career as a construction engineer at NCR, progressed to product development, and soon recruited Kettering, a star engineering student at Ohio State, to help him finish the job of electrifying the company's line of cash registers. Deeds and Kettering saved NCR's dominance of the world market against an onslaught of competitors in the early 1900s. Realizing how well they worked together, the two men decided to join forces on their own. In Deeds's small, two-story barn behind his house on Central Avenue in Dayton, they invented the modern automobile electrical system—both the ignition and the self-starter—and put an end to the back- and arm-breaking business of cranking a car engine. They founded Delco (short for Dayton Electric Company), then sold it to General Motors and quickly became rich from the growth of the automotive giant.

Ohio, particularly Dayton, was a hotbed for inventors and entrepreneurs at the beginning of the century, boasting the Wright brothers in aviation, John H. Patterson and NCR in business machines, Charles Goodrich in rubber goods, and Deeds and Kettering in automotive and electrical engineering. The largely agrarian state of Ohio, unfettered by outdated factories and mills, had been transformed into one of the nation's leading manufacturing areas by the Union Army's nearly insatiable demand for weapons and supplies during the Civil War. By the end of the century, notes historian George W. Knepper, the state "led the way in nearly every new growth industry—automobiles, aircraft, electrical equipment, business machines and scores of others—even as it remained an important farming state."

Deeds and Kettering were familiar with the workings of the military from their development of the water-cooled Liberty engine, which they designed and manufactured in a crash program for the U.S. Army and its allies during World War I; it was considered America's greatest technological contribution to that war. Their newly formed Dayton-Wright Company turned out more than four thousand Allied planes using the Liberty engine. As a member of the Aircraft Production Board, Deeds had divested himself of any financial interest in the company, but his guidance of the fifty-million-dollar program led to accusations—and a federal investigation—of profiteering. Although Deeds was later exonerated, the humiliation of that experience made him wary of ever signing another government contract in which he, or one of his companies, might make a profit.

Deeds went on to be a major force in the creation of the American airline and machine-tool industries and eventually a kingmaker in American corporate finance. Kettering, who disdained business affairs and did many a job on a handshake, continued to tackle technical challenges, inventing ethyl alcohol to solve the problem of engine knock and, with much foresight, a more efficient diesel engine that he thought would help prevent depletion of the world's oil reserves. Kettering also conducted some of the earliest secret experiments with rocket-guidance systems, designing a flying bomb called the Kettering Bug, a technology that was to resurface with devastating effect in World War II as the German V-1 "buzz bomb."

In a classic example of what sociologist C. Wright Mills later described as the inner workings of the "power elite," Bush first made contact with Deeds when the two men served on advisory committees that steered American aeronautical research. Deeds, in turn, introduced Bush to Kettering. Beyond an interest in planes and rockets, the three men also shared a faith in the use of technology to solve

America's problems, including the Great Depression and the massive unemployment of the day. And, like the Navy's Hooper, the trio wanted to modernize the American military.

When Deeds accepted the NCR presidency in 1936 with a mandate to reinvigorate the company, Bush became the company's unofficial technical adviser, pointing NCR's long-term research toward the emerging field of electronics. By early 1937, after the Navy had at last signed off on Bush's proposal for the RAM project, Bush had persuaded Deeds to donate a token but regular amount to MIT and to send a team of NCR engineers to learn from his work on electronics and microfilm.

The chain from Deeds to Hooper to Bush found its next link in Joe Desch. Deeds had asked for Bush's help in staffing NCR's new electronics-research laboratory in 1938, but for whatever reason, Bush didn't send any of his "boys" to Dayton.

NCR's research director, Harry M. Williams, decided to look for talent locally, where there was an abundance of experienced, practical engineers who could balance the more abstract influence of MIT. Desch had already proved at General Motors' radio research division and at Frigidaire that he was especially good at turning ideas into workable products. His experience included work on a radio-teletype system that could link electric typewriters, a device that later drew the interest of the Navy and IBM.

Beginning in 1938, Desch and his few assistants taught themselves about the latest electronic developments and soon became as skilled and knowledgeable as the MIT men. Frequently, Desch, not his advisers at MIT, was first to arrive at new discoveries and to build working machines. In fact, Desch beat MIT to the creation of an electronic digital calculator in 1940, albeit partly because Bush's men were too busy with other projects. The size of a dishwasher and mounted on casters, the NCR calculator marked a milestone in digital electronics. Independent of MIT's related work, Desch's staff also explored the use of microfilm, high-speed printers, magnetic digital recording, and fast-pulsing miniature tubes for counting and tracking. It was in this last area that Desch soon gained a national reputation as an innovator.

Then, just as Desch's work was leading to the development of new products and the promise of a healthier profit margin for NCR, war broke out and Deeds's patriotism ended the company's commercial quests. It wasn't long before Bush's National Defense Research Committee, aware of Desch's expertise in electronics and manufacturing, came knocking on his door in Building 10 at NCR. Powerful and persuasive, the NDRC answered only to the president of the United States.

WHILE DESCH WAS leading NCR into the electronic age, the embryonic new guard at OP20G was struggling to do the same for the Navy. Their first RAM, called the Comparator, drew its power from the Index of Coincidence and the laws of probability, not from the kind of Enigma-mimicking logic the Poles and British were engineering into the early Bombes. It could therefore attack, at least theoretically, any kind of cipher system.

The IC method also could be computed with electromechanical machines, such as a punched-card tabulator. But even with the IBM machines, the process was very slow and labor-intensive; a long message could take days to analyze. Bush insisted he could produce a high-speed machine 150 times faster than the IBM tabulators. He hoped, in the long run, for machines that did at least fifty thousand letter comparisons per minute—and perhaps as many as two hundred thousand. Either punched tape or microfilm would allow the condensing and overlapping of text. Optical sensing devices, such as photocells, would register the matches, and, finally, electronic tubes would tally the results.*

But the theory was far more elegant than the practicalities. Over the next five years, from 1938 through 1943, Bush's MIT students,

---

* In the first version of the Bush design, two strips of punched tape were overlapped and run past each other at very high speeds. The two tapes were shifted ("stepped") one letter at a time until all possible matches of text had been searched. Wherever the text in the two messages lined up, focused light would penetrate the punched holes and their energy would be registered by the photocells. Electronic tubes would then track the number and locations of the light pulses. The logic of the machine was similar to Turing's Banburismus, but both methods were developed independently.

Navy scientists, and finally the best factory engineers in America struggled to make Bush's idea work, and none would produce a reliable machine.*

THE YOUNG MEN from MIT came to that November 3, 1941, meeting no doubt expecting that the RAMs and the pressing need for new technologies to attack Japanese codes and ciphers would dominate the agenda. After all, the Navy had been preparing itself for years to wage an inevitable war against the Japanese in the Pacific. But much of the discussion that day dealt with the "special problems," as they were called at the meeting, faced by Agnes Driscoll and her Enigma team. Perhaps because the young engineers did not have proper security clearances at the time, the term "Enigma" was never brought up.

By this time, Driscoll had been struggling long enough with the German naval code, with so few results, that she humbled herself to seek the help of junior engineers. She may have asked John Howard to explore ways to automate the entries in her catalog and to speed up the search through its millions of records.

But Safford and the other leaders at OP20G failed to follow through on her request. Some two weeks after the meeting in Washington, Howard was sent some additional information on Driscoll's problem but, at the same time, was told it was not of great importance. "Miss Aggie," in essence, had been blown off by her own superiors, a clear sign that she was on her way to being labeled a has-been.

Yet if Joseph Wenger, who was posted in another section of Navy intelligence at the time and absent from OP20G's line of command,

---

* Three separate attempts were made to design and develop a RAM Comparator for codebreakers, using a variety of punched tapes and microfilm. And even though the electronic tubes for counting matches remained slow, bulky, and temperamental beasts as late as 1940, they turned out to be the least of the problems for the machine's design. The biggest and most resistant obstacles were mechanical: the overlapping tapes and their punched holes could not be aligned precisely and reliably enough at high speed to permit accurate reading of their matches. The tapes had to be aligned within one thousandth of an inch. Analyzing a thousand-letter message required a million passes by the reading head, through one thousand different steppings of tape, each time with the tapes in perfect alignment.

had heard about the downgrading of Driscoll's request, he would have been disappointed if not angry. Wenger still believed a statistical and machine-driven attack against the Enigma was the only answer to the German military's constant upgrades of their machines and the intelligence blackouts that often occurred at the most critical moments.

Wenger's belief was based on painful experience, not just theory. As an intelligence staff officer and former ship commander, Wenger had seen Japan suddenly change its code systems, time and again, and then watched in frustration as Navy cryptanalysts took years to reconstruct the new codebooks.

THE MORNING OF December 7, 1941, changed everything.

Finger-pointing immediately followed the Japanese surprise attack. Safford was the crypto officer who took the brunt of the blame. In early 1942, Safford and eventually Driscoll were pushed aside, making room for Wenger and the germ of the emerging M section.

As the new operational head of OP20G, Wenger acted quickly and decisively. He formed a new American Enigma team—with Robert Ely in charge—to explore alternatives to Driscoll's method. Then, a few months later, he pulled Howard Engstrom from his assignment in OP20G's radio wave–studies section and asked him to organize the M section. Engstrom's orders were to mold the disparate collection of mathematicians and engineers into a working team whose goal was to develop new mathematical methods for codebreaking. The team's more immediate task was to launch the Navy's own RAM program, independent of Bush and the NDRC.

Although it seemed that Hooper's and Wenger's dream of giving science, research, and advanced technology a home in OP20G had come true, the times still were not right. The pressures of war did not permit the kind of experimentation and abstract research needed for truly creative approaches. As M was being launched, the Atlantic became a nightmare for U.S. merchant vessels. Those working under Engstrom were instructed to devote their talents to the quickest possible solutions for cracking the four-rotor Enigma, not long-term innovation. Ely's quest for a unique Enigma attack quickly became one based on M's still incomplete knowledge of the British Bombe. And quite soon M's engineers were forced to retreat from Bush's visions of a general-purpose codebreaking machine and to concentrate on the simplest possible devices to help the Allies' hard-pressed cryptanalysts.

In early 1942, Hitler unleashed his U-boats against America, and dozens of freighters were torpedoed in sight of its coastal cities, where residents at times could watch the flaming horror. Within a few weeks, the Führer's Operation Drumbeat did more damage to American ships than the Japanese had done at Pearl Harbor. More ominous still for the Allies, the U-boats were sinking the supply ships in Atlantic convoys at a pace that threatened the survival of Britain.

Wenger asked Engstrom's young and relatively inexperienced group to become the core of the Navy's attack against the U-boat codes and ciphers. To augment M with more experienced engineers, Wenger took the RAM program away from Bush and the NDRC and brought aboard the MIT team—Howard, Coombs, and Steinhardt—as the first of M's engineering adjuncts. The search for more engineers continued, and by the end of 1942 OP20G had recruited many of the leading men in computer electronics, including Joe Desch. Very soon, it was clear that OP20G had become dependent on the nation's industrial might—machines, ones quickly produced and therefore less ambitious in design, were needed in a hurry to replace the old hand methods.

On top of the U-boat pigeon shoot in the Atlantic, there was also the fear that bombing or sabotage might destroy Bletchley's makeshift and very vulnerable facilities.

Thus, in the spring of 1942, the American Navy was ordered to start forging its own Enigma-cracking capability, whether the British liked it or not.

Britain again rushed a group of its intelligence leaders to the States in March to protect its Ultra monopoly. By then, Denniston had stepped down as head of Bletchley Park. Its new commander was Edward Travis, a no-nonsense manager with a bulldog visage who was even less willing to share British technical secrets. The British again assured OP20G that Shark would be beaten, and they agreed to share more Enigma information. But in exchange, they reiterated their demand that the Americans concentrate on the Japanese problems and let Britain manage European intelligence. The British promised the Navy that it would soon create a new Bombe and insisted that the Americans would not have to design their own. They pleaded with OP20G to refrain from launching any crash programs that might lead the Germans to alter their code systems. Britain soon agreed to host a new team of experts from OP20G at Bletchley Park. They were to be shown and told all.

Yet OP20G doubted the British would ever devote enough resources to the Atlantic U-boat Enigma, grappling as they were with German Air Force and Army codes as well. And while the American Navy was under fire at home, the Army's codebreakers resented having to rely on Bletchley Park, especially with U.S. troops about to take part in the Allied invasion of North Africa.

In a memo to his supervisors in April 1942, Robert Ely outlined the need for the Navy's Bombe and its basic design—an all-new, all-electronic machine, without spinning wheels. But Ely's OP20G memo also revealed the Navy's still very incomplete picture of the Enigma, Shark, and the British Bombe. America's experts were able to outline the workings of only the older three-wheel plugboard versions of the Enigma, and they seemed uncertain about the workings of the reflector. Furthermore, the memo contained only the broadest generalities about the British Bombe's logic, and yet it asked a great deal of OP20G's engineers: produce a single, ultrafast electronic marvel that would outdo all the British machines.

Starting in April 1942, the new guard wasted its first six months of Bombe development asking the British for many of the same technical details that had been offered to Driscoll. By May 1942, the Americans still had not adopted key parts of the British Bombe logic—including the cold-point test and the two-way flow of current in the Turing design. OP20G wouldn't even realize the full power of the Diagonal Board until July, when its inventor, Gordon Welchman, explained to American visitors at Bletchley Park how his device could reduce the number of false hits by 60 percent.

Yet the British can't carry the blame alone for the delay in the American Bombe program. Even as late as mid-1942, the Americans were saying they didn't need a copy of the British Bombe, just diagrams of Bletchley's latest machines. They were acting as if they had their own Bletchley Park. Through the spring and early summer, the OP20G engineers continued to explore the possibilities of a high-speed electronic machine—hoping for breakthroughs in technology and counting on advice from the more experienced British. They eventually did receive the needed assistance from Bletchley, learning more about Britain's cryptanalytic methods and how to avoid testing all the Enigma-wheel combinations.

But the Americans didn't want to depend on the British for the captured Enigma wheels, codebooks, and cribs to make their own Bombe method work. OP20G urged its engineers to design and build several powerful new machines that could make statistical and catalog attacks practical, without the need for crutches. The Navy still hoped to attack Shark with Wenger's old dream of pure analysis.

At the start of the summer of 1942, Bletchley Park hinted it had found a solution to M4 Shark. But as the summer wore on, the Navy tired of waiting for the British four-wheel Bombe to work and began laying the groundwork for their own Bombe project. By August, the Americans were determined to tackle the problem themselves—alone if they had to. OP20G informed the British that month it was going to build its own Bombe, and within several weeks it hastily announced that its men had beaten Britain and C. E. Wynn-Williams to the design of a fully electronic Bombe with a two-way electronic wheel.

The apparent design breakthrough was aimed at the Enigma challenge alone, not at creating a general purpose codebreaking machine. The project quickly took shape: Wenger was given all the money and staff he desired plus freedom from the traditional oversight and meddling by the U.S. Navy's Bureau of Ships. NCR's electrical-research laboratory, headed by Joe Desch, was taken over by OP20G to be a research center and possibly a production site for the machine.

Months before, Desch and his men at NCR had been screened for security, and began to move their laboratory from the Building 10 headquarters on Main Street to the old night school in Building 26, where they would be separate and secure from the rest of the NCR campus. In the midst of a late November snowstorm, Desch and his staff carefully stacked crate after crate of their delicate equipment onto the back of a flatbed truck. They stayed there with their load as it was driven at a crawl down three blocks of slippery streets to Building 26. Later, Marine guards with riot shotguns and submachine guns were dispatched to Dayton. A call went out to naval personnel to recruit the best electronic engineers, whether or not they were in the Navy, and Desch was ordered to expand his seventeen-man civilian staff. The M section was reorganized to oversee the electronic Bombe work at NCR. Then, in early July 1942, the Navy approved an open-ended contract that could provide, if needed, millions of dollars for the project.

Now the pressure was on at OP20G, and not just because of what was happening in the Atlantic. The Pacific was still a disaster, even though the victory at Midway in early June signaled a turning of fortunes. That victory was something of an embarrassment for Wenger and those in OP20G who had fought so long for centralized operations and expensive machines. The turning back of the Japanese fleet was in large part due to the Navy's long-awaited reentry into the Japanese naval-operations code, JN-25. But it was a "mustang" officer, Joseph Rochefort—an ex–enlisted man and Dayton native commanding OP20G's tiny outpost in Hawaii—whose unit had stripped off the JN-25 additives and translated the exposed code groups, enabling the Navy to understand key parts of Admiral Yamamoto's impending attack in the Pacific. Worse for OP20G, the Hawaiian outpost did so with only a handful of tabulators and sorters run by Navy bandmembers from the USS *California*, who had little else to do since their ship had been sunk during the attack on Pearl Harbor.

The codebreakers learned that Yamamoto was out to repeat his stunning success at Pearl Harbor by concentrating his best ships, including his aircraft carriers, for a final knockout blow against the American Navy. Rochefort's group was fairly certain that the letters AF in Yamamoto's directive stood for the coordinates of Midway Island, but OP20G's Washington analysts insisted it was the Aleutians.

Rochefort devised a clever test: he had the Navy installation on Midway Island broadcast a message that its desalinators were no longer working and that its supply of freshwater was dwindling. Sure enough, within a day or two the Japanese broadcast their own message that AF was nearly out of freshwater. Admiral Chester Nimitz quickly devised a plan to ambush the Japanese at Midway, and Yamamoto's fleet steamed into a fatal trap.

Rochefort's correct analysis was a blow to OP20G's grand schemes for scientific cryptanalysis. Wenger, Engstrom, and their college men had to show results in the Atlantic if the M section was to survive. But they would soon learn the same hard lessons in humility that Shark had taught the British. The ambitious path they had chosen was to prove much longer and more tortuous than any of them could have imagined.

5

A Giant Leap . . .
and a Step Backward

Summer–Fall 1942—Dayton, Ohio

FOR WEEKS IN July and August, sweltering in temperatures that hovered near ninety that summer, Joe Desch pored over plans for what promised to be a remarkable new codebreaking machine, developed by the Navy's M section of mathematicians and engineers. Even though he had overseen thirteen other military projects at NCR, this, he knew, would be his ultimate challenge: a totally electronic deciphering machine at least one hundred times faster than anything in use. The Navy design might well rely on tens of thousands of the miniature, fast-pulsing tubes Desch himself had invented, pushed to the limits of their capabilities.

Perhaps no man in America knew those limits so well as Desch. Prior to the war, in his laboratory on the third floor of NCR's Building 10, he had created the fastest miniature thyratron tubes of his day. He himself had blown and shaped the tiny bulbs around their delicate cathode wires. The nickel wires first had to be superheated to fifteen hundred degrees in a quartz chamber filled with hydrogen. With the flammable gas leaking from the chamber, "you had to light both ends [of the furnace] exactly right or you had an explosion," recalled Jack Kern, a former NCR engineer who had worked under Desch. "That was the fun part of the day."

The tube assemblies, each about two inches long, were baked again at five hundred degrees to drive all the residual gases out of the glass. Each tube was then injected with a prescribed amount of argon. The inert gas conducted electricity at a very specific threshold of energy, with no partial state in between. Hence, the sealed tubes were ideal "on-off" switches that could be used for counting infinitesimal pulses of electricity—more than one million per second. Desch's tubes had been the first to reach such speeds, in a counter he had designed for the Army's Aberdeen Proving Ground, for precisely timing the flights of cannon shells.

Desch's lab had become a technology showplace for NCR, drawing visitors from all over the world. Edward A. Deeds and Charles F. Kettering often stopped by to check on their pet projects. So did the dean of the Dayton engineering pantheon, Orville Wright. Wright and Desch were climbing the steps to Building 10 one day in 1940 when a bomber flew overhead on its way to landing at Wright Field, the local base that bore the name of Orville and his brother Wilbur. Hobbled by a limp suffered in an early flying accident, Wright had stopped on the steps and was staring up at the plane when Desch worked up the nerve to ask the aviation pioneer if it troubled him that his invention had been used for war.

Wright reflected a moment, then shook his head. "No," he said. "If we hadn't done it, somebody else would have. It was inevitable."

Desch ran into his own inevitabilities in the summer of 1942. The more he went over the Navy plans, the more he bumped up against an inescapable conclusion: an all-electronic machine was impossible. If the electronic American Bombe followed the architecture of Britain's, it would devour more than twenty thousand tubes run at speeds that couldn't be sustained. And a universal codebreaking machine, one that could attack more than just the Enigma, would need thousands more tubes and even higher speeds. Either machine would demand too many scarce resources to manufacture, would generate too much heat to operate reliably, and would utilize more electrical power than could be supplied by conventional means.

Wenger, Engstrom, and Howard's MIT group were devastated, but Desch was highly respected, and his judgment could not be ignored. Yet it meant the entire RAM project was in danger, as was perhaps even OP20G's research section.

OP20G's promised electronic Bombe was now a failure, its second RAM project was stalled, and it was contributing little to the war effort in the Atlantic. There was only one solution: turn the whole problem over to Desch. He would have to be drawn into the tight circle of people who knew of America's and Britain's great secret, Ultra.

How Desch felt about being privy to one of the most important Allied strategic advantages of the war is best gauged by his reaction more than thirty years later, when he learned the British were divulging their role in Ultra with the publication of F. W. Winterbotham's book *The Ultra Secret.* Desch's daughter, Debbie Anderson, recalled that her father launched into a stream of invective against the British, yelling, "I always knew those SOBs would talk!" He took his own part in that secret to his grave.

Later that summer, Desch began receiving new details about the design of the British Bombe, supplied by Robert Ely and Joe Eachus, the U.S. Navy officers who had been installed as the first American codebreakers at Bletchley Park. The two began sending coded telegrams back to OP20G almost as soon as they arrived at Bletchley in June, and the information kept flowing from England throughout the summer.

Eachus, who was thirty-two at the time, was an Indiana native raised in southwest Ohio. After graduating from Miami University, near Dayton, and earning his Ph.D. in mathematics from the University of Illinois, he had been teaching at Purdue and, almost as a lark, taking the Navy's correspondence course in cryptanalysis when the Japanese attacked Pearl Harbor. Soon after, Eachus went into the Navy. A little more than a year later, he was one of two OP20G officers assigned to work temporarily at Bletchley, side by side with Turing and the other British codebreakers. Eachus had no complaints about British cooperativeness: "As a matter of fact, I remember some of the places I visited, the people were anxious to talk about what they were doing because they had almost no opportunity to do so."

One of the first vital pieces of information to come back to the United States was the need for a two-way flow of electricity through the Bombe's commutator wheels, a Turing invention that gave the Bombe much of its problem-solving power. Theoreticians at OP20G believed that two-way electronic tubes could perform the same task, at blinding speeds, but Desch was later to inform them otherwise.

The evidence indicates that the British told Ely and Eachus everything about their existing Bombes, including the cold-point tests that greatly increased their efficiency, as well as what was known at GCCS at the time about the forthcoming four-wheel Bombes. Blueprints for the four-wheel design, as it existed in the summer of 1942, were sent to Washington sometime in September. How much and exactly what Desch was told by OP20G during the summer remains unclear. But on their return from England in August, Ely and Eachus reported to Desch's supervisors in Washington, including Howard Engstrom, and later made trips to Dayton themselves.

Desch and Engstrom had agreed that the Dayton Bombes would follow the general logic and technology of Britain's machines, but how many Bombes were to be built, how they were to be operated, and how much speed and codebreaking capability was to be designed into each machine were topics still under debate. One option was to build 336 of the two-and-a-half-ton machines, to run through all possible Enigma-rotor combinations without changing wheels, thus saving operating time and labor but greatly increasing the cost of the project. Other questions concerned how many Bombes should fit into a single frame and how many Enigma machines to simulate in each Bombe. A greater number of Enigma analogs per Bombe would give them more codebreaking power but also would demand more electrical and mechanical power to drive the additional wheels at the necessary speeds.

A more general question was how many automatic features should be built into the machines. More features would help meet the demands of those who would run the machines and produce intelligence. But fewer would lower the cost of construction and improve reliability and performance.

Each answer would engender a different set of engineering challenges for Desch and his team.

. . .

BY MID-SEPTEMBER, Desch was able to go back to his Navy supervisors with a plan for an original American Bombe that could approach the performance, if not the elegance, of the Navy's all-electronic design. Desch's machine, part electronic but mostly mechanical, would attempt to crack Shark by fusing Britain's Bombe logic with the best of America's high-speed electromechanics. Still, it would have to make use of the labor-intensive British-style commutators, which simulated the Enigma code wheels and had to be changed with each run of the machine. But such a Bombe could be operational by the end of the year, and, more important, production could begin in a matter of months.

Desch's memo of September 15, 1942, outlining his machine in less than twelve pages, is a marvel of clarity and conciseness. Yet it reveals some startling gaps in his knowledge about the workings of the British Bombe and its supporting methods, leading him to wildly overestimate the number of stops or false hits (three thousand for each test of the Enigma's wheel order) and hence to overstate the number of Bombes that would be required.*

No doubt at the request of British codebreakers, Desch incorporated into the design the ability to run three-wheel as well as four-wheel Enigma problems, in case the British should need help against the German Army and Air Force ciphers. To speed the Bombe's operation, he included an automatic feature that would record the locations where the fast-spinning wheels had found a possible hit and, after stopping them, rewind them back to their hit positions for conducting the additional Diagonal Board test. That way, a new search for possible Enigma solutions could begin immediately with no gaps in coverage. "A small motor, in addition to the main drive motor, could perform this function," he wrote. "A rewind speed of about 100 rpm probably could be realized. The bomb then would be completely automatic."

---

* Having never seen the word "Bombe" in writing or in print—by agreement with the British—Desch might also be forgiven for misspelling the word as "Bomb" in his memo.

But the innovative heart of the machine would be its electronic tracking system—a truly original Desch contribution, which he described in just one sentence: "The memory device will consist of two banks of 26 miniature thyratrons each, one tube in each bank being ignited when a hit occurs."

Desch's report estimated that the Navy would need 336 of the costly machines—nearly three times more than later experience was to indicate. The huge error, corrected in the following months, was based on Desch's still incomplete knowledge of the British Bombe. Even so, the Navy brass gave him the go-ahead for the inflated figure in his report, perhaps because, with that many machines, there would be no need for time-consuming wheel changes between runs.

OP20G was desperate and willing to take a huge gamble on the design. The Navy promised everything and anything Desch needed to get the job done as quickly as possible—millions in funding, hundreds of trained personnel, and the highest top secret priority. The old engineering group from MIT was ordered to put the other machine projects on hold until the critical Bombes were ready. Immediately, Desch hired ten more top civilian engineers and put them to work on a trial machine.

In early October, Wenger was so confident of the project's success that he promised the first Bombes by the beginning of 1943. He began negotiations for the land and buildings to house the Bombes once they came off the production line, as well as the hundreds of clerks, maintenance men, and armed guards who would be needed for their operation.

WITH ULTRA AND the Battle of the Atlantic in the balance in 1943, the Bombe project was placed on a fast track, and cost overruns in the millions were accepted without question. The jump from an estimate of two million dollars to one of four million in a few months did not threaten the program. Resources were seldom a problem at NCR, despite the heavy demands from other war industries across the country. At its height, the project employed more than one thousand manufacturing workers and required material and components from thousands of different suppliers. And the greatest efforts were made to keep the project secret and secure, given the fears that even a hint of the project's aims would cause the Germans to alter their code systems. On March 17, 1943, when the German U-boat threat was heightened by another Enigma blackout, the Navy asked Roosevelt for the highest possible priority for the project, the president's AAA designation. He granted it the very next day.

At times, OP20G had to bow to the personnel demands of other branches of the Navy in order to guard the project's security: relying too often on its AAA status might tip off the wrong people to the American Bombe and the Ultra secret. OP20G thus found it almost impossible to persuade the Navy that sailors should be transferred from sea duty to technical detail on an inland project.

The Navy took over the 36,800-square-foot building at NCR and found it an ideal match for its purposes. Erected just four years before, Building 26 was one of the first structures in the country to use steel-reinforced concrete floors. It was strong enough to serve as a factory site for the five-thousand-pound Bombes and roomy enough with its twelve-foot-high ceilings and wide hallways for moving the massive machines, which stood seven feet high, eight feet long, and two feet wide—larger than three modern refrigerators side by side. The building was fireproof and also air-conditioned, thus protecting the Bombes' sensitive electronic components. Not far behind the building ran the old Miami-Erie Canal and a spur of the Baltimore and Ohio railroad line, which quite conveniently led to Washington, D.C., in twelve hours.

Its twenty-three classrooms provided privacy and security for each step of the manufacturing process, as did the glass-brick windows that let in plenty of daylight while blocking out potential snoopers. The project was broken up into units and, where necessary, assigned to different rooms, so that only the top managers knew enough to comprehend the purpose of the project. Each room had a thick wooden door that could be locked. Only if your name was posted on the door could you be admitted to that room. "And many people didn't get in many rooms," Kern said.

The engineers sometimes felt the need to leaven the building's strict need-to-know atmosphere. One day, just as a maintenance man finished drilling a hole from the hallway into one of the secure rooms, engineer Ralph Bruce stooped down and shouted through the hole in a booming voice: "Hey, do you have a pass to get in here?"

Wenger soon got the organization for the project he had wanted, as free of bureaucratic constraints as possible. While the bean counters in the Navy's Bureau of Ships at first controlled the money and were theoretically in charge of all the project's technical details, the bureau yielded more and more autonomy to Wenger, Engstrom, and Desch. The end result was a new Navy entity, dubbed the U.S. Naval Computing Machine Laboratory, that would serve as an umbrella for all the Navy's codebreaking-machine projects. In formal terms, the NCML was the boss of the Dayton operation, but by early 1943 it was really only a source of funding and support for the OP20G engineers and scientists. In essence, OP20G had its own machine-development program at what, in effect, was to become its own secret factory inside Building 26.

It is unlikely that NCR executives at the time had any notion of how much of the company's resources would be tied up by Navy demands as the Bombe project ballooned. In mid-1942, when Deeds ordered NCR to accept a "best efforts," no-profit contract with the Navy, the agreement called for preliminary work on codebreaking machines, not a massive development and manufacturing effort. The effect of the open-ended contract, combined with the formation of the NCML, was to free Engstrom's M section from the hassles of paperwork and bureaucratic interference. But at the same time, it bound NCR to the Navy: before the war was over, NCR executives began to chafe under the no-profit clause.

The longtime cordial relations between Desch and the young men from MIT helped to create an open atmosphere in Dayton. And as luck would have it, the Bureau of Ships found someone they thought would be just the right man for managing a loosely controlled project of engineers and technicians who were unused to taking military orders: Commander Ralph Meader. Although over forty at the time,

Meader was not a member of the bureau's meddlesome old guard. As a Navy reservist, he had spent more than two decades working for the engineering divisions of America's largest electrical corporations, including Western Union, often in a more freewheeling relationship as an inventor. He had earned several patents and a reputation as both a solid engineer and an even-tempered executive. He had learned how to work with, as well as to direct, creative people—perhaps, too, because he had been married to one for twenty years. He met his wife, Janet Clark McLaren—a graduate of the Royal Academy of Music in London—while she was traveling in the States with a theater company. She kept her show-business connection after their marriage and at one point brought her husband into the fold as a stage manager for a Broadway show.

Like Engstrom, Meader had worked his way into the nation's elite academic circles from a relatively modest background. His father was a shoemaker in Lynn, Massachusetts, who lost his shop in a swindle, according to Meader's son, Bruce. Meader's academic abilities gained him admission to the prestigious Boston Latin High School and later, on scholarship, to Dartmouth, where he played tennis and took all the toughest math courses. During World War I, he enlisted in the Navy as an ensign and, afterward, took graduate courses at Harvard and Columbia. Using the money he later earned from his engineering patents, Meader tried a variety of business ventures between the wars, most of them failures, including an import-export business with a Hungarian friend of his wife and an investment in a Florida quarry. He went bankrupt before World War II defending his patents on a repeating pen-and-pencil mechanism against a suit filed by EverSharp.

ALTHOUGH RELATIONS WITH Meader and the Navy began harmoniously enough, Joe Desch and NCR began to feel put-upon after only a few months. It didn't help matters that when Desch's civilian team was transferred from NCR's payroll to the Navy's, they had to wait three weeks for their first paycheck. "For a young family back then, that was a real hardship," recalled Carmelita Ford Bruce, widow of NCR engineer Ralph Bruce.

Hundreds of sailors and WAVES, the Navy's women's auxiliary, would have to be assimilated into NCR's operations to help Desch's team with the assembly and maintenance of the machines. "The sailors were the hardest to control," Jack Kern said,

> because they wouldn't take orders from a civilian, and yet they were given to us to use. This made for a rather sticky situation for us. There were no naval officers in charge—they were all upstairs running Bombes. They were problem solving, testing, whatever one does behind closed doors in their situation. I think that only Joe Desch and perhaps [his assistant and business manager] Bob Mumma ever got in there. The Navy had direct wire connections to Washington and were actually transacting business.

The converse relationship also got sticky—civilian employees having to take orders from the Navy. Once NCML and Meader took over Building 26 in late 1942, pressure was put on the NCR staff to work overtime, including weekends, even though only Desch and possibly Mumma knew the importance and urgency of the project. By May 1943, Desch's team of engineers was placed on a wartime work schedule of fifty-four hours per week, according to payroll records, and many were putting in additional hours even at that. "I know of more than one person who worked twenty-four hours on Sunday and got paid double-time," Kern said. "Saturday and Sunday were supposed to be off, yes, but we usually worked on Saturday."

The Navy's heavy-handed attempts to increase the pace of work weren't always successful, Kern remembered: "If you're doing something mental, trying to overcome a problem or something, you can't work fast, like you could if you were simply putting something together."

Meader, to his credit, eventually recognized that engineers couldn't be managed like factory hands. In a report filed with Wenger after the war, he wrote:

> It must . . . be borne in mind that work being done by engineers in research and development cannot be passed on from

shift to shift. Engineers must personally see their work thru [*sic*] to a conclusion and obviously no engineer could work 24 hours a day nor seven days a week. The advantage of [NCML's] full-time operation was really effective only in the production of parts and the assembly of components.

In that same report, Meader noted that the Navy ran into early problems with NCR when executives tried to sidestep Deeds and the Navy's no-profit contract by letting out most of the Navy work to subcontractors. That approach soon ended, however, when the Navy brass wrote directly to Deeds in January 1943 and then summoned NCR's top executives to Washington for a tongue-lashing on wartime priorities.

"The contract written with NCR was . . . definitely the wrong thing to do," Meader wrote later.

The contractors, as their lucrative fixed-price war contracts increased, were very reluctant to use their personnel and facilities for no-profit work at the expense of increasing their profitable work. We reached a stage where 93 percent of all our specially designed parts were let out to subcontractors. Many of these contractors were incapable of executing precision work and their equipment was such that delays which were intolerable resulted. . . . It was necessary to direct the contractor to prosecute whenever possible the work in his own plant under threat of the Navy exercising its war-time prerogative of taking over.

Sailors who refused orders from civilians "continued to be a bone of contention with the management of the contractor," Meader wrote in his report. But he fired back with his own complaint against NCR's employees for not being more grateful that they had been given draft deferments

solely at the request of the Navy and solely for the purpose of working under this overall project. . . . This situation became critical when certain civilians refused to work overtime even when such overtime was deemed absolutely essential to the successful prosecution of the war. However, nothing actually was done except to handle each case individually and to continually pacify the civilians as much as possible.

The mix of civilians and military personnel in Building 26 led to some intense encounters at times. Marines armed with shotguns and pistols patrolled the hallways and actually lived in the building, doing their bathing, shaving, and laundering in the restrooms and hanging their uniforms to dry on the roof. The leatherneck guards were hardened cases even by Marine standards—all were veterans who had been wounded early in the war and reassigned to Dayton. Some were prone to skittishness, as Lou Sandor, one of the engineers, discovered. "I had a habit of slamming the door to the restroom whenever I went in," Sandor recalled. One day, his habit startled an off-duty Marine, who was shaving at a sink. "All of a sudden, I was staring into the barrel of a forty-five. I don't know who was scared more—me or the Marine who almost shot me."

The local draft board, unaware of the vital nature of the work being done at NCR, could be a major nuisance for its personnel. More than once, Desch had to retrieve one of his charges at the Dayton train station, just moments before the engineer or technician was shipped out for military duty. One NCR engineer languished for three days in the local jail on charges of draft dodging before Desch was able to persuade the authorities to release him.

NO ONE AT NCR, of course, took more orders from the Navy than Desch. When he first became involved in the Bombe project in the summer of 1942, he was told to drop all his other research projects then in progress for the NDRC, the Aberdeen Proving Ground, and the Army. And his personal life came under intense scrutiny for the duration of the war. Even after he had signed a pledge of secrecy the year before as an investigator for the NDRC, binding him "not to disclose any confidential information regarding this research except to others engaged in work on this specific problem," Desch was asked to undergo a second and more grueling security clearance before he could be told about Ultra.

In May 1942, he spent three days in Washington under relentless interrogation by Navy inquisitors who hurled insults and accusations, trying to break him down. The questioning eventually became so abusive that Desch told the Navy he didn't want the job—at which point they relented and told him he was cleared. He was to return to Dayton immediately to begin his new assignment. "Dad told me once he had had it up to here with their bull," Debbie Anderson said. "But he must have calmed down, because he got the job."

With it was to come more stress and more intrusion into his personal life than Desch could have possibly imagined at the time. It meant working fourteen- and sixteen-hour days under mounting pressure from Navy officials and living under twenty-four-hour surveillance by Navy guards, even in his own home.

"You could see it was having an effect on him," Kern said. "He would more frequently get mad in meetings. Of course, getting mad was his way of getting things done . . . of increasing your enthusiasm for you to get your work done. We all noticed that he complained more about things."

And yet because of the top secret nature of the project, Desch could never really explain to his subordinates the pressures he was facing, or even what the machines they were laboring so mightily to perfect would be used for. "We knew that [the machine] was for a decoding activity, but we just didn't know the details of it," Sandor said. Even Desch's on-the-job vocabulary was restricted. "We never heard of . . . Bombe, Enigma, or NCR Navy [sic] Computing Machine Laboratory during the war," Kern said.

Some men might have turned to their families for solace and support, but again Desch was blocked. For the duration of the war, he would be forced to sever relations with most of his German relatives. The Navy was taking no chances with a man who could speak fluent German, who was an avid ham-radio operator and communications expert, and whose mother had been born and reared in Germany.

Desch's mother, Augusta Stoermer, had emigrated at age thirteen from Germany to Liverpool, England, then to an uncle's home in Pittsburgh, where she had rolled cigars for a living, and finally to Dayton, where she met Edward Frank Desch. Homesick even in her later years, Desch's mother had kept in touch with relatives in Europe and had gone back to visit in Germany before the war. Edward Desch died in 1937.

Desch was permitted only limited visits with his mother and two younger sisters, providing the entire family avoided all contact with Desch's half cousin in Dayton, Augusta "Gusty" Burger. Gusty still had a father in Germany who was a member of the Nazi Party, and her husband, Albert Burger, had been known to tune in Hitler's broadcasts on his shortwave radio before the war.* Unable to explain to his family the reason for his infrequent visits and for avoiding Gusty, Desch found his relations with his mother and sisters became strained during the war.

Throughout the war, Desch was never out of sight of his Navy shadows—plainclothes guards who sat in parked cars outside his home and office, waiting to tail him around town. Years later, Desch gleefully told his daughter what fun it had been one night after work to lead the guards on a wild-goose chase through the countryside south of Dayton, before doubling back to his own driveway.

Hardest of all for Desch to swallow was having Ralph Meader quartered in his own home to keep an eye on him. Desch had built the two-bedroom Tudor cottage just two years earlier as a gift to his wife, Dorothy, on a small lot at 413 Greenmount Avenue in the charming streetcar suburb of Oakwood. Even by 1940s standards, it was a cozy home for a young couple, but no doubt a bit too cozy with Meader in the spare bedroom across the hallway. Meader "practically slept in his bed," said Bob Mumma. "I'll tell you, day and night, he couldn't get rid of him. Joe just about lost his mind." Years after the war, and even after his only daughter had taken occupancy of the

---

* The Burger children said they later learned that their maternal grandfather, Friederich Zimmerman, had joined the Nazi Party only to keep his postal job. The children also said that Albert Burger gave his life trying to prove he was a loyal American: he worked extra shifts at General Motors in Dayton during the war, packing graphite powder into bombs, and died from emphysema in 1977 as a result of his exposure.

room, Desch disdainfully referred to "Meader's room," never bothering to remove the large oak desk his boss had used there.

Desch's loathing of Meader had many possible sources, but certainly one was his Navy-bred style of management. Realizing that Desch was the best man to motivate his own employees, Meader applied the Navy's pressure most directly on him and expected it to ratchet down the civilian chain of command. He quickly discovered what worked most effectively on Desch: guilt. Meader told Desch more than once that he was going to be responsible for the deaths of countless American boys if he didn't get the job done.

Anderson believes Meader never suspected the full impact of his guilt-lashings. Her father was a devout Catholic who had been raised to believe in the concept of mortal sin and the eternal damnation of hell for those who failed to live up to their earthly responsibilities. Some of the men who would die in the war included his former ROTC buddies. Desch himself had been excused from the unit because the Navy had needed his talents at home—all the more reason to blame himself as the death toll rose in the Atlantic. "We were losing ships like mad," Mumma said. Desch "felt guilty, I think, because he wasn't active. That's what bothered him."

Desch had been commissioned as an officer in an Army ordnance unit, but when the Navy learned it might lose his technical expertise to the front (and worse, perhaps, to the Army), it pulled his orders, Anderson said. Far from bringing relief, the dispensation induced bouts of guilt in Desch for the rest of the war, and the rest of his life. "Now I know why Dad was really conflicted and angry most of his life," Anderson said, who didn't learn of her father's role in the Bombe project until the mid-1990s, almost a decade after his death. "The Joe Desch I knew carried a lot of anger around. I know it wasn't about me and Mom. And I wasn't sure it was about NCR, either."

IN THE EARLY months of 1943, tension infused the Bombe project from the highest levels down. Desch smoked his Chesterfields, two packs a day, and when the long workday was done, he liked his Scotch and water.

Despite the Navy's constant pressures and Desch's ramrodding of his staff, progress was painfully slow. The design for the pilot model of the Bombe was submitted to the Navy in January. But with spring and an expected U-boat offensive fast approaching, Desch was far from producing a working machine.

The British, wondering whether to rely upon the American effort because of their own problems developing a four-wheel Bombe, sent Alan Turing to Dayton to check on the NCR work. Turing's visit was to provide some valuable insights for the Americans, but his recommendations to OP20G would also add to Desch's mounting burden of stress.

6

The Turing Memo

WHEN ALAN TURING arrived in Dayton's Union Terminal at 2:00 P.M.—his train from Washington, D.C., delayed six hours by a snowstorm—he must have felt himself literally a stranger in a strange land, having entered for the first time the heartland of a culture he found both abhorrent and fascinating. Then again, Turing was a misfit no matter where he found himself.

The thirty-year-old mastermind of the British Bombe had been too much an individualist for the tradition-bound circles of Cambridge, where he first made his mark as a young theoretician. And he had been too much the English gentleman for the competitive world of Princeton, where he pursued his postdoctoral research among the likes of Einstein and John von Neumann. Further placing himself in his own category, Turing was not only gay but an avowed atheist who had devoted much of his adult life to pondering ways of turning human logic into machinery. Turing had laid down the principles of the modern, all-purpose computer, predicting, quite correctly, that one day thinking machines "would play a good game of chess."

Turing's eccentricities were legend during his reign as the top codebreaker at Bletchley Park. He seemed almost to cultivate an image as a rumpled, absentminded scholar, chaining his tea mug to his radiator (mugs were at a premium in England during the war), wearing a gas mask around town to curb his allergies, and riding a broken-down bicycle with a chain that fell off after a certain number of revolutions, both to discourage thieves and because he was fascinated by its periodic pattern.

The visit to NCR was only one part of Turing's assigned tour of the States in the winter of 1942–1943. He had already spent much time with the young cryptanalysts in Engstrom's research section in Washington. Turing had gone on to Dayton with the permission of Bletchley Park, which now had an intense interest in the Navy's Bombe development and other codebreaking machines being explored at NCR. He was visiting not only to offer his advice but to report back to his superiors on the progress of the Americans. The British wanted to know how much they could rely upon the promised American Bombes as well as upon the American pledge to be only helpers in Britain's intelligence battle against Germany. In November 1942, not long before Turing left for the States, his commander, Edward Travis, sent this memo to Wenger at OP20G: "Should be glad if Turing . . . could examine machinery. Make any use you like of him in connection with bombes. Have suggested he stay a week in Washington but if you should like him longer I should be quite willing."

The British had already provided the Americans with much technical detail on their existing Bombes and given the research group at OP20G an outline of their hopes for new four-wheel machines as well as modified three-wheel Bombes. GCCS, in fact, asked that OP20G send a third team to England to learn the details of their first four-wheel Bombes, which they mistakenly believed would be in operation before Turing's return to England in early 1943.

But the advice Turing was able to give the Americans was limited for a number of reasons. Although Desch was still in the beginning stages of his project and had not even a working prototype, the British sensed that OP20G wasn't likely to be receptive to any radical changes in Desch's design, given the Navy's desire to produce machines by the first months of 1943. Turing, who was not known for his diplomatic skills, had probably been told by his superiors to be as discreet as possible and, specifically, not to exhibit any of Britain's anger over the Americans' increasingly independent Bombe policies. The British weren't happy with the American decision to build a Bombe, but without a working four-wheel Bombe of its own GCCS had to accept OP20G's venture. Two months before Turing's visit, the two sides had reached a compromise, signed by a GCCS representative and the head of U.S. Naval Communications, captain Carl Holden, known as the Holden agreement: Bletchley would continue to be in charge of the European and U-boat codebreaking work, but the Americans would now be a full, if junior, partner in the operation.

Knowledge of Turing's visit to Dayton was restricted to a select few in Britain: that a math genius was traveling to a small midwestern city in America would certainly raise questions about the kind of work being done there. Joan Clarke, Turing's fiancée at the time, knew of his travels along the East Coast during the war, but even decades later denied that Turing had ever been to Dayton.

Although there had been hints in OP20G histories that Turing had traveled to NCR and that he had criticized Desch's efforts, the visit was not confirmed until 1999 when federal archivist Lee A. Gladwin found proof among a newly released collection of documents that had been sealed for decades in the Navy's Crane, Indiana, archive. A nine-page memo written by Turing for his superiors in England made the facts indisputably clear from the title: "Visit to the National Cash Register Corporation of Dayton, Ohio."

The memo began with an apology—or perhaps an implicit criticism of American trains—for the lateness of his arrival that first afternoon at "the works . . . where the Bombes are being made." As a result, he wrote, "we did not have quite so long there as we might have had, but probably sufficient."

Turing did not complain about his less-than-elegant lodgings in Dayton, although he may have had reason to. Debbie Anderson said her father mentioned before his death in 1987 that Turing had spent the night on their living-room floor. While there is no proof of this, the Desch home may have been the only residence in Dayton under the protection of plainclothes guards at the time. Perhaps, too, under Dayton's crowded wartime conditions the Desches' offer of lodgings seemed entirely hospitable. The four OP20G officers from Washington who had accompanied Turing on his visit—among them Joe Eachus, who had worked with Turing at Bletchley the summer before—ended up sleeping on a hallway floor in a downtown hotel.

Despite their differences in background, as well as Desch's fears that Turing was there to undermine his work, the two men may have struck a chord with each other, at least intellectually. Desch shared Turing's interests in the concept of real numbers as well as in mathematically based cryptography, Anderson said. Both men claimed to have invented an unbreakable code at one time in their lives. One can only wonder if the two men talked about their ideas over martinis before a crackling fire in the Desches' living room. Then again, maybe they did not. Turing had an aversion to conversation with most Americans, as he had made clear while he was at Princeton, in a letter to a friend in England:

> These Americans have various peculiarities in conversation which catch the ear somehow. Whenever you thank them for anything, they say, 'You're welcome.' I rather liked it at first, thinking I was welcome, but now I find it comes back like a ball thrown against a wall, and become positively apprehensive. Another habit they have is to make the sound described by authors as 'Aha.' They use it when they have no suitable reply to a remark, but think that silence would be rude.

There's no evidence that Turing was outwardly rude to anyone during his brief visit to Dayton, although Bob Mumma once recalled an argument that Turing and Desch had over the wire brushes to be used in the NCR machines. It's more likely Turing was oblivious to those he met or frightened of them and found his refuge in the self-consistent, self-contained world of pure math. Even in the company of mathematicians, Turing was less than outgoing. At a later stop in his trip to the States, new acquaintances there "complained of Alan giving no sign of recognition or greeting when he passed them in halls; instead, he seemed to 'look straight through them.' "

Turing's withdrawn and somewhat cold approach to people wasn't limited to Americans, according to his biographer Andrew Hodges. At

Bletchley Park, Alex Fowler, who was just over forty, took Turing to task about his lack of social skills. Turing was stung and felt the need to explain to Fowler why he struggled with so many aspects of life and social relations. Fowler recalled what the younger man had told him: " 'You know at Cambridge,' he said, 'you come out in the morning and it's redundant to keep saying hallo, hallo, hallo.' " Hodges concluded that Turing "was too conscious of what he was doing, to slip into conventions without thinking."

Turing's problems with social relationships and, later, his entanglement in then-illegal homosexual affairs, led to his being marginalized at Bletchley during the last years of the war. In 1952, the same year he was awarded Britain's highest civilian honor for his wartime service, the Order of the British Empire, he was arrested, put on trial for homosexuality, and, as a result, placed on probation. Two years later—and two weeks shy of his forty-second birthday—he committed suicide. In a scenario reminiscent of one of his favorite movies, Walt Disney's *Snow White and the Seven Dwarfs,* he dipped an apple in a mixture of jam and cyanide. Then, without writing a note to explain his actions, he took several bites and passed away.

HOW MANY TIMES Turing came to NCR remains uncertain. Anderson believes he made more than one trip to Dayton, based in part on her father's comments and those of his assistant, Bob Mumma, years later to a Smithsonian historian. If Turing had found time to tour the city, he would have encountered a community that, although not threatened with bombing as were the cities in England, was nonetheless stressed by war.

By 1943, the war economy dominated the working and family life of industrial cities like Dayton to a degree that is hard to imagine today. In addition to the rationing of meat, gasoline, sugar, and even coffee, some sixty war-production industries employed nearly half the city's population—about 115,000 workers—and turned out products that were sent to nearly every Allied front. Another 45,000 men and women were employed at the three military air bases in the area: Wright, Patterson, and McCook fields.

Starting in 1941, the peacetime production of Dayton's factories—cash registers, automotive parts, refrigerators, and tires—had been quickly converted to meet the needs of fighting men. The Inland Division of General Motors was turning out the M-30, considered one of the best rifles of the war, as well as a one-pound pistol called the "Little Monster," to be air-dropped to resistance fighters in Europe. GM's Frigidaire division switched from building refrigerators to turning out giant propellers for the B-29 and .50-caliber machine guns for defending the B-17 Flying Fortresses. NCR built the carburetors for both the B-24 Liberator and B-29s, as well as shell fuses, computing gun sights, a rocket motor, and a variety of gun parts and shells. GM's Delco division cranked out tank treads, special shock absorbers for Army trucks and tanks, bomb fuses, and the Allison liquid-cooled engines used in Bell Airacobras, Curtiss P-40s, and Lockheed P-38 interceptors.

By 1943, the forty-eight-hour workweek was standard in Dayton and many other industrial cities, and most factory hands worked much longer. The long hours meant that many workers had little time to shop for necessities. In an era when family life was still valued above convenience, downtown stores usually closed at 5:45 P.M. and all day Sunday. Dayton retailers may have been the first in the country to extend their hours until 8:30 P.M. on Monday and Wednesday nights. Even banks began to keep their doors open on Friday nights so that factory workers could cash their checks.

With thousands of men off to war, labor shortages were critical. To ease the shortage, some plants created "buddy shifts" in which high school students filled in after school starting at 7:00 P.M., allowing full-time workers to break for dinner before returning to their jobs at 10:00 P.M.

The almost insatiable needs of the war plants triggered unprecedented efforts to expand the Dayton labor force. More than ninety-three thousand registration cards were mailed, one to every home in Dayton and Montgomery counties, urging women to join the workforce. The number of women in the Dayton workforce nearly doubled between 1942 and 1943 alone. Recruiters were dispatched to surrounding rural areas and as far south as the hardscrabble hills and isolated hollows of Appalachia, where they touted the wages and benefits to be earned in Dayton plants. From a population of 211,000 in 1940—then the fortieth largest city in America—Dayton swelled by another 43,000 by the end of the war.

The city's infrastructure showed the strain. Hotels needed a week's notice for reservations, traffic snarled, trailer camps ballooned, and more than 2,500 temporary housing units went up all over town. And with so many fathers overseas and mothers working outside the home, juvenile-delinquency rates jumped almost overnight. From January through March 1943, the number of first-time offenders brought into Montgomery County juvenile court—407 cases in all—nearly doubled over the same period the year before. As one distraught judge observed, most of the growth in new cases was occurring among eleven- to fourteen-year-olds. To address the problem for the duration of the war, city commissioners signed a petition in February 1943 calling for a voluntary curfew of 10:00 P.M. for children ages twelve and under and of midnight for high schoolers.

Given Turing's inward-looking temperament, it's doubtful he noticed how much the war effort was transforming America. Eachus said he remembered little of Turing's reactions, except that the mathematician had noted with ironic interest that the NCR site housing the U.S. Bombe project "was Building 26, and that there are, of course, twenty-six letters in the alphabet." Eachus said he never found Turing to be arrogant in his dealings with Americans.

But some in Dayton at the time felt otherwise. Phil Bochicchio, a Navy mechanic who did much of the troubleshooting maintenance on the Dayton Bombes, said British visitors in general "acted like they knew everything more than we did. Maybe they did. But they were as peculiar as hell, and, like God, they were way up there looking down on us."

The Navy's reluctance to reveal to the staff in Dayton all that OP20G knew about the British machines and methods probably caused some of the resentment at NCR toward the British. Although Desch left no written comments on his encounters with the British or with Turing, he did complain in a 1973 interview with Smithsonian historian Henry Tropp that "it was a one-way street. The British came over and visited me and looked at everything I was doing, but I could never see anything they were doing. And when you mention Turing, he was one of them that came over here very frequently."

Anderson discovered among her father's wartime memorabilia a photo he had taken at a July 1943 outdoor gathering at NCR, where a young man who looks remarkably like Turing is standing with his arms akimbo in a dark tweed jacket among U.S. naval officers in dress whites. Desch left no identification of anyone in the photo, though Ralph Meader is easily recognized in the crowd.

Turing's memo to GCCS about his visit to Dayton seems rather evenhanded, especially given his somewhat indelicate writing style as well as the tardy and meandering development of the American project. Turing provided valuable insights for Desch and his team, but by swaying Desch's superiors at OP20G to make last-minute changes in their approach he also complicated Desch's already daunting assignment. Desch and John Howard, now the Navy's supervising engineer on the project, scrambled to include the changes in a second Bombe design even as they rushed to construct the first prototype.

Turing began his critique of the December 1942 American Bombe by arguing against one of Desch's most prized features: the automatic rewind. Turing didn't think the feature extravagant or superfluous, but he thought a faster, more ambitious design would eliminate having to stop the machine at all. The British, in fact, had hoped to avoid the cumbersome stops for the Diagonal Board test in their own high-speed version of the four-wheel Bombe. In this context, Turing's doubts about Desch's rewind feature seem reasonable.

> We were given a demonstration of how the motor was able to reverse and be going full speed in the reverse direction in a fraction of a second, with the full load: however, this seems to me hardly to prove that all will be well when one tries to reverse the Bombe itself, e.g. the gears might get distorted under the strain. They say that the whole machine is being built sufficiently strongly [sic] to withstand such strain. Possibly the real objection to this method is that the time taken over each stop is fairly considerable, viz 15 seconds, and of course it seems a

pity for them to go out of their way to build the machine to do all this stopping if it is not necessary.

Engstrom originally had liked the rewind feature, but apparently Turing persuaded him to lobby Desch to drop it. Desch refused—and, as it turned out, he was right. His mechanism performed admirably throughout the war, while the British failed in several attempts to produce a working nonstop Bombe.

Turing expressed a more valid criticism about Desch's idea of using a commutator wheel of different size to simulate the first and fastest wheel on the Enigma. Desch worried that he might not be able to drive the fastest of the wheels at the necessary speeds (three thousand rpm) unless it was smaller than the rest and could therefore withstand the additional torque and centrifugal force. To head off the anticipated problems with overheating and distortion, Desch had wanted to use two smaller wheels instead of one large wheel. Smaller wheels were less likely to warp and chip as they whirled at high speeds.

But Turing realized that different-size wheels made sense only if the Americans went through with their plans to build 336 fixed-wheel Bombes. If not, Turing's experience told him that having to change two different kinds of wheels would be a logistic and operational nightmare for hard-pressed Bombe clerks. Adding another sixteen wheels to the sixty-four needed for each setup would significantly increase the changeover time between runs. In fact, Turing became a bit sharp in his comments about the idea: it made him "smile inwardly at the conception of [British] Bombe hut routine implied by this programme."

Turing's point scored well with Engstrom, who had already realized that different wheel sizes would add considerably to the cost of the Bombe program. Those brass-and-copper wheels, sandwiched between heat-resistant Bakelite, were hard and expensive to manufacture. Worse, their 104 contacts had to be wired by hand and by trained military personnel who could be trusted not to talk about what they were doing. Providing the eleven thousand or so commutators OP20G required during the war did, as Engstrom feared, prove to be one of the greatest manufacturing and security challenges of the Bombe project.

In a January 20 memo, Engstrom asked Meader to "advise Mr. Desch of the urgent necessity" of using a one-size-fits-all wheel. But on this point, Desch sided with his engineering instincts rather than the needs of codebreakers. His first two prototypes—Adam and Eve—both used different-size wheels.

Turing, however, was able to predict at least one engineering pitfall that Desch and his team had not: laboratory testing alone could not anticipate all the problems with the high-speed brushes used to sense the commutators' electrical connections. The British knew from their more advanced trials that the brushes had a tendency to bounce over the contacts—a glitch that caused numerous false hits and misfirings. Just as Turing had done at Bletchley Park, the Americans had first tested the contacts on an oscillograph and not detected any problems. In his memo, Turing cited the British experience with "brush bounce": "Such a demonstration was made by Commander Travis and Flowers and myself [using an oscillograph] at Malvern, and yet when it came to the point of lining [our Bombe] up for a trial menu, it failed on account of bounce."

Engstrom passed the warning on to Meader in a January 5 memo, as well as some more general advice from Turing, who knew all too well how suddenly and dramatically the Germans could change their Enigma systems. Engstrom put the NCR team on guard to keep the Bombe design as fluid as possible "in order to permit the addition of new features, or the change of those already incorporated, from time to time as rapidly as possible."

Turing's memo was not all negative. He gave understated praise to a Desch innovation that eliminated the need for a circuit breaker on the Diagonal Board and possibly reduced the number of false stops at the same time. "I think they have got something here, but it remains to be seen how great are the transients [stops] that remain," he wrote. Desch's idea of using electrical switches on the Diagonal Board rather than plugs and a circuit breaker was even more remarkable in

Turing's view, given that the Americans had proceeded much on their own. "Starting from scratch on the design of a Bombe, this method is about as good as our own," he wrote.

What the Turing memo makes clear is that the Desch machine already was different enough from the British Bombes—in its central drive and gearing system for spinning the commutator wheels, in its menu setup, rewind feature, and particularly in its electronics—to label it a truly original American machine, not just a colonial knock-off.

The British had used a system of electrical relays in their first Bombes to identify the positions of the wheels when a hit was made. The system had proved reliable, but Desch had felt that for a more powerful machine a relay system would be too slow. He turned to his experience with the NCR electronic calculator and created a digital electronic tracking and control system that amazed the Navy's engineers. In his final version of the Dayton Bombe, his system of several hundred tubes did more than record the position of a hit, it acted as a control center for the machine. It was able to track the wheel positions, signal the motor and the clutches, then return the wheels to their hit positions. Electronics again played the central role in testing for stecker contradictions. At that point, the wheel locations and steckers were printed and the operator could signal the machine to restart its search.

While Wenger, Engstrom, and other top officials at OP20G no doubt read Turing's report and passed on what they might have learned, Desch himself was never shown the memo, to protect his morale—a delicacy of consideration that later amused Desch. "After the war, they showed me the reports and they weren't very complimentary," he told Tropp in his 1973 interview, then added, chuckling, "[The British] must have had to swallow hard because we had to build 100 machines for them." In fairness to the British, Bob Mumma spoke up in that same interview: "They never dreamed they might do like we did given their limited resources."

But the truth is, the British tried with their limited resources to take the same machine-intensive approach. Desch and his team didn't realize the British had already built fifty three-wheel Bombes by early 1943 and were manufacturing almost two per week, albeit with limited success against the four-wheel naval Enigma.

THE TEMPO AT NCR picked up as spring of 1943 approached, but the men in Dayton were not keeping pace with the war. Desch still was bogged down in the Navy's highest-priority project, nowhere near achieving his goals, while brave young men were dying in the icy waters of the Atlantic.

7

Troubles with
Adam and Eve

March 19, 1943—Dayton, Ohio

AS ONE OF the first maintenance technicians assigned by the Navy to the U.S. Bombe project, Phil Bochicchio, who was to become the project's floor supervisor, arrived in Dayton in March 1943 with orders to report to the U.S. Naval Computing Machine Laboratory, no street address given. But when Bochicchio's train pulled into Union Terminal, no one at the USO lounge there had ever heard of the laboratory, nor was there a listing for it in the phone book. Bochicchio, a twenty-year-old machinist's mate from New Jersey, wasn't shy about asking. He walked the two blocks north from the train station to downtown, then the five or six blocks around to the police and fire stations and the Navy recruiting office. None had heard of the lab, either. Finally, at the Dayton Municipal Building, a Chamber of Commerce official offered to drive Bochicchio out to NCR, where the man knew the Navy had several other projects in progress. At NCR, Bochicchio promptly reported to the Navy liaison officer, but the officer seemed clueless as well, Bochicchio recalled: "He looked at my orders and said, 'I don't know what to do with you.' I said, 'Well, great. Just give me something to do.' "

For the next two or three weeks, Bochicchio designed tools at NCR before he learned anything about the project that had summoned him to Dayton. Unknown to him, the Navy and FBI were completing a thorough background check before giving him his orders. "Finally, I got a letter from my dad saying [to] call home as soon as I can. When I called, my dad said, 'What kind of trouble are you in, boy? The FBI has been here, naval intelligence has been here. All the neighbors are wondering.' "

Bochicchio wasn't in trouble, but he was in for a lot of hard work over the next two years. As floor manager, he was in charge of setting up and debugging the sensitive decrypting machines. Unlike the later production models, which stood more than seven feet tall and weighed two and a half tons each, the first two prototypes, Adam and Eve, were small enough to stand on sawhorses, but like all complex, unproven machinery, they were prone to seemingly endless glitches.

Bochicchio said a big part of Desch's engineering headache was trying to please both the Navy theoreticians, who designed the logic of the machine and insisted on speed, and the Navy codebreakers, who wanted something reliable and easy to operate and maintain. "The mathematician thinks one way, the cryptologist thinks another. And you're sitting in the middle, and you have to try to figure out how in the hell to give them both what they need from the machine."

Following Turing's visit, debate between Navy engineers and codebreakers reached its height over the design of the fast wheel on the machine. In March 1943, Engstrom repeated his "request," in no uncertain terms, for a one-size wheel design. This time around, Desch complied with his boss's wishes, although the stresses on the single fast wheel proved to be a source of continuing frustration for him and his design team, even after the first machines went into production.

OP20G's September 1942 memo requesting money for the Bombe project had promised to deliver the first NCR machines to the Navy in February 1943—a promise that was unrealistic but nonetheless backed by Desch himself. A month after the approval of his design, Desch had written to Meader on October 23, 1942, that he would need close to sixty sailors for assembly and repair work on the Bombes, beginning at the end of the year, "so that they will be thoroughly trained in the servicing of the equipment when it is ready for use."

If Americans suffered from any universal flaw during World War II, it was the belief that Yankee industrial know-how could work miracles overnight. Hence, if the first British Bombes were designed and produced in eight months, why then American industry ought to be able to do the same, even with a far more complex machine, in little more than half the time.

But by February 1943, after five months of intensive development, all Desch had been able to fashion were two wheezy prototypes that were prone to oil leaks and breakdowns after only a few minutes of operating at the speeds demanded. A month later, when the German U-boats unleashed their fury against Allied shipping in an all-out effort to turn the war, Desch still hadn't produced a working machine.

AS THE SPRING U-boat offensive opened, the Germans changed some of their codes and tightened up their procedures so that the Allies were again shut out of the submarine code systems. They remained blind for more than a week during what became the worst month for the Allies in the Battle of the Atlantic. More than twice as many Allied merchant ships (ninety-five) went to the bottom in March as in February.

The destruction might have been even worse had another surge of insight among the British codebreakers not allowed the three-wheel Bombes to be useful again. U-boats were required to report the sighting of any Allied convoy to Admiral Dönitz's headquarters, using a special short-signal code so that Allied direction-finding equipment wouldn't have time to home in on their transmissions. However, the British had a copy of the latest codebook for those short signals, captured from U-559 in November 1942. The codebooks, plus an order to U-boat skippers to report weather conditions and convoy sightings in the Enigma's simpler three-wheel mode, allowed Bletchley's Hut 8 to solve Shark for 90 of the 112 days between March 10 and June 30, 1943.

Although the decryptions were by no means immediate, with many keys taking weeks to solve, old-fashioned cryptanalysis had again saved the day, and it was a good thing. The British were having as little luck as the Americans with their two separate designs for a four-wheel Bombe. During tests in April, the projected fast-wheel speed of one prototype had to be drastically reduced from three thousand rpm to twelve hundred. The first production models, introduced in June, were to prove less than reliable as well.

By mid-1943, with its ongoing problems as well as OP20G's promise to let the British oversee its Enigma efforts, England wished all the best for the NCR program. After all, the British reentry into Shark had been based on such an unpredictable foundation—captured materials and enemy error—that Bletchley Park didn't dare accuse the Americans of wasting resources on developing a four-wheel Bombe. The NCR Bombe offered perhaps the best hope of a consistent break into Shark.

Despite all the setbacks in Dayton, OP20G had no choice but to continue its investment in the project, and it bet millions of dollars more that Desch and his engineers could overcome the next set of technical hurdles. They instructed him to rush to the production stage and stand ready to build as many as three hundred machines to tackle what the British feared most—changes in the Enigma systems that might call for all 336 wheel orders to be tested, and with only weak cribs to help.

While Desch and his men fretted over the final design of the Bombes, other sections of NCR were setting production records, something that made the Navy optimistic about the Building 26 project, if and when it moved into the manufacturing phase. Despite its early problems meeting Navy demands in 1941, NCR went on to establish one of the best corporate records of the war. In January 1942, NCR earned the first of its five "E" awards from the Army and Navy— an honor given to companies that were deemed to have gone beyond the call of duty. Only one other company in America, Dayton's Frigidaire, earned an equal number of E awards.

Part of NCR's success was due to the company's improved ability to direct outside subcontractors. By mid-1943, the engineers and technicians in Building 26 were amazed at how quickly they could get anything they wanted from NCR and the hundreds of subcontractors on the project. Thousands of different precision parts were produced for each Bombe. "From an engineering standpoint, it was wonderful," said Lou Sandor, one of the NCR engineers assigned to Desch's team.

The abilities to produce reliable precision parts and to deliver them on time were to be essential to the complex assembly and testing operation. Gears would have to be made to specific tolerances and be hard enough to withstand high speeds, sudden braking, and intense stresses. The commutators would have to be exactly balanced so that they would not distort while spinning. Their embedded metal contacts would have to be cut and milled to exact lengths so that electrical pulses to the rest of the machine were perfectly timed. Even the miles of electrical cable for each machine would have to be specially designed and ordered.

Secrecy requirements made the supervising of subcontractors tricky. They could not be told the why of their work, and every effort was made to prevent them from guessing. For instance, the number 26 was never used on parts specifications. The manufacturers of the commutators were told to number their contacts from 00 to 25. The cable manufacturers were told to make the cords in twenty-eight, not twenty-six, different colors.

Even when the secrecy problems were overcome, creating a functioning Bombe was a tall order, especially when the first wheel of the machine was designed to rotate at close to two thousand rpm—down from a hoped-for 3,440 rpm in September 1942 but still as fast as a car engine cruising at highway speeds. At such velocities, keeping the wheels in balance and in their original shape was a formidable task, especially since Engstrom had nixed Desch's idea of different-size wheels.

The Adam and Eve prototypes were prone to sparks and short circuits that ruined decoding runs and oil leaks that created maintenance nightmares. The technical hurdles continued as Desch moved during the spring and summer of 1943 to his second set of prototypes, Cain and Abel, and then to his production machines. To make proper contact with the spinning wheels, the sensing brushes on the face of the machine had to be kept oil-free. Power from the five-horsepower electrical motor had to be distributed evenly through a labyrinth of motors, shafts, gears, and clutches, or the resulting stresses would cause the machine to overheat and grind to a halt. The line shafts had to be beveled to precise tolerances so that the rewind mechanism would return the machine to the exact location of the hit. In short, the NCR Bombe was like a high-performance race-car engine being pushed to its limits—before anyone even knew for certain it would work.

BESIDES GRAPPLING WITH the Bombe's technical flaws, Desch also had to contend with his boss and unwanted houseguest, Ralph Meader. The project's naval supervisor was constantly on Desch's back. Mumma said the pressure on Desch "just got worse and worse. . . . We worked seven days a week, you know, and pretty long hours. One Easter Sunday, I know, I laid off and didn't come to work and Joe was awful mad about it." Vince Gulden, another member of Desch's engineering team, remembered working ninety-hour weeks that spring. "Meader was on the quarterdeck with a whip and he was giving us stories about [the Battle of the] Coral Sea—how it wouldn't have happened if you guys had been there and finished earlier. We heard that more than once." The Bombe, of course, would not have helped the Americans against the Japanese code systems in the Pacific, so Meader was either bluffing or ignorant about the purpose of the NCR machines. The former seems more likely.

Guilt was a common method for motivating workers in war plants all over the country. Posters on bulletin boards, next to time clocks, on factory walls, and in break rooms often showed factory workers shoulder to shoulder with soldiers and sailors. The idea was to create an attitude in workers that they were "production soldiers" on a par with the men fighting on the front—and to remind them that, unlike those in combat, they were not risking their lives and should therefore pull their weight by working harder. The factory-worker-as-warrior message was so prevalent by 1944 that an official of the National Association of Manufacturers was moved to quip, "The boys in the foxholes would, on their return, be forced to employ a press agent to convince the public that soldiers, too, had something to do with our victory."

When he could get away for an hour or two, Desch liked to retreat to his garden plot off Wilmington Pike, near a local dairy at the time, where he grew everything from corn to kohlrabi, his daughter said. And he loved to whistle, mostly Sousa marches, snatches of classical music, and romantic movie scores. But the supersecrecy of his work kept him from confiding in the one person who might have been able to help him handle the stress: his wife, Dorothy.

Desch had a surprisingly romantic and sentimental side. His letters to Dorothy were always addressed to "Sweetie-pie" and often ended with strings of Xs for kisses. On a business trip to New York in 1938, three years after their marriage, he wrote her two letters on the same day, morning and evening, both telling her how much he missed her.

When he could find the time, he loved to go out dancing with Dorothy. He was an excellent ballroom dancer, especially at waltzes, Debbie Anderson said. "Mom said more than once they cleared the floor" at the Biltmore Hotel, a popular Dayton nightspot at the time. But by spring of 1943, a night out with his wife had become a rarity: Desch was captive to the top secret work inside Building 26.

Despite the endless hours of work both in Dayton and Washington, the Americans still had not made their hoped-for decisive contribution to cracking the U-boat codes. That was evident in the round of intelligence negotiations between Britain and the United States in May 1943. The U-boat onslaught in the spring and the delays in both Bombe programs strained the GCCS-OP20G relationship. So had demands by America's Admiral Ernest J. King that his ships and planes be allowed to attack the special refueler U-boats, called "milk cows" (*Milchkühe*), even if the pinpoint attacks might raise German suspicions that the Enigma was being read.

Wenger fretted over the future of OP20G. Without the American Bombe, his agency would have no real contribution to the European war and no way to prove the need for his machine-driven approach to cryptanalysis. The M section, with all its technical expertise, was reduced to using hand methods against the easy parts of the Enigma keys already broken by the British. On the rare occasions when the Americans did solve a key, it took the group an embarrassing average of six hundred hours. Moreover, OP20G had to organize itself to deal with a two-front war. Most of its people and resources had to be focused on the Japanese problems: the Navy was engaged in a death struggle with the Japanese, and OP20G had promised Britain that it would carry the codebreaking burden in the Pacific.

JAPAN WAS A very different cryptanalytic enemy from Germany. Although Japan used some automatic encrypting machines, such as Purple, its vital naval messages made use of rather old-fashioned paper-and-pencil code-additive systems like the ones OP20G had tackled during the 1930s. Message clerks started with code groups of numbers for specific words and terms, then added or subtracted another set of numbers from another book. A machine program for tackling the Japanese additives had begun even before the Bombe project. But until OP20G's research crew was freed from the Bombe effort, the Japanese project was the child of IBM, not NCR. Attacking a code system via machine called for lots of memory, and stacks of punched cards, such as those used on IBM tabulating machines, were the most practical mass-memory devices of the era.

One of the central attacks on additives was based on trying various "subtractions" from the code to see if the results matched any known high-frequency code groups. Tabulators and their kin were obvious choices for the enormous task of sorting and listing the thousands of different code groups. With much labor, they could be used to find strings of repeated text in different messages and, hence, point codebreakers to their underlying meanings.

With IBM already a major supplier of tabulators and other equipment to codebreakers, it was natural for OP20G to turn to Thomas Watson's company for help in tackling the Japanese codes. IBM agreed to help design and build a range of special "tabs" to supplement the hundreds of standard machines leased by OP20G during the war. In fact, OP20G became one of the two largest users of IBM machines in the Washington area during the war. The other was William Friedman's Army group, which had moved across the river from OP20G's new Nebraska Avenue headquarters.

Engstrom and Meader may have felt some competitive pressure because of IBM's ability to deliver its products quickly, but they maintained their faith in NCR and Joe Desch, explaining to their superiors how the Bombe was a much more challenging engineering project.* They might have also mentioned that IBM was making a healthy profit from codebreakers through its leased tabulators and punch-card sales while NCR was working on a no-profit basis. Navy and Army codebreaking operations were each paying close to one million dollars per year to IBM.

Still, if the NCR project was to survive, it had to produce working machines and useful intelligence very soon, if not immediately. In late May, Wenger ordered Desch to ready the two temperamental prototype machines for use on Enigma intercepts to be sent from Washington to Dayton. The results were to be forwarded to the British as examples of America's new abilities. Worried and hopeful, a Navy delegation from Washington—including the head of naval communications, Admiral Joseph Redman—arrived in Dayton near the end of the month, just as a secure communications line was set up between Building 26 and OP20G in Washington.

But even with the most attentive coaxing from Desch and his team, Adam and Eve were feisty and unpredictable. They could be made to perform now for up to several hours, rather than minutes, before breaking down, but oil leaks and faulty electrical contacts continued to plague them. Problems as basic as the carbon brushes splintering from their contact with the high-speed commutator wheels seemed intractable. As the summer of 1943 drew near, the Bombe again seemed to be too much of a challenge, even for the talented Joe Desch.

NOT LONG AFTER lunch on May 28, in a secured inner room at NCR's Building 26, Phil Bochicchio was conducting a test run on

---

* While IBM could deliver its standard machines quickly, it took them many months to produce the first complex version of the special Navy tabulator equipment.

Adam when its high-pitched whine suddenly died, and the machine shut off. At first, he thought it was just one more electrical short.

But then, as it was designed to do, the Bombe came back to life and began slowly to rewind. That stop suggested that a solution might have been found, but more testing was needed to see if a possible Enigma key had been identified.

Each Bombe solution was the result of a two-step process. To begin a test, the operator first set the starting positions of the wheels to match a codebreaker's menu—that is, the suspected pairings between the plain and cipher text and their positions within the message. When the Bombe was started, electrical energy raced through the ever-changing circuits of its spinning wheels, trying all the thousands of various settings that might satisfy the letter patterns in the menu. While the Bombe was going through the many unsuccessful settings, all of the electrical wires were "hot." But if the conditions of the codebreaker's menu were fulfilled, one circuit would become "cold."

At that point, the machine stopped, rewound back to the suspected setting, and in about fifteen seconds made a second or hot test. It polled the Diagonal Board, looking for inconsistencies, such as two letters being steckered to the same letter. If no such contradictions were found, the Bombe would print a "story," giving wheel positions and possible steckers. With that in hand, a cryptanalyst used an Enigma mock-up to see if the story led to the cipher message becoming sensible German plain text. If so, a Jackpot was declared.

On cue, Adam began printing out its results during Bochicchio's test run. Still, he was skeptical. He had a fellow mechanic, K. P. Cook, run the same menu through Eve. Eve shut off in precisely the same rotor positions, went through its hot-point test, and printed out the resulting sequence of settings.

"We concluded that both machines were working, because they both gave us the same printout," Bochicchio said. "But we didn't know what it meant because we hadn't been cleared that far" for security reasons. Whatever its purpose, he said, "I thought to myself, 'That's a hell of a machine.' "

Bochicchio immediately went to the naval offices and gave the printout to Meader, who then cabled the results to Navy intelligence in Washington, using Building 26's new high-security encryption machine.

Three or four days later, Bochicchio said, Meader heard some exciting news back from Washington. "They told us that one hit had been worth the entire cost of the project," Bochicchio recalled.

That first hit must have seemed like redemption for Desch and the others who had labored so long and so hard on the NCR Bombe, but it didn't provide information, as Meader had been told, that the Navy could use. The test menu that had been fed into the two machines had been based on an Enigma intercept that was perhaps weeks old and, OP20G would soon learn, had been decrypted first by GCCS.

Nor had the NCR team overcome all the technical hurdles still in its path. As Dayton entered its steamy summer months, the engineers were still struggling with the machine's most basic parts. Those large rotors seemed doomed to overheat, lose their shape, and create faulty electrical signals. The carbon sensing brushes also seemed to have been meant only for slow and dependable tabulators. As quick fixes were made to those parts, more oil leaks developed on the prototypes. Those problems raised such fears about the production model's design that assembly was halted and all message testing was suspended.

Meanwhile, in the vast expanses of the Atlantic, the battle of men, ships, and wits couldn't wait. The tide already was beginning to turn—without the help of the American Bombes.

$$8$$

U-boats on the Run

June 5, 1943—Azores area, Central Atlantic

IT WAS A choice morning for submarine hunting—calm seas, a gentle southerly wind, and just a hint of sea haze on the horizon—as Lieutenant "Goose" McAuslun and Lieutenant Richard S. Rogers each flew their U.S. Navy aircraft over the vast, empty reaches of the Atlantic, midway between Jacksonville and Morocco. McAuslun's Avenger torpedo-bomber carried four 250-pound depth charges set to detonate at fifteen feet below the surface, just deep enough to catch a submarine in the midst of crash-diving. Rogers's Wildcat fighter was equipped with six .50-caliber machine guns, an effective armament for clearing the decks of any surfaced U-boat. But in order to defeat their elusive prey, the pilots had something just as important as their weapons: up-to-date intelligence information, in this case from the British, locating a line of seventeen German U-boats, codenamed "Group Trutz," lying in ambush for a slow, eastbound convoy of thirty-one Allied merchant ships.

The pilots' mission: kill the subs before they could sight the Allied vessels. The pair was on the last leg of a five-hour patrol, seventy miles from their escort carrier, USS *Bogue,* when McAuslun spotted *U-217* cruising placidly on the surface about seven miles to their right. McAuslun signaled Rogers, who immediately banked his Wildcat and dove. "He just tore off and left me in his smoke," McAuslun recalled. After Rogers strafed the sub three times, killing several gunners and starting a fire in the conning tower, the U-boat commander decided to dive. That's when McAuslun dropped his tubby Avenger down out of the sun.

Leveling off at an altitude of one hundred feet, he released all four depth bombs on either side of the sub's submerging hull. The explosions lifted it out of the water and split it nearly in two. The sub sank in just thirty-three seconds, with Rogers strafing the upright stern one last time before it went to the bottom.

If Rogers dispatched his duties with a bit more fervor than might have seemed necessary, his excitement was understandable. *U-217* was the first Nazi submarine destroyed by the U.S. Navy in a purely offensive action. The day before, making use of the same communications intelligence, pilots from the *Bogue* had damaged and scattered three other U-boats from Group Trutz. Those two days marked a turning point in the Battle of the Atlantic: the Allies were no longer just detouring convoys to evade the submarines, and their escorts were no longer waiting for the wolf packs to attack. They had evolved the organization and the means to pursue the subs before they could strike. The Allies were no longer the hunted, but the hunters.

The Allies sank forty-one German submarines in May 1943, a nearly threefold increase from the fifteen sunk the month before. By May 24, Dönitz had had enough: he licked his wounds and pulled his subs out of the North Atlantic convoy routes. While Dönitz and the German cryptologists refused to believe that their Enigma codes were being read by the Allies, they were mostly correct in blaming two other key factors for their submarine war's demise: the superiority of Allied detection equipment and the omnipresent air cover in the Atlantic.

The U-boat skippers could run, but they had nowhere to hide. In the four months from May through August, the Allies dispatched 106 Atlantic U-boats to the bottom—21 more than in all of 1942. Of the 42 sunken subs credited to the Americans in the critical summer months of June through September, 21—or half—had transmitted or received messages revealing their locations to the Allies. But Shark decrypts at the time were still inconsistent and slow in coming, limiting their usefulness to sub hunters. In fact, that summer the Americans sank only five U-boats within two weeks of their locations being decrypted, and they were still almost wholly dependent on Ultra intelligence from the British, who relied on their three-wheel Bombes, years of cribbing experience, and captured German short-signal code-books to break into Shark.

OP20G did not yet play a major role in Enigma codebreaking. Although Desch's prototype produced their first real Jackpot in late June, the U.S. Navy did not have the machines, the methods, or the trained people it needed to be a true codebreaking partner for several more months.

As the summer progressed, Desch and his engineers relied on old-fashioned tinkering to get their machines to behave. They found better ways of protecting the Bakelite wheels from heat, perhaps by improving the Bombe's ventilating system, which on the early production machines consisted of little more than smokestacks. They also improved their methods of polishing, smoothing, and adjusting the spinning rotors so they were less likely to distort. Phil Bochicchio served up a few important tricks, including soaking the machines' leather seals in oil before installation, so they would swell and prevent leakage, and installing a circuit tester that checked for opens and shorts prior to running the machines.

Tired of OP20G's apprentice role to the British, Wenger and Engstrom pressured Meader, and in turn Meader pushed Desch even harder. If OP20G was too late to be the savior of the Atlantic, there was still much to do to vanquish the U-boats. Despite the period of calm after the spring U-boat offensive, no one was certain of the safety of the convoys—all the more troubling given the massive buildup of men and matériel that would be needed for the planned invasion of Europe.

Even after the heavy losses of U-boats in May 1943, Hitler and Dönitz showed no signs of scaling back their sub offensive. At a Führer Conference on June 3, 1943, Hitler declared: "There can be no talk of letup in submarine warfare. The enemy forces tied up by our submarine warfare are tremendous, even though the actual losses inflicted by us are no longer great."

The Kriegsmarine wasn't the only worry for Allied codebreakers. Germany's Army, Air Force, rocket-development team, and police agencies might switch over to four-wheel Enigmas. And those German systems that continued to use a three-wheel machine might easily broaden the blackout by changing their procedures or making more sophisticated use of their plugboards.

Worse, there were fears of dangerous new Nazi technologies, including a new breed of bigger, faster U-boats and sub-launched rockets that could rain terror on U.S. coastal cities. As Samuel Eliot Morison wrote:

> Although the turning point had been passed by the end of May 1943, it was by no means a foregone conclusion that it would not turn again. First one side would obtain an advantage with a new weapon or tactics; then the other would produce a new device or defensive weapon to counteract it. And always there was bright expectations for the Germans, and apprehensions for the Allies, that . . . secret weapons would burst forth like monstrous messengers from Mars, to sweep Allied shipping from the sea.

In the summer of 1943, the U-boats faced a new frustration in their attempts to locate and destroy Allied shipping. The two-year, nearly unbroken run the Germans had enjoyed in reading British naval Cypher Number 3, the primary code for the convoys, came to an abrupt end in June when the Allies switched to the more secure Cypher Number 5—a move long urged by OP20G's Laurance Safford.

The switch in codes was a classic example of the machinations of spy versus spy. Ultra's early and limited breaks into Shark more than hinted to the British what they had refused to hear from the Americans as early as 1941: that the Germans had information on convoy locations that could be obtained only through codebreaking. The

American suspicions had been confirmed in March 1943 when Lieutenant Mahan, an OP20G analyst in Washington, noticed a German intercept in which Dönitz had abruptly canceled an order of a few hours before and ordered a dramatic change of course for his U-boats. Mahan left his post at the OP20G complex near Tenley Circle and rushed downtown to the convoy-routing department in the Main Navy Building, where he insisted on seeing the latest Allied orders to the convoys. After some bureaucratic haggling, he got his way and soon found the detour order for the convoy that had triggered the change of course by Dönitz.

If any more proof were needed, the switch from Cypher Number 3 to Cypher Number 5 had instant and dramatic results for the fortunes of Allied convoys. Although the U-boats sank forty-one merchant vessels in May 1943, it was the last good month of hunting for Dönitz and his wolf packs in the Atlantic. From that June until the end of the war, the Germans never sank more than fourteen merchant ships in any one month.

Allied intelligence victories weren't the only factors that turned the tide in the Atlantic, nor perhaps even the most important. Much credit must be given first of all to the valor, skill, and persistence of the British Navy and Air Force, particularly for waging a devastating air campaign in the Bay of Biscay—the gauntlet that U-boats had to traverse between their bases in western France and their hunting grounds in the Atlantic.

But beyond the human factor, a host of improvements in antisubmarine warfare converged against the U-boats: improved air cover, weaponry, and detection; better training and coordination among antisubmarine forces; new methods for analyzing U-boat movements; and more aggressive tactics, including those of the new escort class of carriers like the *Bogue*.

By 1943, the fusion of science and the military that Vannevar Bush had sought through the National Defense Research Committee began to pay big dividends for the war effort. Allied technical developments came fast and furious in the antisubmarine war. The old "ashcan" type of depth charge, dropped with a wish and a prayer from the sterns of destroyers, was replaced with a rocket-propelled design with a streamlined casing and a contact fuse. The new depth charges—a larger version called the "Hedgehog" for destroyers and the smaller "Mousetrap" for chase vessels—were grouped on the foredeck and launched in deadly patterns ahead of the ship, before the ship's sonar passed over the U-boat and contact was lost. Unlike the old depth charges, which detonated at a preset depth, the new projectiles did not explode unless they hit something. Their contact fuses eliminated both the danger to the ship from a shallow, premature explosion and the roiling underwater noise that overwhelmed sonar operators trying to maintain contact with the submarine.

A variety of new weapons were introduced to enhance the air attack as well: powerful five-hundred-pound depth charges, deadly rockets, and the small homing torpedo known as "Fido," which could chase submarines with devastating accuracy as they began their dives.

Just as important as the development of new anti-sub technology was the Allied ability to adapt their training and tactics to put those new weapons to best use. In May 1943, the U.S. Navy at last created an organization to pull its fragmented campaign against the U-boats into focus: the Tenth Fleet was the new central command for protecting the convoys and coordinating the attack against the subs. The new fleet, which had no ships, was basically a reshuffling and regrouping of existing units that had sprung up haphazardly during the war in response to specific needs. Under the command of Rear Admiral Francis S. Low, "a tough, conscientious, intelligent and hardworking officer," the Tenth Fleet cleared the way not only for improved coordination but for uniform training of personnel, faster dispersion of new anti-sub devices, and better instruction in their use.

The Germans tried to counter the Allied technological advantage with new weapons and new tactics of their own. As early as April 1943, the Nazis had begun equipping many of their subs with powerful new antiaircraft weapons, usually a group of four twenty-millimeter machine guns placed in the conning tower and a thirty-seven-millimeter antiaircraft cannon mounted on a platform (dubbed a "bandstand" by the Allies) behind the tower. The combination proved daunting for many Allied aircraft, including the heavily armed long-range bombers.

Dönitz eventually made a "fight-back" strategy an edict for his sub crews in September 1943. The subs were to cross heavily patrolled areas in teams, then circle and fire back with antiaircraft guns whenever Allied planes swooped in. Dönitz reasoned that the U-boats were most vulnerable, particularly to air-dropped depth charges and Fido homing torpedoes, during the thirty seconds to a minute that it took them to crash-dive.

In turn, the Allies countered the "fight-back" strategy by sending out patrol planes in pairs. By staying on the surface to fight, the U-boats only improved the chances of one of the two planes scoring a hit. It is no surprise then that the success rate of Allied aircraft attacks doubled in the last half of 1943, with one in four resulting in sub sinkings and 40 percent causing damage to their targets.

The Allies also found better ways of detecting U-boats, including more powerful and accurate sonar—the supersonic echo-ranging equipment for finding subs underwater. In addition, small high-frequency direction-finding sets, known as HF/DF or Huff-Duff, were installed on ships to widen the existing land-based net for homing in on radio signals from surfaced U-boats and tracking their general direction. To search for submerged U-boats from the air, pilots could drop sonobuoys—floats equipped with hydrophones and radio transmitters.

The single most significant improvement for detecting surfaced submarines was the introduction of microwave anti–surface vessel (ASV) radar, which was more accurate and reliable than conventional radar and took up less space and weight so that it could be installed in aircraft. The Germans, who struggled until the end of the war to develop a submarine that could stay submerged indefinitely, considered airborne ASV radar the biggest reason for their defeat in the Atlantic.

Allied air coverage for the convoys was nearly universal by the spring of 1943. To fill in uncovered regions, such as the notorious "black pit" in the central Atlantic near Greenland, more long-range and very-long-range aircraft were based in Newfoundland and Iceland. Meanwhile, the role of the small escort carriers like the *Bogue*, known also as CVEs, was expanded so that they could hunt and kill submarines as well as provide continuous air coverage for the convoys. Converted from merchant vessels, the "baby flattops" could transport up to thirty planes and reach speeds of more than eighteen knots—faster than most Nazi U-boats, even while surfaced.

Admiral Low planned to attack the Nazi U-boat fleet when and where it was most vulnerable: the 1,600-ton milk cows. The big U-tankers allowed the combat U-boats to stay far out at sea. Eliminating the German ability to refuel in mid-ocean would reduce the number of U-boats on patrol. With the promised help of timely breaks into Shark, the Navy's antisubmarine forces planned to attack the rendezvous points of refuelers—with the chance of surprising multiple subs as they cruised the surface looking for one another or as they were refueling.

As the British warned, however, the opportunity also brought with it a great risk: too much success in sinking the milk cows would lead the Nazis to question the security of their submarine codes and perhaps put an end to Ultra. But Admiral King insisted that the potential benefits were too great. In an April 27, 1943, telegram to the British Admiralty, he wrote: "While I am equally concerned with you as to security of 'Z' information it is my belief that we are not deriving from it fullest value. The refueling submarine is the key to high speed, long range U/boat operations. To deprive the enemy of refuelers would at once decrease the effectiveness and radius of entire U/boat deployment."

In mid-June, the escort-carrier commanders—once given the signal that their convoys were within coverage of land-based aircraft—were free to attack known concentrations of U-boats. Along with his new orders to the escort commanders, Low later wired that he would release special intelligence "that will enable you to more quickly and positively" find U-boat targets.

Much of that special intelligence was expected to be generated by the U.S. Bombes, but their operational usefulness was still several months away. OP20G's own history claims that a test run on a Bombe in Dayton found the Shark keys and broke the messages that helped guide the *Bogue* and McAuslun's Avenger to *U-217* on June 5. But log sheets for the Shark keys that month show a British solution, and the official OP20G war diary says the Dayton Bombe didn't tap effectively into Shark for the first time until June 22—decrypting a May 31 message.

Regardless of who gets the credit for the Allied successes in early June, the British and Americans were by then collaborating closely to break into Shark, sharing keys, cribs, and equipment and providing each other with all U-boat-related intelligence. Bletchley solved the toughest parts of the Shark keys, such as the wheel order and steckers, then let the Americans clean up with the easier task of finding the lower-level keys, such as the starting positions of the wheels and ring settings. But even then, the Americans, often relying on hand methods, rarely beat GCCS to the easier keys.

The British continued to front the attack against Shark all through the summer of 1943, even though it was a bad time for reading U-boat transmissions. In July, the Germans introduced a new reflector on their four-wheel machine, and Dönitz's withdrawal from the North Atlantic gave the codebreakers fewer messages to work with. In June, the British solved fourteen days of Shark keys, all within a week's time, while the American Bombe program continued its struggle.

Yet by summer's end, America's role as junior partner in Ultra began to change.

THE JUNE 18 order from OP20G to Dayton must have seemed like a frightening case of déjà vu. The Navy wanted to scratch the existing Bombe design for a whole new codebreaking machine, with a semi-automatic method of switching rotors and greater machine speeds— all without delaying production. Desch was stunned. In effect, the Navy wanted a machine approaching the complexity of what we now call a modern computer. Leading theorists knew even then that electronic digital processing would become the basis for computers, but more practical types like Desch, who realized the limits of industrial production, also knew it would take years to put such a machine into operation. Desch had told the Navy as much in the fall of 1942, but here they were again with their electronic pipe dream.

Desch went to Meader and pleaded his case. There simply was no practical, high-speed substitute for the many hardwired rotor wheels that could be rearranged on the Bombe's drive spindles. Thousands of tubes in very dense circuits would be needed to imitate all the possible rotor wirings of the sixty-four wheels on a Bombe. The energy requirements and the strain on precious war materials would be staggering. And the tubes would generate so much heat that the machines couldn't be depended on to operate reliably.

Meader, who normally went along with whatever his naval superiors wanted, was quick this time to back Desch. He dashed off a message to Engstrom that same day, arguing that too much money, manpower, and scarce materials had already been invested in the first Bombe model, which was now so close to production it deserved a chance. The Navy had little choice but to renew its faith in Desch and hope that his hundred machines, when they finally reached Washington, would do the job.

By the last week of July, fifteen Bombes had been assembled at NCR, but none would work properly for long. "We were plagued with false stops or with no stops at all," said Gilman McDonald, one of five naval officers assigned to Building 26 in mid-May to study how best to operate the Bombes. Both Desch and Howard "were completely mystified" by the behavior of their production models, he said.

It was perhaps Desch's darkest hour. If the Navy scrapped the project, a year of intensive work and millions of dollars would be declared a waste, and he, along with Wenger and Engstrom, would take the brunt of the blame. But Desch relied again on his practical side, and at the very last minute he made a discovery that revived hope: the faces of the rotors still were not flawlessly smooth, causing the sensitive brushes to bounce and trigger false stops. "All rotors were then sanded with fine emery cloth on a flat metal surface" to smooth out the distortions, McDonald said.

But solving one problem immediately led to another: the machines failed to arrive at the correct stops. The tiny copper slivers from the sanding of the rotor faces were bridging the near-microscopic gaps between the rotor contacts—a mere twenty-thousandth of an inch—and shorting out the legitimate stops.

To solve both problems, Desch insisted on a rigorous program of preventive maintenance: all rotors and brushes, on each bank of every Bombe, would be sanded and cleaned of copper slivers on a regular basis. The maintenance crew developed tiny tools and blowers for cleaning out the minuscule gaps between the commutator contacts. Desch requested that an entire new maintenance staff and routine be established to make sure the delicate tasks were done right.

Again, the Navy trusted in Desch's judgment, and the project was saved.

August 3, 1943—Central Atlantic

AFTER NEARLY FOURTEEN weeks of hunting in the Americas, with two kills to their credit off the East Coast, the crew of U-66 was more than halfway home, skimming along the Atlantic's sun-dazzled surface 457 miles west-southwest of the Azores. Thinking the worst of their mission over, the watch crew was caught off guard when the sub was spotted by a Wildcat-Avenger team from the escort carrier USS *Card*. The pilots had not found the U-boat by accident. They had been alerted by the Tenth Fleet that U-66 would be in the vicinity to rendezvous with U-117, a milk cow, and refuel for the trip home—information gleaned from Shark intercepts.

Wildcat pilot Arne S. Paulson bore in on U-66 and strafed the deck and conning tower, instantly killing the deck officer. The sub's skipper, Kapitänleutnant Friedrich Markworth, ordered battle stations and refused to submerge until Avenger pilot Richard L. Cormier followed in to drop his depth charges and Fido homing torpedo. Both weapons, however, failed to release. Markworth dived and resurfaced to fight again, only to be wounded in the stomach by more of Paulson's strafing. Cormier made a second run in his Avenger, this time unloading all his bombs. Though badly damaged, U-66 dived a second time and managed to escape once again.

But inside U-66, the crew was in turmoil. In addition to Markworth, the first watch officer and a midshipman had been seriously wounded. The men waited patiently until the cover of night, when the sub could resurface and radio headquarters for help. Dönitz ordered the sub to a nearer rendezvous point with *U-117*, but once again the Allies decrypted the time and location.

Four days later, the two subs met in the early-morning hours. *U-117* sent over its doctor to tend to the wounded and its first watch officer to fill in for Markworth. As daylight broke clear and bright, the tanker started refueling *U-66*.

Just minutes later, Avenger pilot Asbury H. Sallenger found the two submarines, about five hundred yards apart. Both subs let loose with their flak guns, but Sallenger attacked anyway, bombing *U-66* and squeezing off a few machine-gun rounds at the deck of the milk cow. Sallenger hovered out of range for twenty-five minutes until more planes from the *Card* showed up. When *U-66* started to dive, Sallenger went in again to drop a Fido but missed the smaller sub as *U-117* opened up with its guns. Two arriving Wildcat pilots strafed *U-117* "unmercifully," according to ship logs, before two more Avengers bore in with depth charges and Fidos, finally sinking *U-117* with all hands.

U-boat headquarters was still unaware of the loss of *U-117* when it ordered the tanker to cancel its New York harbor mine-laying mission and to serve as a refueler west of the Canaries. But the only U-tanker in the Atlantic that month was now debris. The submarines that had counted on it for fuel were forced to limp home. All in all, the sinking of *U-117* was a persuasive example of King's offensive strategy.

As planned, the Allies did indeed nearly wipe out the Nazi U-tankers in the summer of 1943, sinking nine of twelve milk cows in operation at the time. Shark decrypts played an important role for the Americans: two of the three refuelers sunk by U.S. escort carriers were located with the aid of radio intelligence. Still, most of the milk cows fell victim to the intense air campaign waged by the British in the Bay of Biscay.

The Kriegsmarine may have been on the run, but it was far from giving up. Dönitz ordered the U-boats back into the North Atlantic in September, armed with more powerful antiaircraft weapons, new decoys, and the T5 acoustic torpedo (the Zaunkönig), which could home in on the propeller sounds of escort vessels. But the Zaunkönig failed to give the Germans the upper hand, partly because the Allies were already towing the Foxer noisemaker to divert the torpedoes.

The American Bombes were too late to help turn the tide in the Atlantic that summer, but the battle there and the war itself were far from over. Despite their successes, the Allies were still projecting a net increase in the number of U-boats by year's end. What's more, they still rightly feared that Dönitz would try to renew the war against Allied shipping with newer, faster U-boats and more deadly weapons.

Enigma decrypts would be vital to helping the Allies keep track of updates in the U-boat arsenal, including the development of engine snorkels that allowed the subs to stay submerged longer, new microwave equipment for detecting Allied radar, and still more powerful antiaircraft guns. Dönitz especially clung to the hope that a new generation of faster, longer-submerging U-boats would be able to attack Allied ships and speed away without detection. He believed the new U-boats could turn the tide back in favor of the Nazis—if only his embattled crews could maintain their fighting spirit to the end. Even late in the war, he was rallying his U-boat commanders to carry on the war with renewed intensity. In a report transmitted and intercepted on October 22, 1944, Dönitz told his sub fleet that "a new U-boat war must and shall be our most important goal in the war against the western powers. The Navy and its equipment services must work for that end with fanatical energy."

Through the summer of 1943, the engineers and technicians at NCR continued their fight as well, their long hours unabated. In July, the Navy's faith and insistence that Joe Desch could work out the glitches in his Bombe paid off, and the early production models began to show that they could do the job. By August, the machines scored their first useful break into Shark, within a week of message transmission.

IN AUGUST 1943, Bletchley's worst fears about American security seemed to be confirmed: British codebreakers decrypted a stunning message to the Abwehr, Germany's intelligence department, that pointed to a traitor in the highest civilian ranks of the U.S. Navy Department. The decrypt read: "On August 10, the following message came from KO Switzerland: 'For several months coded German orders to operating U-boats have been read. All orders are being read. Addendum: Source: a Swiss-American in a high position in the U.S. Naval Department.'"

Fortunately for Ultra, German security officials once again pooh-poohed the notion, as they had so often in the past, that the Allies were breaking into the Enigma with any kind of regularity. The message went on:

> Chief MND [Military Intelligence Service] excludes the possibility that radio traffic is being read on a continuous basis by the opponents. Naturally, the possibility is always open that a complete set of code equipment with an adjusted key fell into the hands of the enemy from a lost boat. Protection should be given against this possibility by a change of the key word "Andromeda."

There are no records that the Navy ever accused or attempted to prosecute anyone for leaking the Ultra secret to the Nazis via a Swiss agent. But the list of possible civilian suspects within the Navy was very short, leaving open the question of whether the suspect was in a high enough position of status and power to elude prosecution. Regardless of the identity of the man who may have sought to betray the Ultra secret or whose loose lips may have done the same, he couldn't stop the U.S. Bombe from entering production in the fall of 1943 and ultimately shortening the war.

STANDING GUARD ON the night of September 11 by a railroad siding in an empty field behind NCR's Building 26, Navy Midshipman Raymond Torchon kept watch as huge wooden crates were rolled on dollies from a truck bed and into a waiting baggage car. In all, six sealed crates, each several feet taller than a man and longer than a pickup, were brought from a warehouse at the rear of Building 26.

Torchon had no idea what was inside the giant boxes, and he had sense enough not to ask. "All I knew, it was NCR, and I thought they were cash registers," he said in an interview in the fall of 2001. "What did we know? Nobody knew—not for fifty years."

Torchon was one of four Navy sailors assigned to guard the baggage car and its top secret cargo until a train engine arrived at 5:00 A.M. the next morning. The guard detail was then to escort the shipment to Washington, D.C., delivering the first six of some 120 U.S. Bombes to OP20G's codebreaking annex near Tenley Circle. Every week, the same size load left from the same railroad siding, with Torchon and his fellow guards sometimes catching up on their sleep atop the giant boxes. Hidden inside each was a mammoth N-530 production Bombe.

Torchon recalled his meager training for guard duty with laughter. "The day before, the lieutenant [in charge] took us out into the woods and put up some targets. We had .38-caliber guns, and we started shooting. I think we killed two squirrels. I don't know. I thought, 'What the hell is this going to prove?' "

But for the engineers and managers on the NCR project who knew what was inside those crates, those early fall days of 1943 weren't the stuff of nostalgic, carefree memories. Although enough of the bugs had been worked out, no one was as yet certain the Bombes would work over the long run. Perhaps least certain of all was Joseph Wenger, who was overwhelmed by the awesome responsibility of the Bombe project late that summer. To recuperate, he decided to take himself and his family to Florida in September. For the next six months, he relaxed with his wife and son in a cabin in Clearwater, not far from his parents' retirement home. There, he built kites, walked along the beach, and took up again the drawing and sketching he had eschewed for a career in the Navy.

Wenger was still in Florida in November 1943 when the turning point came for the American Bombe. By December, the average time to decrypt a Shark key was just eighteen hours with the help of the new machines. It was seldom more than forty-eight hours until late 1944, when a dearth of messages and a splitting of the U-boat keys lengthened break times for several months. But until the end of the war, the U.S. Bombes were breaking the keys for all Shark messages and most of the German Army and Air Force codes.

After a hospital stay and an OK from his superiors, Wenger returned to work in Washington in April 1944 with his faith in Desch and NCR justified. The Bombes had proved their worth. With no downtime, save for minor repairs and scheduled maintenance, the Bombes were running twenty-four hours per day, every day.

The fact that the Bombes eventually did perform reliably and as promised is a tribute not only to the engineers who designed them but to the skills of the men, and women, who built them.

9

The WAVES Come Aboard

May 1943—Dayton, Ohio

AFTER NAVY BOOT camp at the Hunter College campus in the Bronx and three weeks of background checks, testing, training, and indoctrination in Washington, D.C., seventy young women boarded trains at Union Station in Washington for a top secret assignment they were told they could never discuss, even among themselves, at a destination described to them only as "out West."

They were bright, adventurous, patriotic women, most of them in their early twenties, who had enlisted in the women's naval auxiliary—Women Accepted for Voluntary Emergency Service (WAVES). Selected from "good families" all over America, from the biggest cities to the smallest towns, it's easy to understand how, as their train steamed westward, many of the recruits entertained fantasies of a tour of duty in southern California—with movie stars, sunny beaches, pleasant climes. But those dreams were abandoned when they disembarked later that day at Union Terminal in Dayton, Ohio.

"It rained and rained and rained that month. I thought, 'Oh my gosh, it's going to rain here forever,' " said Catherine Convery Racz, who had been a telephone operator in Boston. She was one of the first among six hundred WAVES in all who assembled Bombes in

Building 26 in 1943 and 1944. Their skills and their pledge of security were desperately needed to offset the wartime shortage of men.

The WAVES may have guessed at the nature of their work, but few had more than an inkling of its significance, even those who went back to Washington in the fall to operate the codebreaking machines. One of them was Evelyn Hodges Vogel, a plucky Missouri native who had lied about her age to enlist in the WAVES at age eighteen. Recruits were supposed to be at least twenty, but Vogel's father, a Navy man himself, had signed the papers against her mother's wishes.

Vogel said the women had been warned by their commanding officers in Washington that they would be punished just as severely as the men if they violated security requirements. "They told us they would shoot us at sunrise if we talked about what we were doing," Vogel said. "And we did keep our mouths shut. Men always think women have big mouths, but we didn't. We were so proud to be serving in the armed forces and doing something women had never done before."

The WAVES organization, less than one year old, had been born in controversy. Concerned about the extra cost and administrative problems, the Navy brass had resisted strong political pressures to enact a women's service until spring of 1942. But once Congress passed the enabling legislation in June, the Navy quickly set up a program, using the leaders of America's elite women's colleges as the top officers to assure the public—and the recruits—that the WAVES would be respectable, ladylike members of the armed services.

Any concerns that the women might be made to ape their male counterparts was dispelled when Parisian couturier Mainbocher was asked to design the WAVES uniform. Donating his work to the Navy, the Chicago native insisted on a simple, proper, but form-fitting and feminine design that proved to be a worthy recruiting tool. A savvy advertising campaign by former journalist and publicist Louise K. Wilde emphasized the glamorous aspects of naval service—fashionable uniforms, training on college campuses, unusual work, and opportunities to meet men—and attracted a large number of enlistees.

Desch and Meader had felt the Bombe design and the refinement of its components were far enough along to justify taking the final steps toward large-scale manufacturing. The second set of prototype machines, Cain and Abel, which were much like the final production Bombes, were under construction, contracts were being let to suppliers, and there were no hints of the technical problems that were to emerge in June and July. While Desch scrambled to find skilled civilian workers, Meader scoured the Navy for more electrical engineers and put the final touches on a program for training the many codebreaking clerks who would be needed for the expected rush of U-boat intelligence once the American Bombes arrived in Washington.

THE NAVY KNEW that, in order to compete with the much higher wages offered in the private market, it would have to supplement its meager salaries for women volunteers with plenty of amenities—comfortable living quarters, decent food, and, where possible, recreational facilities and dating opportunities. The WAVES leaders were able to void the Navy's antifraternization rules, allowing the WAVES and male Navy officers to date and even marry.

The WAVES recruitment strategy of demanding class while offering perks worked well. They met their quotas, avoided any serious scandals, and could afford to be selective. The WAVES wanted quality rather than numbers alone, and their enlisted personnel were older (ages twenty to forty-nine), more skilled, much more highly educated, and more socially acceptable than the men in any of the armed services or the women recruited to the Army. Not surprisingly, the Women's Army Corps fell short of its recruitment goals. One of the WAC leaders, Jeanne Holm, blamed the corps' early failures, in part, on the Army's insistence that the military women be treated no differently from the men, subjecting them to unattractive uniforms, bland food, and lack of female amenities in the training camps.

In contrast, the WAVES leadership took an almost maternal interest in their young charges. While the enlisted Navy men on the Bombe project were left to fend for themselves in Dayton's crowded wartime housing market, the WAVES were quartered at Sugar Camp, a private compound of rustic cabins nestled among the wooded hilltops overlooking the NCR campus. NCR gave the Navy full use of the thirty-one-acre site, which had been built in 1894 as a training center and retreat for the company's sales force.

The conditions at Sugar Camp, especially in the cold months, weren't always the height of comfort, however. The WAVES bunked as many as eight in cabins that had been designed to house just four—two guests on each side, with a shower, a toilet, and a pair of sinks in between. The unheated structures were rustic and charming—built entirely of wood, with latticed windows and built-in closets and beds, each with its own writing table, goosenecked lamp, and fan. But during that cold, rainy spring of 1943, the fans were of little use. "Oh my goodness, it was cold. We slept in the same bed, or we put newspapers in between the blankets," recalled Joan Bert Davis. In the fall, heated barracks were built.

Despite the spare lodgings, Sugar Camp offered a dining hall, infirmary, recreation center, auditorium and theater, baseball diamond, and a large outdoor pool. "It felt like a little country club," said Sue Unger Eskey. "We were more or less like a bunch of overgrown Girl Scouts. We loved it." Jimmie Lee Long, a Texas native, said Sugar Camp was a breath of welcome air after boot camp. "We had been cooped up with so many girls at boot camp. We weren't used to this mass of people. And when we got to Sugar Camp, we had a chance to go off and curl up somewhere on a log or on a bench and read a book. You could find a little peace and time to think and write letters."

Still, there was plenty of work to be done. During peak production of the Bombes, the Sugar Camp bunks never grew cold: one shift of women worked while another slept. Shifts ran eight to twelve hours long, twenty-four hours a day, and were rotated weekly.

The WAVES found their lives carefully regimented, as did the Navy men, with a midnight curfew (often violated, the women said) and a strict dress code. Their civilian clothes were sent home, and even their sports attire was furnished by the Navy. Those who married during their tour of duty were given seven days off, which were subtracted from their annual leave, and had to get permission to wear their wedding gowns for their big day.

To maintain discipline and esprit de corps, the WAVES marched in full uniform, their hair pinned neatly beneath their hats, to meals,

The four-rotor Enigma machine, introduced by the German Navy in early 1942 and shown here with its casing open, overwhelmed British codebreakers with its message-scrambling capabilities. The new naval system, called Triton by the Nazis and M4 Shark by the British, led to a near blackout in reading U-boat radio messages until December 1942. *Photo courtesy of the National Archives*

A WAVE adjusts a commutator wheel on a U.S. Navy Bombe, designed to attack the German Navy's four-wheel Enigma. The American Bombe was developed and built in a top secret crash program in 1942–43 at the National Cash Register Company in Dayton, Ohio. *Photo courtesy of the National Security Agency*

Alastair G. Denniston (left), head of the Government Code and Cypher School at Bletchley Park until 1942, displays his usual dapper appearance along a London street. Denniston visited U.S. Navy codebreaking headquarters in August 1941, prepared to tell the Americans everything the British had learned about breaking the German Enigma codes. *Photo courtesy of the National Archives*

Agnes Meyer Driscoll, shown here in a rare photo taken a year before her retirement in 1957, was the U.S. Navy's top codebreaker in 1941 when A. G. Denniston offered to share Britain's hard-won expertise. Convinced she had already arrived at an old-fashioned paper-and-pencil solution to the Enigma, Driscoll rejected Denniston's historic offer. *Photo courtesy of the National Security Agency*

Captain Laurance F. Safford, Agnes Driscoll's former student, was head of the Navy's codebreaking operations in 1941. Safford strived to build the Navy's OP20G division into an American version of Britain's elite codebreaking group. He was removed from his position in a Navy shake-up soon after the attack on Pearl Harbor. *Photo courtesy of the National Security Agency*

Admiral Stanford C. Hooper was the prime mover in leading U.S. Navy cryptanalysis into the modern machine age. Hooper and his Navy protégé, Joseph N. Wenger, believed that the introduction of electric ciphering devices, such as the German Enigma, would force codebreakers to become mathematicians, statisticians, and engineers—not just linguists with a bent for puzzle-solving. *Photo courtesy of the National Security Agency*

Joseph N. Wenger became head of the Navy's OP20G codebreaking division soon after Pearl Harbor. OP20G developed some of the most advanced electromechanical machinery of the day, including the U.S. Bombe, to attack Japanese and German naval ciphers and codes. *Photo courtesy of the National Archives*

Sir Edward Travis, who replaced A. G. Denniston as head of Bletchley Park in 1942, was a no-nonsense manager who at first put little trust in America's ability to keep codebreaking secrets. By the end of the war, however, he had helped forge a remarkable alliance between American and British codebreakers. *Photo courtesy of the National Archives*

Joseph R. "Joe" Desch, chief engineer for the U.S. Naval Computing Machine Laboratory at NCR, was the leading designer of the U.S. Bombe. Desch had been recruited by the Navy in large part because of his pioneering work in the development of fast-pulsing miniature gas tubes—the silicon chips of their day. *Photo courtesy of the NCR Archive at the Montgomery County Historical Society*

Personnel of the U.S. Naval Computing Machine Laboratory, including Desch (front row, left), on the steps of Building 26 at NCR, where the U.S. Bombes were developed and built in a top secret program equal in priority to the Manhattan Project. Commander Bruce I. Meader (front row, third from left) was the on-site naval officer in charge of the program. *Photo courtesy of the NCR Archive at the Montgomery County Historical Society*

Young Joe Desch (second from left), who grew up in Dayton just blocks from where the Wright brothers invented the airplane. The son of a wagonmaker and a German immigrant mother, Desch would become NCR's chief of electrical research. *Photo courtesy of the NCR Archive at the Montgomery County Historical Society*

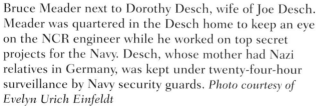

Bruce Meader next to Dorothy Desch, wife of Joe Desch. Meader was quartered in the Desch home to keep an eye on the NCR engineer while he worked on top secret projects for the Navy. Desch, whose mother had Nazi relatives in Germany, was kept under twenty-four-hour surveillance by Navy security guards. *Photo courtesy of Evelyn Urich Einfeldt*

This aerial photo of the NCR complex in Dayton, Ohio, taken in 1952, shows Building 26 separate from the rest of the main campus, in the very bottom right of the photo. Note the railroad spur behind the building, which was used to ship the completed Bombes to Navy codebreaking operations in Washington, D.C. *Photo courtesy of the NCR Archive at the Montgomery County Historical Society*

U.S. Navy WAVES, hundreds of whom helped build the U.S. Bombes, march through the main gate at Sugar Camp, the NCR retreat center where they were housed during the war. WAVES marched in full uniform through the streets of Dayton to and from Building 26. To protect the secrecy of the operation, WAVES were instructed to tell the curious that they were training on business machines. *Photo courtesy of the NCR Archive at the Montgomery County Historical Society*

A WAVE relaxes in one of the rustic cabins at Sugar Camp. The cabins, though cozy, were unheated and, until more permanent quarters could be constructed, were filled with bunks. *Photo courtesy of the NCR Archive at the Montgomery County Historical Society*

WAVES line up to use the phone at Sugar Camp. WAVES swore never to talk about their work at NCR, even among themselves, and were told that they would be "shot at dawn" if they violated their oaths. For more than fifty years, none of the hundreds of WAVES involved in the Bombe project divulged the secret. *Photo courtesy of the NCR Archive at the Montgomery County Historical Society*

WAVES stand by the old woody station wagon that was their only means of transport while staying at Sugar Camp. The Navy-issue car often broke down and had to be pushed. *Photo courtesy of Evelyn Urich Einfeldt*

WAVES in black armbands march on the grounds of Sugar Camp to protest strict new curfews in November 1943. What the protesters didn't know was that the tighter security measures were imposed after a potential spy was found to be working in Building 26. *Photo courtesy of Evelyn Urich Einfeldt*

19

An aerial view of the Naval Communications Annex near Tenley Circle in Washington, D.C., in the 1950s. Formerly the Mount Vernon Seminary for Girls, the fifteen-acre complex was converted to house the 120 U.S. Bombes as well as the WAVES who would operate the machines around the clock. *Photo courtesy of the National Security Agency*

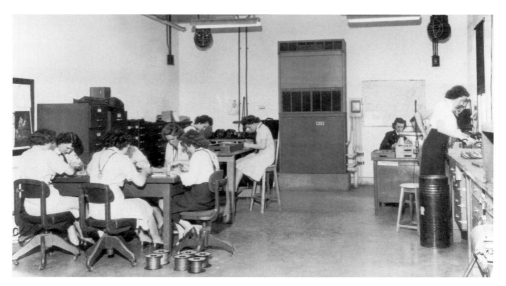

WAVES perform delicate work on some of the commutator wheels used on the U.S. Bombes, shown in stacks on the floor. The 104 contacts of the brass-and-copper wheels, sandwiched between heat-resistant Bakelite, had to be wired by hand. Maintaining the 11,000 commutators the Navy required during the war presented the greatest manufacturing and security challenges of the Bombe project. *Photo courtesy of the National Security Agency*

A WAVE keeps watch over a bank of U.S. Bombes inside Building 4 of the Naval Communications Annex. When a Bombe stopped running, it meant that it had arrived at a possible solution, often called a "hit" or a "strike." Lights on the machine would flash, a bell would ring, and a probable key setting for an Enigma message would print out at one end of the machine. "We'd take the sheet of paper down the hall and knock on a door," one WAVE operator recalled. "A hand would come out; we'd turn over the printout and go back and start all over again." *Photo courtesy of the National Security Agency*

WAVES at the Naval Communications Annex conduct some of the further testing and refinement of Bombe solutions needed to decrypt Enigma messages. Codebreakers used various hand methods and simple machines such as the M-9 (an Enigma simulator that helped find remaining steckers and the ring settings) to complete the Enigma keys, then produced a fully decrypted message. *Photo courtesy of the National Security Agency*

Circular splashes mark the spots where Ensign Edward R. Hodgson's machine-gun bullets hit near *U-603*. In this attack on June 4, 1943, one of Hodgson's depth bombs bounced off the U-boat's jumping wire before exploding. The submarine eventually escaped. The U.S. Bombes began playing a major role in helping break U-boat radio messages in September of that year. *Photo courtesy of the National Archives*

Joe Desch in his new lab inside Building 20 after the war, where he spent years trying to improve his fast-firing miniature gas tubes. After nearly two years of fourteen-hour days and impossible production deadlines, Desch walked quietly out of Building 26 in August 1944 and off the job. Navy officials persuaded him to return six weeks later. Desch continued to grapple with Japanese codebreaking problems but stepped down as the Navy's chief project engineer. *Photo courtesy of the NCR Archive at the Montgomery County Historical Society*

Desch, pictured here in a 1950s portrait, continued to give technical advice to the Navy and the National Security Agency long after the war. In a secret ceremony at the Navy Department in 1947, he was awarded the National Medal of Merit—the highest civilian honor for wartime service—for his work in developing the U.S. Bombe. Desch could tell no one of the nation's gratitude, not even his daughter, Debbie, who would puzzle over the significance of her father's award for the next fifty years. Desch died of a stroke in 1987 at the age of eighty. *Photo courtesy of the National Security Agency*

to classes, to their factory shifts. "We were marched all the time, every day, no matter what the weather," Racz said. Each morning, traffic was halted on Main and Stewart streets as two hundred WAVES strode four abreast the mile or so from Sugar Camp to NCR's Building 26. They were hard to miss, especially for enlisted men looking for female attention. "I'm afraid the sailors were not very well-liked by the WAVES," recalled Robert Shade, who had been a Navy machinist mate stationed at NCR. "I had a Model A roadster and I used to drive 10 sailors to work. . . . Of course, the WAVES were marching along and we would count cadence with them—if you can picture 10 sailors hanging on a Model A roadster."

In Building 26, the WAVES worked from blueprints and diagrams to wire, solder, and assemble parts of the massive Bombes—each task performed in a separately guarded and locked room, so that no one could identify a whole machine or even a component. A WAVE never met any of the other workers in Building 26, other than those assigned to her room. The Navy often sacrificed efficiency to secrecy: one WAVE would be given the wiring diagram for one side of a commutator wheel, while a second WAVE worked on the other side of the wheel in a separate room.

"We never talked about our work or asked about other activities being carried out in other parts of Building 26," Sue Unger Eskey wrote in a letter many years later to Joe Desch's daughter, Debbie Anderson, who organized a reunion of the Dayton WAVES in 1995. "We had no knowledge that the Bombe was being conceived and built directly over our heads on Floor 2."

Even so, Eskey had an idea of what those rotors she was soldering so carefully might be used for. "If you had any intuition or deep thoughts about it you could sort of figure it out. There's 26 wires and 26 digits on the wheels and, oh yeah, the alphabet has 26 digits, too. . . . I knew absolutely nothing about codes or anything, but I had that thought. And, of course, I didn't share it with anyone because we were not allowed to talk about anything."

The work could be both exacting and boring, especially on the graveyard shift. "Bonnie Skinner would sing to us half the night so we could stay awake," Eskey recalled. "She had a beautiful, operatic voice." Dorothy Firor, who was in charge of one of the rooms in Building 26, remembered that not everyone came whistling to work on the morning shift. "I would stand at the door and say good morning as the girls came in. One of them would always say, 'What's good about it?' "

Vogel worked in Firor's room:

> The loveliest thing was that when we would have lunch hour or rest period, we would all put our heads down on our work table and Miss Firor would read to us the *Bobbsey Twins* or *Little Women*. She would read us all these childhood books, and just lull us into relaxation. Then when the time period was up she would close the book and say, "Well, I'll start on the rest of it later." We were her flock.

It was a testament to the WAVES' skills that the machines eventually proved so reliable: sloppy soldering was a major problem for other early computer prototypes, but not the NCR Bombes. Inside each rotor that imitated the fastest wheel of the Enigma machines was complex internal wiring that had to hold up under speeds of two thousand rpm, generating centrifugal forces that warped or cracked many of the wheels. The scores of electrical connections on each wheel had to be meticulously matched and circuit boards soldered, sometimes using a microscope. A single mismatched connection or a weak solder point could lead to hours or even days of wasted efforts by cryptanalysts and engineers. The Bombes demanded more than eleven thousand such precision wheels. Even so, "There was no room for mistakes. Now I understand why," Long said in a letter to Anderson.

Although the WAVES had been carefully screened in Washington, not all of them were up to performing the delicate soldering and assembly work. Those who failed at those tasks were trained to assemble wire harnesses for the machines' circuitry, said Phil Bochicchio. "We laid out plywood board with nails, and each wire had a color code that went to a particular nail. Then they had to lace all those wires together with wax string. Finally, the girls that were adept at soldering nested those lacings into place."

More than one of the WAVES working on the Dayton Bombes cracked under the stress and tedium and had to be reassigned, despite their knowledge of the project. One tired WAVES member committed every codebreaker's worst nightmare: she absentmindedly walked out of the secret Bombe-decryption room carrying both an original ciphered message and its plain-language equivalent. Both were recovered before falling into the wrong hands.

A more delicate problem arose when officers learned that a WAVES member was pregnant. She was released from service, but not before she was sworn to secrecy about anything she had done for the Navy.

Less serious personnel matters cropped up throughout the war, usually involving requests for transfer out of OP20G and minor disciplinary infractions. In mid-1944, the officer in charge of morale reported that some twenty WAVES per day were coming for help with personal matters. As a result, the officer requested more staffing and a separate office so that private conversations could be held with WAVES who were "emotionally upset or wishing to discuss a highly personal problem."

The Navy found ways to help the women relax. Once their shifts ended, the WAVES were free to enjoy themselves, either on or off the Sugar Camp grounds. Curfews were seldom enforced. There were ball games and poolside activities just outside their cabin doors and movies and skits in the Sugar Camp auditorium. The camp cafeteria never closed. "The food was excellent," Racz recalled. "I know we had a lot of good beef—things people on the outside didn't have during the war." Firor recalled the special advantages of living next to the Sugar Camp pool. "We went skinny-dipping in between the times the night watchman made his rounds."

Getting around town was never a problem for the WAVES, even though the camp's Navy transport—an old woody station wagon— often broke down and had to be pushed. "Wherever we were going, people would stop and ask us if we would like a ride," Vogel said. "Of course, in those days, nobody ever harmed us. The Age of Innocence was still intact." Firor recalled a polite young farmer on his way into town who offered a ride to her and another WAVES member as they were walking to the opera. The women asked the farmer if he would like to go to the opera, too. "I'd as soon hear pigs squeal," he replied.

The WAVES were pet oddities in Dayton, both as women in uniform and as Navy personnel in the town where the Army Air Corps tradition had originated with the Wright brothers themselves. If anyone asked about their work at NCR, they were instructed to say they were training on adding machines—a story that matched the project's cover name, the Naval Computing Machine Laboratory. "People must have thought we were pretty stupid to be there all that time learning how to run adding machines," Evelyn Urich Einfeldt said with a laugh.

Many NCR families made a point of "adopting" individual WAVES, inviting them to their homes for Sunday meals and to their churches for services, providing an escape from the regimented life at Sugar Camp and a gathering place as well for those who wanted a more familylike atmosphere for parties and social affairs. In those times of rationing and shortages, "even the people in the department stores were lovely to us," said Dorothy Braswell. One downtown store owner in particular made a point of ringing up Sugar Camp as soon as he received a new shipment of nylons, so that the WAVES always had the first pick of what had become a scarce wartime item, she recalled.

Many WAVES remembered how Joe and Dorothy Desch, older and more sophisticated, had floated in and out of their lives at Sugar Camp for Sunday dinners and other festivities—always in the company of Ralph Meader. "We were all in awe of Joe and Dorothy, because they were beautiful people in appearance—like movie stars. And always dressed so fashionably," Vogel said.

Betty Bemis Robarts remembered Mrs. Desch as "a beautiful woman—tall and elegant, just like she stepped out of *Vogue*."

According to several WAVES, Desch had an even more compelling reason not to like or trust his naval supervisor: Meader was a well-known flirt. There were times, Desch knew, when Meader was in his home with Dorothy. Debbie Anderson said that, even during the roughest times in her parents' marriage long after the war, her father had never accused her mother of an affair with Meader. But she said her father was infuriated that Meader would often flirt with Dorothy.

Alvida Lockwood, a member of the WAVES who did repair work on the Bombes, chuckles whenever she recalls Meader. "He liked the ladies," she said. Vogel concurred: "He wasn't what you would call an attractive man. Actually, he reminded me a little of Santa Claus. But he had a twinkle in his eye all the time, and I think he made women— the girls—happy. I think they were attracted to him in a way."

Lockwood said she never saw Meader abuse his relationship with the WAVES. "He wasn't the kind of man you were afraid would pinch you," she said. Other WAVES viewed Meader as a "fatherly type," Vogel said. "He was easy to talk to. He always called us 'his girls.' We weren't in awe of him as we were of Joe."

Despite what would now be called his sexist bent, Meader saw the value in recruiting women to the armed forces, Einfeldt said. "There were a lot of higher-up people who didn't want women in the service, but Commander Meader did. He appreciated what the women were doing. He ran a tight ship, though. You didn't step out of line."

Many of the WAVES who assembled the Bombes now consider themselves groundbreakers and pioneers in expanding the work roles for women. But at the time, their motivation was to serve their country more than their gender. "We didn't join for any reason other than patriotism," Einfeldt said. After the war, "most of the women I knew didn't even know they were veterans and could take advantage of GI benefits—because you did it for the patriotism."

In the process of serving their country, many of the women were encouraged to take bolder paths after the war—paths that might never have occurred to them without having been in the WAVES. Esther Hottenstein, Desch's executive secretary during the war, left behind her old teaching job following her service and went on to medical school.

Robarts, who had never been away from her parents' home in the small town of Nashwauk, Minnesota, said her experience in the WAVES forced her to grow up in a hurry. "I must have cried the first two weeks of boot camp. I was awful homesick," she said. "All these girls were talking about how great it was to get away from their parents, but I was just devastated." After the war, she went off on her own to Butler University in Indiana, where she became a competitive diver and reached the NCAA championships.

For many of the WAVES, the months at NCR passed almost as if in a dream. In fact, until top secret documents were declassified in the mid-1990s, it was as if they hadn't been in Dayton at all. "There was no record I was ever in Dayton," Racz said. "For years, I couldn't understand why. All the important people who were there, and we still didn't know what was going on." Even their assigned rank in the WAVES, "Specialist Q," was cloaked in mystery, she said, "although a lot of people joked that it stood for 'cutie.'" Navy officials told the WAVES the classification involved work in communications but nothing more.

Veronica Mackey Hulick, who had received a Navy Unit Commendation Ribbon and a personal letter from Secretary of the Navy James Forrestal for her work in operating the Bombes during the war, tried repeatedly in the late 1970s to access her records. A written response from a rear admiral in March 1978 informed her that

> if pertinent files were maintained at the time, apparently they were destroyed after the war. Existing records do not show what specific duties you performed [in Washington] or at the National Cash Register Company in Dayton. The oath that you took in 1945 has not been modified by published accounts speculating as to activities carried out by personnel located at the Naval Communications Annex.

The WAVES leaders realized that their enlistees wouldn't always be focused on the war effort or their careers. That became clear to OP20G chief Joseph Wenger early in the American Bombe project. Even before production began in Dayton, Wenger had busied himself with finding the right location for the WAVES to operate the machines. In October 1942, he believed he had found the perfect spot and said so in a memo to his superiors. But the WAVES commanders, who were intent on attracting a high class of recruit, had other ideas, as well as the political clout to back them up.

Wenger's preferred site was a secluded Chautauqua camp, just fifteen miles south of NCR along a wooded, two-mile front of the Great Miami River, complete with all the amenities that the WAVES leadership thought essential to recruitment: a large hotel and auditorium, cottages, swimming pool, skating rink, tennis courts, Tom Thumb golf course, movie theater, and coffee shop. The site in Miami Township was rural but not isolated by any means: nearby traction-company lines, accessed from the camp by crossing the river over an iron footbridge, provided speedy service to Dayton and other towns in the area.

In his memo, Wenger ticked off all the other advantages of the site: it was close to NCR, for ease of delivery and maintenance of the machines; in an area not likely to be attacked and that would therefore need no bombproofing; and far enough removed from other well-known OP20G activities so as not to raise enemy suspicions. What's more, he estimated it would cost one hundred thousand dollars to renovate the site to meet Navy requirements, as opposed to one million dollars if the operation was based in Dayton.

Wenger toured the site with a WAVES officer, Lieutenant Lawrence, and representatives from both the Bureau of Ships and the Bureau of Yards and Docks. The site was found "highly satisfactory" by the two bureau representatives but not by the WAVES lieutenant, "whose main objection rested in the fact that the site was about 15 miles from Dayton and, therefore, somewhat inaccessible," Wenger said. "Moreover, Lieutenant Lawrence seemed greatly concerned over the fact that there was no prospect of suitable male companionship in the immediate vicinity." In other words, the site was too far removed from the officers at NCR and Wright Field.

Wenger ended his memo by strongly recommending that the Navy lease and develop the Chautauqua site and "if the WAVES raise objection to locating there, that we man the project with men." Certainly the WAVES must have known that Wenger was bluffing: persuading the Navy brass to allocate hundreds of sailors to nonsea duties was nearly impossible by late 1942. And by that time as well, fears that Washington, D.C., and other major urban centers might be bombed had subsided. The WAVES also had plenty of political clout, given the elite background of its leadership and the strong support of Eleanor Roosevelt in the White House.

The WAVES had their way: the operational site for the Bombes would not be in the rural splendor of southwestern Ohio but in the urban excitement of Washington, D.C.

In November 1942, OP20G had notified the Mount Vernon Seminary for Girls, the oldest girls' boarding school in the District of Columbia, that it was about to be taken over for "special training" of a secret nature. At the end of its fall semester, having been paid a sum of $1.1 million, the seminary vacated its nine ivy-covered brick dormitories and classroom buildings and its cozy chapel, clearing the way for Navy personnel to begin their move there in early 1943. The new site, later dubbed the Naval Communications Annex, was at Massachusetts and Nebraska avenues, near Tenley Circle, five miles from OP20G's original location in the Main Navy Building on Constitution Avenue downtown.

The fifteen-acre campus was chosen, according to a Navy brochure, for "its location at one of the highest points in the District of Columbia, with clear lines of sight to the Pentagon, Fort Meade and other military installations [and] away from tall buildings" and also because its buildings and spacious grounds could be converted easily to military use. Early in 1943, part of the land was used for the construction of two new high-security buildings to house the Bombes and other codebreaking machines.

By fall 1943, Washington was ready to become part of Ultra.

10

A Well-Oiled Machine

December 1943—Washington, D.C.

MARY LORRAINE JOHNSON, one of several hundred WAVES who faced long hours and uncomfortable, even dangerous conditions running the Bombes, remembers mostly the deafening noise inside Building 4 at the Naval Communications Annex near Tenley Circle. Scores of American Bombes were lined up on two open floors, whirring and clacking as they raced through the millions of permutations possible on the Enigma machine. "The noise factor was something else," she said.

> When this machine started running, it was so loud . . . all of us got to the point that we wanted to scream that it hurt so badly. I think that it affected different girls to different degrees. We soon learned we had to tune the noise factor out—mentally tune it out. It took us about six weeks because we would sleep and still hear that awful noise. . . . Some girls were having ear problems, and going in [to Navy doctors] and saying, what is wrong with my ears and I have an awful buzzing in my head.

In the Washington summers, the WAVES sweltered in the intense heat generated by the machines. "We had [a] constant sauna," Johnson said. "Our officers were very strict watching us and would pass the salt pills around because we would go in with a fresh uniform and after two hours we would be wringing wet. . . . Occasionally we would have a girl pass out or feel woozy and a salt pill would bring her out of it and she would be OK." A fast-spinning commutator wheel, made of copper, brass, and Bakelite and weighing nearly two pounds, could take off an operator's limb if loosed from its spindle. "The safety of operating these machines was intense," Johnson recalled. "One time a wheel came off, a bottom wheel, the one that is going so fast, and it just missed my legs by a fraction of an inch. Fortunately, there was a wall there and it went right into the wall."

On the Bombe's gray metal face were two rows of black disks with a rotating brass pointer that could be set from 00 to 25 around the circumference. Each number represented a different letter of the alphabet to be tested according to the menu for the Bombe run. Below the knobs, both on the front and back of the machine, were four rows of eight commutator wheels, for a total of sixty-four wheels.

Setting up the machines for each run called for intense concentration. The menu instructions for mounting the different wheels and setting their starting points were not easy to follow, and a slight mistake could lead to a missed solution and a severe reprimand. Some types of Bombe runs were physically tiring, especially those designed to handle possible Enigma wheel turnovers within a crib. On some of those "Hoppity" runs, as they were called, the machine had to be stopped and the wheels reset an average of fourteen times, at exactly the right points during the run.

The WAVES had plenty of much-needed opportunities to blow off steam. Recreational activities included tours to Mount Vernon and Annapolis, dances at naval stations and Army bases, picnics at Rock Creek Park, bike rides along the Potomac, roller-skating, and free concerts. There were classes in ballroom dancing, dramatics, bridge, and hobby crafts. Organized sports included swimming competitions in the station pool, tennis, archery, badminton, softball, basketball, bowling, horseshoes, croquet, Ping-Pong, billiards, and golf at a course in Maryland. WAVES interested in music could join the glee club, string ensemble, quartets, or orchestra, with their instruments furnished by the Navy.

Despite the many leisure-time opportunities, secrecy restrictions and the long work hours often kept many WAVES from taking advantage of them. More often, socializing took the form of spontaneous after-hours gatherings of the kind that moved local resident and attorney James D. Mann to write to the commander of the annex:

> For some time it has been impossible for the people living on the north side of Van Ness Street, between Nebraska and Wisconsin Avenues, to sleep between 11 p.m. and about 2:30 a.m. This is due to the unusual amount of noise made by the young men and women stationed at the Communications Annex. I suppose they work at night and go to the Hot Shoppe on Wisconsin Avenue between the aforementioned hours. . . . One morning this week about eight WAVES walked up the middle of Van Ness Street at 1:30 in the morning singing. In about five [or] ten minutes, two Marines came along singing at the top of their voices. It is nothing unusual for there to be six to a dozen instances of noise like this after midnight.

BREAKING SHARK WAS not just a matter of building and operating machines but of inventing processes and organizing human resources. Codebreaking, like modern invention, had outgrown the days of one man or woman sitting down with a pencil and paper and waiting for inspiration to strike. It had become an elaborately cooperative effort involving numerous steps, the skills of hundreds of people, and a division of labor that could capitalize on those proficiencies.

American and British field stations intercepted U-boat radio messages and relayed them by special Teletype lines to the Traffic Group, a dozen or so people whose around-the-clock job was to see if any of the intercepts fit into known Enigma networks, such as Shark. Identifying networks (or systems) was not a simple matter. The disguised message indicators that specified the network had to be unraveled and identified, sometimes with the help of the radio frequency or the time and place of origin of the transmission.

Once its network was identified, the message was usually forwarded to another OP20G subsection for radio fingerprinting—that is, a means of telling exactly which German station or U-boat sent the message—and also to the decryption section for Atlantic problems, known as GY-A. A copy of the message was transmitted to the British at Bletchley Park as well, so that both countries could compare the intercepts in case problems arose in decrypting them.

If the message had been transmitted on a system with an already fully solved daily key, processing was relatively straightforward. The Communications Group used an Enigma analog machine, known as the M-8, to decode the message by simply setting the machine to the known keys, much the same way a German Enigma operator receiving the same message would have done, and typing in the transmitted letters.

If the message was from a system or day whose key was not fully solved, it was sent to the Decryption and Crib groups. When only minor parts of the keys were missing, the codebreakers used various hand methods and simple machines such as the M-9 (an Enigma analog that helped find remaining steckers and the ring settings) to complete the keys and then produced a fully decrypted message.

The Decryption Group sometimes faced a greater challenge: finding the starting position of the wheels. To do this, they called upon their voluminous catalogs of matching plain and cipher text and, when required, the RAMs, the Bombes, and their attachments.

Once the decryption was completed, the plain-text message was forwarded to the translation section, known as GI, where German naval language was turned into useful English. From the translators, the message went to OP20GI, whose job was to compile fragments of information into plain intelligence. Huge historical files had to be built up to enable the analysts to understand a translated message. The history of each U-boat and each of their captains, for example, helped pull meaning out of a translated message. From "GI," the intelligence was disseminated to those responsible for military and diplomatic decisions.

If the message was from an Enigma system that had not been solved, it was sent to the Crib Group, whose members had perhaps the toughest job among the codebreakers: to sift through the many intercepts to find a message in which they could safely presume to know a significant portion of the underlying plain text. Those working in the Crib Group needed an intimate knowledge not only of German military and Enigma procedures but of the circumstances under which the message was sent. That meant constantly staying on top of the latest developments by reading as many past and current messages as possible. Even more so than translating, cribbing was an art, one dependent on intimate knowledge of many German systems and the habits of those transmitting the messages.

Many useful cribs for Shark and the other networks the Americans were attacking by the end of 1943 came from other, better-known systems already tackled by the British. That meant that the Americans were at a disadvantage and dependent on GCCS for good cribs throughout much of the war. As well as having a long head start on Shark, GCCS was reading dozens of other German systems. The British knew the habits of U-boat captains and their Enigma operators, and they were reading higher-level systems, such as Dolphin, which carried messages repeated on Shark.

Following the spring 1942 accord between GCCS and OP20G, the British not only set the priorities for which messages were to be processed in America but frequently sent the "Amirs" (the codename for cribs) to be used on the Bombes and the long reencodements from other systems that could be used as a source of cribs by the Americans. Throughout the war, the Americans received a flow of Amirs from England, sending only a few of their own crib suggestions, codenamed "Rimas," to GCCS.

It took quite some time for the Americans to become adept enough at cribbing and menu construction for their test solutions to match the power of those sent by GCCS. The British were years ahead in the indexing of points of reference—the meanings of thousands of abbreviations and military terms and the names of German commanders and their units. At times, minor conflicts arose over the Allied agreement to run jobs using British cribs and menus ahead of those found by OP20G's Crib Group. The Americans occasionally felt that the British were sending weaker cribs (thus weaker menus) for the U.S. Bombes than GCCS was using on its own machines, thus giving England an advantage in breaking the system.

The next step performed in the Crib Group was to see whether the assumed crib would set up enough restrictions on the possible Enigma keys that it could be used as a menu. Once the menus were constructed, the Crib Group then determined which wheels and wheel orders were to be tested and in what sequence.*

The menus and the wheel lists were sent to GYA-2, the Bombe Operations Group, where the machines and their crews of WAVES were assigned their tasks. Generally speaking, menus for more urgent messages or those more likely to lead to a solution of the day's keys were assigned to more of the machines. Depending on the type of problem, it took the WAVES anywhere from a few minutes to more than a half hour to follow the menu orders and mount the proper wheels and starting positions on a Bombe. Once the machine was started, a full test of a Shark key typically required twenty minutes, exclusive of stops.

Veronica Hulick, one of the WAVES who operated the Bombes, told Smithsonian historians that when the machine arrived at a hit, lights flashed, a bell rang, "and a probable key setting would print out" at one end of the machine. "We'd take the sheet of paper down the hall and knock on a door. A hand would come out; we'd turn over the printout and go back and start all over again."

The final step in the Bombe process, short of reading the message, was performed by the print testers. These WAVES used simple machines, such as the M-8 and M-9, to test the limited number of so-

* The British explored a statistical method, based on the patterns and habits of German wheel selection over time, to reduce the number of orders to be tested. They eventually turned away from the method, thinking that the Germans had discovered their own predictability and had taken measures to correct it. But then one of OP20G's new breed of codebreakers, William Randolph Church, decided to take another look at the German wheel orders. After much labor, he and his crew found a pattern of selection and were able to send, along with the menus from the Crib Group, lists of the most likely wheel selections. This narrowing of the possibilities doubled the efficiency of the American Bombes—saving what amounted to fourteen full months of Bombe time over the duration of the war.

lutions suggested by the Bombe. From them they selected what seemed like the Jackpot. Once obtained, the keys were sent to the Decryption Group, which did further handwork to arrive at a full solution. The Traffic Group was then notified so it would forward any new messages in the same system to the correct department.

Such a complex system needed careful coordination to prevent errors. All of the groups worked under the supervision of a watch officer, who managed the flow of traffic and solutions.

Security at the Naval Communications Annex was just as tight as it had been at Building 26, again with armed guards stationed outside every room. The WAVES who operated the machines were never told the purpose of their work. Even WAVES officers were denied access to codebreaking aids and procedures, unless they were carefully screened. Only a handful of WAVES were assigned to work with confidential and secret materials and to supervise the assembly and operation of the Bombes. The Navy, always conscious of social class, chose women for the job "who, because of their background, reputation and family connections, are suitable for assignment to secret duties in Communication Intelligence," said an April 1943 request from Vice Chief of Naval Operations William J. Lee.

Hulick said the WAVES had much to prove back then. "If you were good-looking, you were dumb. And if you were blond, you were even dumber. And, of course, no woman could keep a secret. That's what we were up against."

The WAVES not only proved that women could keep a secret, but that they could do it better than most men, said Peg Fiehtner, who was the assistant chief of staff for the Naval Security Group Command at the Communication Annex before retiring in 2000. Never in the history of American intelligence had so many people kept a secret for so long, she said. "It was one of the few secrets kept during the war. It was never compromised."

But the American Bombe project narrowly escaped a very different history. In November 1943, seven months before D Day, one man working quietly in Building 26 almost betrayed the entire Ultra operation.

$$11$$

An Enemy Within?

JAMES MARTIN MONTGOMERY, JR., worked the night shift in the laboratory in Building 26 where the top-secret Bombes were now being built at a rate of six per week. A tall, slim, bespectacled young man of Appalachian descent, Montgomery was perceived as something of an odd bird by his coworkers and supervisors—he was a self-educated, self-proclaimed electrical engineer who never said much to anyone and was perhaps a little on the cocky side. But he was hard-working, bright, and reliable, all traits that had earned him promotions from assembler to checker to lab technician in less than two months since his hiring in August, along with a near doubling of his salary from sixty to one hundred dollars a week. For a twenty-three-year-old man one generation removed from the hardscrabble hills of eastern Kentucky, that was good money in 1943. Odd bird or not, Montgomery was enough of a company man to register with NCR's share-a-ride office, offering space in his 1937 Chrysler coupe to fellow workers who lacked transportation.

At the end of his shift on the morning of November 5, Montgomery and his rider found each other. Montgomery told the man he'd meet him out in the parking lot, after he paired up with his wife,

Lillian, who worked the same shift as an assembler in another part of Building 26.

It was almost 6:00 A.M. on this damp, chilly morning as Montgomery's coworker headed out to the parking lot behind Building 26. No records are available on what exactly happened next, but it's easy to imagine that when the rider reached Montgomery's car, he opened the passenger door and slipped inside to warm himself. Once settled, he pulled out a cigarette, poked it in his mouth, then instinctively reached for the matches in his shirt pocket. Empty. He tried his jacket pockets. No matches there, either.

Desperate for a smoke, the coworker must have pulled open the glove compartment to the car. As he rooted around in the loose papers there, he found no matches, but what he did find must have given him reason to pause—a small stack of three-by-five white index cards, filled with the typewritten names of foreign people and organizations, most of them obviously German and Japanese. Hermann Schwinn. Captain Fritz Wiedemann. Deutsches Haus. The German American Bund. The Japanese minister to Mexico. An officer in Japanese naval intelligence. There were nearly forty listings in all, on thirteen separate cards.

He rooted around some more and found a folded letter. When he opened it and started reading, he found more to stir his worst suspicions. It was on letterhead from the German embassy, addressed to James Montgomery. It read: "Referring to your letter of January 10, 1941, I beg to inform you that this embassy is not in a position to comply with your request." At the bottom of the letter had been typed the names of eleven more foreign names and organizations.

Hastily, the coworker slipped everything back into the glove compartment, trying to arrange the items exactly as he had found them, and waited for Montgomery and his wife to arrive.

He probably said little to the couple as they drove him home that morning while his mind and emotions churned with questions. Should he call Navy security when he got home? The FBI? By the time his shift at NCR started again at 7:00 P.M., he knew exactly what he had to do. He found his supervisor and asked if he could speak to him in private. The supervisor suggested they step into his office. There, the man spilled out what he had found.

In fulfilling his patriotic duty, the coworker had no idea of the top secret tug-of-war that would ensue that day and for months to come between Navy officials trying to protect Ultra and law-enforcement authorities trying to protect the constitutional rights of the accused.

The supervisor nodded and took it all in, but he may have wondered if the informant had overreacted to what he had seen. Why would anyone in his right mind keep a list of spy contacts in their glove compartment? Besides, managers at NCR had no reason to suspect Montgomery of anything. He was a valued employee—never late, did his work, kept his mouth shut.

Perhaps the supervisor thought the man was jealous of Montgomery's series of promotions or suffering from overwork and an overactive imagination. For whatever reason, records show that the supervisor waited until 8:00 A.M.—two hours after the end of the shift that night—to call Ralph Meader.

Meader had a very different reaction to the coworker's story. Here was a threat to everything the Bombe project had struggled to achieve, and just as OP20G was at last becoming an equal partner with the British in tackling the Shark problem. Meader immediately called the local representative of the Office of Naval Intelligence, the agency in charge of security at the plant. Meader must have inwardly winced as he did so. Since the 1930s, the ONI and the Navy's code-breakers had been drifting apart and engaging in increasingly frequent and bitter turf battles. In fact, the ONI had been effectively shut out of Ultra, and only a few of its highest officers knew of the top secret codebreaking operation.

Meader raced his beat-up, Navy-issue Nash Rambler as fast as it could go to Building 26, where he got on the secure cable line to Washington and began typing an urgent message to Captain Earl F. Stone, assistant director of naval communications in the Office of the Chief of Naval Operations.

Meader and Stone could tell the ONI representatives only that an important secret project was at stake. Without being able to supply the details, they struggled to persuade the ONI that drastic action was needed, now.

WHEN JAMES AND Lillian Montgomery left their shift the following morning, plainclothes ONI investigators tailed the couple to their home in Franklin—a small paper-mill town hugging the Great Miami River twenty miles south of Dayton. The town and the surrounding areas in southwestern Ohio were home to thousands of recent migrants from the small farms and coal towns of eastern Kentucky; the parents of both Montgomerys were from Harlan County.

Montgomery completed tenth grade at the Dayton area's Carlisle High School—far more schooling than his parents had ever achieved. But given his social background, his personality, and the Great Depression, he was virtually unemployed for more than three years after he quit school. During 1940 and 1941, all he could find was a series of menial, temporary, and underpaid jobs, at one point working as a driver for the wife of an executive at the Armco steel plant in nearby Middletown, where his father worked as a pipefitter.

James Jr.'s early life had been unstable and filled with tragedy. When he was six years old, his mother died at age thirty, from acute appendicitis and a massive infection. She had been seriously ill for more than ten days, but a doctor was not called until two days before her death, perhaps because of her family's fundamentalist beliefs, which included faith healing and speaking in tongues. A year later, his father found another Kentucky woman, a divorced machinist named Martha Trent, who was willing to become a homemaker and gave much attention and affection to seven-year-old James and his two brothers. The family was just settling into the relationship when, in 1931, Martha died of typhoid fever.

The boys spent most of the next five years under the care of the elder Blantons, their mother's deeply religious parents. Then, when James turned sixteen, a new stepmother appeared, but immediately she and the boys were at odds. By the time James was twenty, she had gotten her fill and disappeared from the scene without leaving a trace.

During those troubled teenage years, James pursued grand dreams for the future: he spent much of his spare time at the Middletown Public Library, where he read every book he could find on the rapidly growing fields of electrical engineering and electronics. Like young Joe Desch, he had tinkered at home and, in 1938, at the age of eighteen, was convinced that he had invented a revolutionary new type of electrical generator—an idea he tried in vain to sell to the U.S. government. He wrote to the governments of England, France, and Germany. Only Germany responded—with a rejection.

At age twenty, James Montgomery began courting eighteen-year-old Lillian Culbertson. Although the two were from the same background, Culbertson's parents strenuously objected to Montgomery. He persisted, however, telling her of the bright future he planned, which included his own radio-repair business.

In October 1940, young Lillian, who had just graduated from high school the previous summer, ran away with Montgomery to Kentucky, where marriages without parental approval were easier to arrange. The newlyweds moved into an apartment with Montgomery's uncle in Cincinnati. Despite his uncle's help, Montgomery found little work, and the months there were stressful: Lillian became pregnant, her mother was fighting cancer, and Montgomery had the local draft board breathing down his neck.

Montgomery registered for the draft in October 1940. But how forthright he was with his draft board is open to question. His registration card had an incorrect birth date, his local employer's name was misspelled, and the signature on the card does not appear to have been his own. Nevertheless, his card and information were accepted, and the board began to process him.

By early 1941, Montgomery and his wife had moved from Cincinnati and in with Lillian's parents in Middletown, where Montgomery was still without a job. Perhaps his frustration and idleness were what led him to shift his library reading from electronics to espionage and, in January 1941, to write a second letter to the German embassy.

We don't know the contents of Montgomery's 1941 letter, which elicited the terse response discovered in his glove compartment, but its context was certainly different from his letter of 1938. By 1941, the United States was embroiled in a very public and heated debate over foreign policy because of the war raging in Europe and Japan's brutal advances into China. The Midwest was a center of isolationism, and few of its residents could have avoided the debate over whether the United States should entangle itself in world war.

Where Montgomery lay in the political spectrum of the period is impossible to determine. He had been a loner most of his life, family members say, and seldom discussed his politics or his religion. According to the family, he "always kept to himself. . . . I just couldn't communicate with him. Nobody could." His family reported that, in his later years, Montgomery belonged to no political organizations and expressed no religious convictions, although it was clear that he had long ago come to abhor his mother's and his grandparents' severe brand of fundamentalism. "He hated those ministers, those Church of God ones," one family member said.

The rejection letter from the German embassy apparently did not end his interest in espionage. He seemed to have kept track of news items and books about the subject through at least the early months of 1941. But with a child on the way, he could no longer focus on such matters. In March, despite his education, skills, and ambitions, he met the fate of most of his Appalachian neighbors, taking a manufacturing job with harsh working conditions. He began what became a two-year stint in the dust-filled filter room of a Miamisburg furniture company. He soon quit abruptly for an even lower-paying job at a local paper company.

He and Lillian had their first child, a boy, in July 1941. The prospect of being drafted and leaving a young bride and small child at home loomed over Montgomery until early 1942, when he was given a 3-A deferment based on family hardship. However, his two brothers, who had been classified as 1-A, were soon drafted.

Lillian decided that she needed to bring in a steady income for the family, despite her young baby. She learned that perhaps the best employer in the region, National Cash Register, had many war-related openings and in late April 1943 took a job with the innocuous title of "assembler" in Building 26. Then, some two months later, Montgomery also was hired as an assembler in Building 26. The couple's two incomes enabled them to move into their own apartment for the first time—half of a small, one-story house near downtown Franklin, in the shadow of the levee.

The future for the family was at last looking up. Montgomery and his wife both had a foothold in a blue-chip company with a long tradition of taking care of its employees.*

At NCR, Montgomery began working with advanced electronics. At last, his knowledge and his skills were being recognized by professional engineers, and he was soon moved to the inner sanctum of Building 26. He must have known he was involved in something very important to the war effort, quickly guessing that it had to do with codes and ciphers.

He could do more than just advance his career. He could do something that might change the course of history.

THE NAVY INVESTIGATORS who spent the day of November 7 parked outside 124 South River Street in Franklin observed nothing out of the ordinary. No visitors. No trips to the post office or even to the grocery store. Just a young couple with a toddler spending a quiet day at home. Investigators also talked with the local postmaster, the chief of police, and a former chief of police in Franklin. None was even aware of Montgomery, though his house sat just three blocks from the town's Municipal Building.

Nevertheless, at 7:00 P.M., when they reported for work at NCR, Montgomery and his wife were immediately taken into custody by naval-security officers and placed under Marine guard inside Building 26. They were held there for questioning, without benefit of an attorney, for at least two days, and Montgomery may have been held there as long as a week, completely isolated from the outside world.

Rumors began to circulate in the building. "I remember they put

* NCR founder John H. Patterson had been a pioneer in employee welfare programs, offering free hot lunches, company-paid trips to the seashore, and picnics on his estate. By the time of World War II, NCR provided employees not only with health insurance and sickness benefits but with medical and dental clinics, a recreation park and pool, and an on-campus office for issuing state fishing and drivers' licenses. There were free night-school classes, free movies three times a day in the NCR auditorium, and even free umbrellas when it rained.

him in a room there, across the hall from where I worked," said Don
Lowden, an NCR engineer, in an interview nearly sixty years later.
Lowden never knew the identity of the man being held in the room,
but there was talk "that he may have taken some special tubes from
that machine," which only the top managers knew was called a
Bombe.

The WAVES working in the building were kept in the dark as well,
but they soon felt the impact of the security crisis: an 11:00 P.M. curfew was imposed on their off-site activities for the next two weeks.
Scores of WAVES, used to coming and going from the Sugar Camp
complex as they pleased, staged a protest one evening by turning their
black Navy ties into armbands and marching around the grounds.
"Certainly, at the time, it didn't do any good," Evelyn Einfeldt said.
"But it was probably all in fun anyway."

In a move that stretched even the loose ethics of wartime command, Ralph Meader took the investigation into his own hands. He
interrogated Montgomery one-on-one the night of November 7 and
into the next day. According to Meader's son, Bruce, his father slipped
a tube into Montgomery's pocket in hopes that its discovery would
force the young man to confess to theft and other crimes. If he did
not confess, there would be little chance that Montgomery would be
set free, even for a few days pending trial.

With Montgomery's permission, the Navy searched his car and,
indeed, found the letter from the German embassy and the index
cards.

Meader later informed his superiors that Montgomery had broken down and confessed during the two-day examination. According
to Meader, Montgomery told him that he had been able to guess the
nature of his top secret work at NCR, that he had stolen vital parts
from the codebreaking machine, and that he was willing to offer his
services and knowledge in any capacity to both the Germans and the
Japanese.

If this was true, Meader faced a dilemma of unnerving propor-
tions. How could the Montgomerys be arrested and prosecuted for espionage without alerting the press and blowing the lid off the top
secret work at NCR? It seemed impossible. Yet if he let them go free,

they would surely deliver the Ultra secret into the hands of the enemy. Worse, Montgomery's skill with radios raised the specter that he could contact agents by shortwave.

Further heightening the tension for Meader and OP20G, a British delegation from Bletchley Park had arrived just a few days before in Washington, D.C., to work out the final details on sharing Ultra secrets. A major publicity leak or breach of security couldn't have come at a more inopportune time.

Meader got on the phone to the assistant director of naval counterintelligence. He, in turn, suggested that Meader have Montgomery arrested on charges of theft of government property and immediately placed in jail. In that way, Montgomery could be locked up without tipping off local law-enforcement officials about the work at NCR.

But there were still the problems of what to do with Lillian Montgomery and of keeping Montgomery quiet while he was in jail. Every path seemed fraught with risk, yet Meader could no longer keep both Montgomery and his wife under wraps in Building 26 on just his own authority. No doubt the couple's relatives, who were caring for their small son, were growing impatient for answers.

AT 3:00 P.M. on November 8, Meader reluctantly called the Cincinnati office of the FBI, launching a relationship between the bureau and OP20G that came to rival the U.S.-British collaboration on Ultra in uneasiness and complexity. Meader and Navy investigators had no doubt carefully rehearsed what they would tell the FBI agents: just enough about Montgomery's threat to national security to be taken seriously, yet not so much that they would reveal the exact purpose of the NCR project or give away the Ultra secret.

Relations between the Navy and J. Edgar Hoover's G-men had not been very cordial in the first years of World War II. Hoover had wanted a full place in American foreign intelligence and cryptanalysis during the war, but a compromise fashioned by the White House between the FBI and Navy intelligence leaders had left the FBI frustrated with a limited role and no clue about Ultra.

That night, FBI and Navy investigators, including Meader, drove to Montgomery's home in Franklin and conducted a thorough search. They believed they didn't need a warrant: Lillian Montgomery had given them written permission and agreed to accompany the investigators. But she must not have had any idea what her husband had hidden beneath her nose.

In the couple's tiny bedroom, wrapped in a large sheet, Meader said he found sketches of assemblies that would reveal the purpose of the machines and electronic tubes—"of such nature that they couldn't be used [for] . . . any other purpose than on the project." That tube was likely the four-diode device developed specifically for the Bombe, said Don Lowden. Only two-diode tubes were available at that time on the open market.

Montgomery had lifted mundane items from NCR as well, including several neon glow lamps, one condenser, and two circuit sketches, plus several electrical items that could have been purchased on the open market, at least in peacetime.

Meader and the FBI soon held a "discussion" with Montgomery about the most secret tube. They instructed the young man to testify that he had stolen only three of the nonspecial tubes, for a total market value of less than thirty-five dollars.

THE NEXT AFTERNOON, November 9, the FBI fingerprinted Montgomery and took him out of Meader's control. All the more frightening for Meader and his superiors, the FBI released Lillian, insisting there was no evidence that she had stolen anything or even knew about the items hidden in the house. She seems to have been too naïve or too frightened to think of contacting a lawyer for her husband.

But the Navy's dilemma was far from resolved. Even if convicted in a secret trial and locked away until the end of the war, how could Montgomery be kept from revealing his secrets to other inmates? Meader wrote to Earl Stone in a secret telegram earlier in the day, "His admitted readiness to serve the enemy, together with his knowledge of certain parts of our machine, makes him potentially extremely dangerous."

FBI Special Agent Belmont wasn't convinced that the Navy had made its case for espionage. Under FBI questioning, Montgomery denied having told Meader that he planned to offer his services to the Japanese and Germans. As for the electronic parts he had stolen from NCR, Montgomery told the agents the items were intended for use in his radio-repair shop and that he had stolen them a month before his arrest, on October 8—a date that happened to coincide with his birthday. Belmont was certain they could file a charge of theft of government property against Montgomery, who seemed "very scared and he will probably take a plea," according to a November 9 FBI memo.

Belmont took his case that day to the U.S. attorney in Dayton.

IF EVER THERE was a prosecutor with a history of standing up to outside pressure, it was U.S. Attorney Calvin Crawford. A feisty and eloquent Democrat of independent views and incorruptible integrity, he had grown up in Greenville, Ohio, and had gone on to graduate from Ohio's Miami University and Harvard Law School. In 1944, when former governor James M. Cox—then the national Democratic Party boss—refused to back his reappointment, Crawford very publicly blew the whistle on Cox's strong-arm tactics in the very newspaper Cox owned, the Dayton *Journal Herald*. "I am by no means the only object of his [Cox's] displeasure," Crawford was quoted as saying by the paper. "All of us together whom he has sought to banish make up quite a goodly company. For it is his habit to decree the defeat of party leaders and candidates who do not chance to please him."

Although he was sensitive to the Navy's demand that the affair be restricted to a small circle of security-conscious officials, Crawford felt the need to contact the attorney general's office in Washington for advice on how to proceed. He turned to Assistant Attorney General Tom C. Clark, the Justice Department's specialist in security matters.

At age forty-four, Clark was on his way to becoming the U.S. Attorney General and, later, a justice of the Supreme Court. By 1943, his government service had included not only steering several espionage cases but orchestrating the questionable legalities of relocating thousands of Japanese families on the West Coast to detention camps and helping then-senator Harry Truman investigate the war industries. Clark already had a taste of what was in store in the Montgomery case, having been involved in the handling of a newspaper reporter's leak concerning the top secret atomic-bomb project. Clark had advised Leslie Groves, head of the Manhattan Project, not to press charges against the reporter since the Constitution forbade secret civilian trials and the project could only be hurt by a public trial.

Clark also knew that the overreaction to threats of espionage and treason during World War I had led to a tightening of laws and procedures after the war. Civil libertarians had made it much more difficult to secure convictions against American citizens, restricting the use of secret indictments and trials to foreign agents and those in the military.

Clark, Crawford, and the FBI evidently dismissed Meader's claim that Montgomery had confessed to him alone on the night he was seized. Besides, Crawford feared, even a secret indictment for espionage might be enough to trigger the interest of the press.

Crawford and Clark no doubt scoured the overlapping and often redundant U.S. Code for applicable sections and found one perfectly suited to the crisis: section 100, title 18, "Embezzling public moneys or other property." The law made no mention of the value of the government property embezzled—it could be any amount, even a mere thirty-five dollars—while its penalty allowed for jail time of up to five years. Certainly, the FBI could make an embezzlement charge stick—hadn't Montgomery been employed in a position of trust with the Navy?

On the same day, November 9, that Montgomery was taken into FBI custody, he was arraigned in federal court on charges of government embezzlement and held in jail on five thousand dollars' bond—not surprisingly, an amount too high for his family to afford.

BUT THE DANGER of exposing the NCR project was only just beginning to take shape. The case had to be presented to a grand jury so that Montgomery could be indicted and stand trial. The Washington

office of the FBI called Belmont on November 11 and told him to tell
the judge that Montgomery must be held in jail quietly, with no publicity whatsoever during his trial or pleading. Belmont must also try to
find a way to muzzle Montgomery in court. If that were not possible,
Washington authorities told him, Belmont must call in every reporter
likely to cover the proceedings and talk with them about their patriotic duty to keep the case quiet—a plea the FBI had used before with
good results.

As for Montgomery's wife, Lillian, the Navy seemed to have decided that the best course was to continue her employment at NCR,
where she could be watched. Indeed, she was to remain in her job
throughout the war.

Although the Navy had dropped out of the investigation, it was
still vested in the outcome. In a November 13 memo, the Navy
warned Hoover's office that, if Belmont and Crawford failed to get a
government theft conviction, it would "take the matter into our own
hands . . . and thereafter [assume] the responsibility" for handling
the case as one of espionage.

The FBI fired back a long memo on the same day: if the Navy really wanted to keep Montgomery quiet, why not draft the man? By
pressing Montgomery into service, the Navy could isolate him for
the rest of the war, perhaps even placing him on a deserted
island. The memo went on to cite instances where judges had given
criminals the choice of jail or enlistment. The Navy took almost a
week to reject the FBI plan, and then never explained its decision.
In the midst of fighting a war, however, perhaps Navy officers were
not interested in baby-sitting a potential traitor.

Two FBI agents interviewed Montgomery in jail on November 13
and again two weeks later. They persuaded him to plead guilty to theft
of government property, but he insisted again that he was innocent of
espionage.

Meanwhile, with the grand jury running a week behind schedule
in considering the embezzlement charges, Montgomery was removed
from custody in Dayton to the Clinton County jail, some thirty miles
southeast in the small town of Wilmington. He remained incommu-

nicado, but the smaller jail meant that he could not always be kept from the other prisoners.

The record does not explain why Montgomery was transferred to the more rural county, but it is safe to assume that Meader and Navy intelligence officials wanted to draw attention away from his connection to NCR and distance him from relatives and friends who might begin to question his treatment. The jail keeper in Clinton County did his best to keep Montgomery isolated from other prisoners and "forgot to mail" two letters James had written. Montgomery's oral request to see a lawyer likewise continued to slip the jailer's mind.

The slowness of the grand jury prompted the FBI and Crawford to come to their own agreement independent of the Navy: they would continue to investigate the possibility of espionage but not pursue the charge for now, even if it could be done secretly, for the simple reason that it would take too long. Any more delays in the case ran the risk of making Montgomery uncooperative and talkative.

"I trust this will adequately dispose of the case in the event a guilty plea is entered," Crawford wrote to Tom Clark and James McInerney in the attorney general's office on November 18. "If he should stand trial, of course, we shall have further problems to deal with."

JUST WHEN IT seemed the Montgomery case might be under control, the local press began asking questions about the man being held in isolation in the Clinton County jail. Alarm spread through the Navy and Justice departments. An internal FBI memo on November 18 stated that Crawford "had already received inquiries from the press that . . . [a man named] James Thompson had been picked up by the FBI as a German agent." The reporters had gotten the name wrong but most everything else right. They knew, for instance, that the suspect was from Franklin.

Meader hoped that some hints from the FBI about the needs of national security might keep the papers quiet. In the main they were, but the Franklin *Chronicle* could not resist printing a short front-page article about Montgomery's arraignment in federal court. While not mentioning spies or espionage, the article ended very cryptically by saying that "Montgomery's arrest three weeks ago led to countless unconfirmed rumors that were circulated widely throughout the community."

Crawford immediately presented Montgomery's case to the grand jury the next day as a simple charge of embezzling government property, although no information was given to the grand jury about Montgomery's work at NCR and very little about the items stolen, other than to say that they were three gas tubes. The grand jury returned the indictment against Montgomery four days later. The case was now bound for public trial.

As Crawford envisioned the publicity in an open court case, he again called Meader and asked if the Navy would reconsider drafting Montgomery and making life easier for everyone involved. Meader called Washington, then telephoned Crawford. The answer again was no.

By November 26, Justice Department officials were beginning to wonder if they had enough evidence to prosecute Montgomery. An FBI check on him found no previous criminal record—and given Montgomery's relative youth, his wife, and his small child, a judge might well look upon a thirty-five-dollar theft as unworthy of a long sentence, even if it had been of government property.

To help strike a deal with Montgomery and his lawyer, Thomas H. Ryan, McInerney told Crawford to leave open the term of Montgomery's jail time to a decision by the court: if the circumstances were right—and the Navy agreed—Montgomery could be freed after serving fewer than five years.

The Navy agreed. Crawford and the FBI agents visited Montgomery in jail and offered him the deal. Montgomery, believing he might get as little as a year in jail, went along. But the Navy was to fail to live up to its end of the bargain.

FEDERAL CASE 1842, *U.S. v. James Martin Montgomery Jr.*, was heard on November 27, 1943, in the federal court for the Southern

District of Ohio in Dayton. With his court-appointed attorney present—whom he had met for the first time that morning—Montgomery pleaded guilty, as promised. The hearing was quick, simple, quiet—everything according to plan.

Montgomery had no statement for the court. There were no reporters present and no indications that Lillian or any other member of Montgomery's family was in attendance. Sitting secretively in plain clothes at the back of the courtroom was Francis M. Seaman, of the Navy's Judge Advocate General (JAG) Office, who was there to make sure everything went according to the Navy's wishes. He reported back to Washington that it had.

Judge Robert R. Nevin sentenced Montgomery to five years in prison, but agreed that Montgomery's sentence could be reduced later, if it seemed appropriate.

The Justice Department and the FBI moved to keep their promises of tight security to the Navy. McInerney notified James V. Bennett, the head of the U.S. Bureau of Prisons, that precautions had to be taken to keep Montgomery from revealing secrets to other prisoners. That meant high-security lockup. But Bennett balked, thinking it an unusual request for someone who had committed such a slight offense. Instead, prison officials followed the assignment rules for young, first-time offenders and, on December 6, sent Montgomery to the federal facility at Chillicothe, Ohio—an "industrial reformatory" that was more a youth training camp than an Alcatraz.

The Navy fumed. It contacted Bennett and insisted Montgomery be kept completely isolated. Bennett, in turn, complained to the top echelons of the prison bureau about the Navy's unwillingness to supply an explanation for its demands and for not passing its request through regular channels.

Undaunted, Navy officials demanded that Montgomery's mail be intercepted, checked for codes, censored, and copied to them. When he learned of the Navy's hounding of Bennett and the prison bureau, Edward A. Tamm—J. Edgar Hoover's right-hand man—told Navy officials of his growing irritation with their meddling. But he must have been persuaded to back up their demands anyway—thanks, in part, to a Navy deception. For the first time, OP20G revealed something to the FBI about the nature of the NCR work, although it was deliberately false. Tamm informed Bennett in a memo that the Montgomery case involved a supersecret electronic device necessary to record accurate shipping information—a lie Tamm had been fed by the Navy.

Despite their many misgivings, the FBI and Bureau of Prisons eventually cooperated with the Navy. Montgomery was moved into the most isolated part of the reformatory, and all his mail was intercepted and checked for hidden messages. He had little chance of contact with the outside world.

AS MONTGOMERY LANGUISHED in isolation over the next few weeks, the unhappiness among prison officials over his treatment percolated up through the Justice Department. In a December 18 letter to Clark, Crawford said he had just heard from the warden at Chillicothe, who complained that he had no way of keeping Montgomery as secure and isolated as desired and that "Montgomery could only be kept in present status for several (3–4) months" without suffering psychological consequences. It was the second such complaint from the warden.

On December 29, Montgomery was transferred from Chillicothe to the more secure federal prison in Terre Haute, Indiana. He was isolated as soon as he arrived there and allowed no visitors. Prison officials continued to fear for his mental status. In a memo that may have been sent directly to Hoover, Tamm wrote that Bennett had contacted McInerney in the Justice Department and told him that no individual could stand such treatment for long. Tamm said he agreed with McInerney's skepticism about the Navy's case: "[McInerney] stated the Navy may have conjured up the whole thing and have become unduly excited in the matter."

LESS THAN TWO weeks later, on January 10, 1944, Ryan asked for a reduced sentence, thinking he had every chance of success, given the deal made at the time of Montgomery's sentencing. But Ryan's request was flatly denied. He was not informed of the exact reasons and certainly not of the behind-the-scenes role of OP20G in blocking the request. But that was not the end of the protests. A new and surprisingly effective advocate emerged for Montgomery: his wife, Lillian. Despite the fact that her husband hadn't been entirely honest with her, she lobbied the FBI and Justice Department for his release.

J. Edgar Hoover made the first move. On February 17, he ordered the Cincinnati FBI office to drop the espionage investigation against Montgomery, despite a startling new revelation: Montgomery had at one time used an alias, "Gerald Walters." Regardless, Hoover decided to write off the case in part because an FBI investigator had discovered that some of the names on Montgomery's lists of foreign agents simply matched those in the book *Armies of Spies,* found in the downtown Dayton library. Overlooked was the fact that there were other names on Montgomery's lists and that he must have spent considerable time searching other sources. Hoover didn't declare Montgomery innocent but argued that any further investigation threatened the Navy's desire for utmost secrecy.

Meanwhile, the Justice Department began inquiries to see if Montgomery's sentence should be reduced. A special agent was sent to Dayton and also to Terre Haute to meet with the prisoner.

Montgomery, it seems, was a new man. Perhaps the few letters he had just been permitted to receive from his wife had bolstered his spirit. Perhaps, too, he finally realized that the government was not going to keep its promise of an early release. When he met with the Justice Department investigator in early March, Montgomery was, for the first time, aggressive—though not entirely truthful—in defending his innocence. He strongly protested his sentence as excessive. He denied the Navy's charge that he was a spy. He drew a sad picture of his early life, especially his having to leave home because of his second stepmother. He emphasized that his two brothers were overseas in the armed forces.

Montgomery claimed that his only contact with a foreign power was the 1938 letter to the Germans. He omitted any reference to later letters, nor did he mention the stolen parts found in his home or the list of agents in his car. Montgomery then stretched the truth of his personal life to the breaking point. He claimed he had been a good member of a Presbyterian church but that he had been unable to attend church the last few years because he had been working seven days a week. He exaggerated the number of years he had worked at his furniture factory job in Miamisburg and left out entirely any mention of the time spent in Cincinnati or the temporary work he had done over the years. He even supplied an incorrect starting date for his job at NCR.

Although the investigator mentioned afterward in his report to Washington that Montgomery's file hinted at possible espionage, he was clearly sympathetic and failed to catch many of the inconsistencies and outright lies in what Montgomery had told him.

Another compromise was soon reached: the Navy agreed to inform the Justice Department every month on whether it was necessary to retain Montgomery in isolation and immediately when the NCR work was no longer a secret. But the Navy continued to demand that Montgomery's mail be sent to the FBI's codebreakers, now revealing to Hoover's office that Montgomery had some knowledge of cryptology.

Lillian managed to send her husband nearly four letters a week—his only contact beyond the confines of his cell, other than two letters sent from his father, during his entire time in jail. Montgomery may not have known that his younger brother, Billie, had been killed in action in October 1944. Billie had been carrying wounded men from a rice paddy on Leyte in the Philippines when a sniper shot him. Certainly, Montgomery was unaware that his own draft status had been quietly altered and that his name had been placed on a secret security-risk list—a tag that followed him and his son through the cold war, according to the family.

World War II had been over for six weeks when the Navy at last relented: Montgomery was released on parole on October 11, 1945. But even then, the Navy refused to reveal the true nature of the work at NCR to anyone beyond the tight circle of Ultra. Contradicting its earlier lie in 1943, that NCR was building an electronic device that kept track of shipping, the Navy told Clark another lie: that Montgomery had worked on the Navy's proximity fuse, a radar-triggered artillery shell for bringing down aircraft.

What the British were told about the Montgomery affair remains unknown. None of the archives in either nation contains any indication that the Navy informed GCCS about the breach of security, despite the 1943 pledge to report all such cases.

Whether or not Montgomery had planned to contact the Nazis about the NCR codebreaking machines may be open to question. But what is certain is that Montgomery and his wife never fully recovered from the ordeal. After his release, Montgomery drifted from menial job to menial job, perhaps because he was blacklisted, as his family members have suggested.

It wasn't until 1953 that Montgomery got a break. He was hired for his first real job in more than a decade as a service repairman for the Jackson Instrument Company. But Lillian began suffering a series of nervous breakdowns, and Montgomery remained uncommunicative and unable to handle his family hardships. In 1967, they were divorced.

Montgomery seems never to have revealed the NCR secret to anyone. He died in Miamisburg on September 24, 1970, a couple weeks shy of his fiftieth birthday. He left behind a 1965 Dodge Monaco valued at $750 and a child-support debt to Lillian for their two daughters of $740. Lillian was able to find the $1,100 needed for his cremation and burial in Dayton's Woodland Cemetery.

Montgomery would have died alone except that Lillian had taken him back into her home to care for him in his final days. The records show he died of a heart attack at 4:00 P.M., brought on by a combination of choked arteries and years of diabetes. His family believes he was killed by a past that haunted him to the end.

12

Triumph!

February 1, 1944—South Atlantic

EN ROUTE FROM Bordeaux to the South Atlantic for another raid on
Allied shipping, Korvettenkapitän C. C. Buchholz, skipper of *U-177*,
received a radio transmission from U-boat Control: "Attention. Japanese submarine in vicinity of your outbound course at 00-09 North,
25-45 West." Ironically, that warning triggered the beginning of the
end for Buchholz and the crew of *U-177*, one of the most successful
submarines in the German fleet. Commissioned in February 1942, it
had sunk at least six Allied ships over the ensuing two years and perhaps as many as twenty-seven, if German broadcasts at the time are to
be believed. But its fortunes were to change dramatically with the
broadcast from Berlin.

The encoded radio message was copied by an Allied intercept station and sent to OP20G's communication annex, where almost ninety
Bombes were now in full operation. With the help of the American
Bombes, the Allies were finding Shark and related keys within a day
or two. Codebreakers reduced that to half a day by early summer of
1944, so that many Enigma messages were being read virtually at the
same time as the German clerks receiving them.

On February 6, 1944, at 7:00 in the morning, two B-24 long-
range bombers lifted off from Ascension Island in search of *U-177*.

Visibility was good—up to fifteen miles—with scattered cumulus clouds drifting above moderate, sunlit seas. Spotting the sub would be relatively simple: the intelligence information guiding the bomber crews was current enough to pinpoint its location. Better still, the planes had no need to use their radar, which might tip off enemy detection equipment to their approach.

Three and a half hours later, Lieutenant Carrell I. Pinnell's B-24 was just below the clouds at 2,600 feet when the bow gunner spotted the heavy wake of a fully surfaced submarine about twelve miles away, bearing seventy degrees from the course of the plane. Pinnell immediately radioed his wing partner, who was miles behind, then told his crew to man their battle stations and test their equipment before he hit full throttle on the four-engine Liberator and banked out of the sun in fast pursuit.

Two miles from *U-177*, Pinnell ran into heavy fire from the sub's flak cannon and twin twenty-millimeter antiaircraft guns. The exploding flak "was so close it sounded like a sledgehammer pounding the cabin," Pinnell recalled. "There was dust falling down from the ceiling."

He took evasive action, wobbling the big plane up and down as he dove, but finally was forced to pull up. "It broke my heart to do that. I thought, 'Boy, this is a good way to get hit, and we haven't even dropped our load.' "

Pinnell could have called off the attack and waited for his wing partner but he feared the U-boat would slip away. Instead, he attacked again about three quarters of a mile from the sub—an act of heroism that earned him the Distinguished Flying Cross. This time, the B-24's bow gunner quieted the sub's guns just long enough that, at one hundred feet, Pinnell was able to straddle the sub's hull with three depth charges on each side.

As Pinnell completed his pass, machine-gun fire flashed at the B-24's exposed belly—but not for long. By the time he had banked and started his second pass, the force of the depth charges had lifted the sub's hull out of the water and ripped it apart. As *U-177* sank, the water above it was a roiling stew of debris, with only its conning tower still visible a few feet below the surface.

Pinnell dropped his remaining three depth charges, flew off, and returned again to find fourteen survivors struggling in the water. The B-24 crew dumped a life raft for them, then radioed their position for ships in the area. Pinnell roared back to Ascension Island.

Despite their late arrival in the war, the American Bombes were making a significant contribution to the destruction of the Nazi U-boat fleet by the fall of 1943. *U-177* was the third sighting of a sub in as many months by Pinnell's squadron alone, all without the aid of radar. Clearly, the decrypts were giving pilots accurate information on their targets.

November 1943 was when the U.S. Bombes at last began breaking the keys to the Shark code on a routine basis. By December, the average time for gaining entry into Shark was thirty-six hours—down dramatically from the embarrassing early months of 1943 when the Americans had needed an average of twenty-five days to break Shark, mostly by hand. The new average was also better than the British Bombes had been able to do during their best times in 1943.

By March 1944, the British trusted the Americans enough to transfer the major responsibility for deciphering the Shark keys to OP20G. With new shipments of Bombes coming from Dayton every week, the Americans now had nearly one hundred in operation at the Naval Communications Annex, where the workforce was at last up to speed. It was not only a matter of trust: the Americans had demonstrated that the NCR four-wheel Bombe was more reliable and more adept at getting the job done than the British models.

The timing was fortuitous, because the job of cracking Shark only got tougher in the months that followed. Admiral Dönitz had decided to end the wolf-pack attacks in the North Atlantic and had dispersed his fleet to hunt vulnerable Allied ships on their own, thus greatly reducing the number and quality of U-boat messages to and from headquarters. Even so, the Americans continued to conquer Shark as well as make contributions to the attacks on several other German naval systems. By the summer of 1944, hundreds of submarine messages were being read the same day, some within minutes of their transmission, giving Allied antisubmarine forces a fresh bead on the subs' whereabouts.

With the faster decrypt times generated by the U.S. Bombes, the percentage of U-boats sunk with the aid of Ultra intelligence climbed steeply. In 1943, Ultra decryptions had a role in just 10 percent of sub kills, but they were a direct factor in almost 30 percent of the U-boats dispatched by American forces in 1944, and 25 percent in 1945. Although British sub sinkings are more difficult to categorize, the Ultra-assisted percentage of sub kills rose from 20 percent in 1943 to 26 percent in 1944.*

It was payback time for the dark days of 1942 and 1943. In May 1944, the Allies sank more than half the operating U-boats—destroying them at a rate faster than the Germans could replace them. Over the next three months that summer, the percentage of operating U-boats sent to the bottom reached a high of 76 percent. More important, the loss of Allied merchant shipping to U-boats remained low throughout the year—with almost no casualties in the Atlantic—in large part because of the more secure British Cypher No. 5.

According to a jubilant and perhaps overstated July 14, 1944, OP20G memo, written when the American attack against Shark was at its high point,

> the effect of the U.S. "bombes" on solving the Atlantic U-boat cipher has exceeded all expectations.... For the last half of each day, we can read messages to and from Atlantic and Indian Ocean U-boats simultaneously with the enemy. In fact, during these hours the translation of every message sent by a U-boat is at hand about 20 minutes after it was originally transmitted. At present, approximately 15 percent of these keys are solved by the British and the remainder by OP20G.

---

* Naval historians have overestimated the percentage of sub sinkings assisted by Ultra intelligence, claiming it was as high as 70 percent of all U.S. sub kills, in large part because they assumed a direct link between any sunken U-boat and any type of radio or communications intelligence. But a closer examination shows that many sub kills were credited to the aid of codebreaking even when the U-boats were sunk many days or even weeks after the location date given in the U-boat's message. In other cases, the credit given to decrypts was actually the result of radio direction-finding or, perhaps, traffic analysis. Although the corrected figures are less dramatic, Ultra intelligence still played a significant role in the Battle of the Atlantic.

The American contribution to the victory over Shark and other Enigma naval systems was hard-won but still far from secure. Wenger, Engstrom, Desch, and their crews battled a stream of near-constant upgrades to the Enigma and its use. While the Germans did not make frequent and significant changes to their cipher systems—their math-beguiled cryptologists were too smug about the theoretical challenges of the Enigma machine to force such radical changes—they did see the need to improve their systems on a regular basis. At times, too, the German military had enough nagging doubts about the security of the Enigma to make larger adjustments—such as introducing a double turnover ring between the fast rotor and the second as it did in 1944. But given the cost and logistics of modifying hundreds and even thousands of Enigma machines scattered around the globe, the Germans took the conservative course, in part because many in the military believed that the Allies' superior radar was the prime culprit for their U-boat troubles.

New German systems and, later, Japanese codes, along with Germany's latest Enigma innovations, kept OP20G off balance and in a reactive mode until the end of the war. Although there were attempts to move far ahead of their adversaries, the bright young theoreticians in Engstrom's M section and the engineers in charge of machine design did not have the time to turn their most advanced ideas into hardware. Desch and the other engineers had to continue to build the types of machines that could be produced fast enough to meet crises, with the risk, of course, that they soon would be outmoded.

The Navy engineers did not have the time to design a more automatic and general-purpose machine—a luxury available during the war only to the Army's codebreakers. With the British decoding a nearly unbroken stream of German Army and Air Force messages, the U.S. Army was able to step back and design its more adventurous Madame X and Superscritcher machines, albeit with unimpressive results. Even though Madame X used thousands of telephone relays to attack the three-wheel Enigma—more relays than the telephone exchange for a town of eighteen thousand people—it nonetheless proved very slow after its completion in 1943 and was used mostly as a research machine. Plans for a four-wheel version of the machine were scrapped because it would have needed another five hundred thousand relays, then in short supply. The Superscritcher, a more advanced design that used vacuum tubes and electronics rather than relays, wasn't ready until after the war.

Unlike the Army machines, Desch's Bombe needed skilled humans to change the wheels, switches, and cable connections for each run. The setups took as long or, at times, longer, than it took a Bombe to find a solution. But Desch's choice was wise given the alternative: a much more complex, unpredictable, and hard-to-manufacture device.

The machine's balance of speed, power, and reliability paid off. The American Bombes were far faster than the British three-wheel machines and faster and more reliable than GCCS's new four-wheel Bombes. On four-wheel runs, the American devices could complete their task in one twentieth of the time needed by the older British models. When setup times for runs were included, however, the American advantage in speed dropped to about a threefold edge over the British, depending on the number of wheels to be changed and switches to be reset. The American Bombes also were faster than the British four-wheel version, by about 50 percent, and much less prone to break down.*

The power of the 120 or so American Bombes was equal to or greater than that of the 220 British Bombes at Bletchley Park. The British, who were charged with attacking many more German sys-

---

* Some of the limitations of the early American Bombes were spotted soon after their design was set in early 1943. First was the realization that the Bombe needed modifications if it was to be efficiently used as a high-speed version of a "locator"—that is, a means of finding the message setting after other parts of the keys of an Enigma message were known. Borrowing on ideas from the British in the spring of 1943, John Howard outlined the first of the so-called Grenade attachments for the Bombes—a five-foot-long, twenty-pound attachment containing a series of electrical switches. By the end of war, some six different types of Grenade attachments were constructed, each performing a more sophisticated set of functions.

More limitations of the Bombes were recognized in the summer of 1943 when the British warned the Americans that the Germans were about to make changes to Shark. With only a vague idea of what the Germans were up to, Engstrom ordered his mathematicians to think both of new methods of attack and of the outlines for a new type of Bombe. But by the time the first ideas were generated, it was discovered that the changes to Shark were less daunting than thought. The Germans had simply added a new fourth rotor that was to be changed only once a month. Although that prevented the reading of Shark during the first half of July 1943, GCCS soon found ways to identify the new rotors and helped OP20G to master the techniques.

tems than were the Americans—including the three-wheel Army and Air Force Enigma traffic known as Bovril—asked for time on the American Bombes.

Fortunately for the Allies, Desch had had the foresight to design the Bombe with the flexibility to attack both three-wheel and four-wheel Enigma problems—all it took was a flip of a switch on the machine. That simple feature became a major blessing. In part because the Desch Bombes were so successful against the four-wheel Shark traffic, they soon developed excess capacity that could be diverted to help the British with their three-wheel problems. During the last two years of the war, more than 60 percent of the U.S. Bombes' running time was devoted to Bovril traffic.*

Bovril was still predominantly a British operation, however. GCCS sent over the intercepts, cribs, and even menus and lists of priorities for runs on the American machines, sometimes to the frustration of Engstrom and Wenger, who wanted to focus OP20G's efforts in the hunt for U-boats. The German Army and Air Force problems were divided into many different systems and produced a deluge of messages for cryptanalysis. Hoping to solve as many keys as quickly as they could, the British kept the easier problems to themselves and delegated the stickier ones to Washington—a move that displeased the Americans.

As the Americans began to help with other Enigma systems, they made further adjustments to their Bombes. Two cipher systems that linked the German and Japanese navies as well as their attachés and blockade-runners—Seahorse and Sunfish—required a Bombe that could handle a long string of menu letters. The Desch machine, whose sixteen banks of simulated Enigmas could handle up to sixteen menu letters, was inadequate for the job. Too embarrassed to have to ask for time on the larger British Bombes, Howard Engstrom requested in the summer of 1943 a new double-unit Bombe with thirty-two banks, dubbed Granddad. Driving twice as many Enigma banks at the speeds required for the fast wheels and also supplying those banks with enough electrical current to keep track of their move-

---

* OP20G had been working on Bovril problems by hand and tabulator methods since early 1943 and began running them on the Bombes as early as September 1943.

ments was a major task for NCR's engineers. Joe Desch and his staff soon found solutions: they substituted a larger motor and a belt drive for the geared shaft in the regular Bombes and silver brushes for copper to carry more current through the banks.*

ALTHOUGH THE BRITISH continued to work on Japanese systems at GCCS and smaller centers in Ceylon and Australia, the United States bore the brunt of codebreaking duties in the Pacific and was the senior partner in the alliance, just the reverse of the European Ultra arrangement. The Navy's Pacific codebreakers had relied on traditional approaches and hundreds of IBM tabulators, including the specially designed NC (Navy Change) IBM machines. Then in November 1943, just as the Navy was about to launch its toughest series of attacks yet against the Japanese-held islands in the Pacific, codebreakers asked for help from OP20G's M section and the team at Building 26.

The Japanese naval systems presented challenges different from, and in some ways more demanding than, those of the Enigma. With few exceptions, they used codes, not ciphers, and many were additive systems, such as the main Japanese naval code, JN-25.†

At times, the Japanese problems were more frustrating and de-

---

* Much more limited in its application—and developed much earlier than Granddad—was the inverted Bombe. Following British advice, OP20G soon recognized that some German problems demanded that the wheel order in the Bombes be reversed so that the slow rotor became the fastest. That allowed the analysts to deal more easily with rotor turnovers within a crib. By the end of 1943, several of the Bombes had been inverted for such use, receiving the name "Fire Engines." In addition to standard Bombes, the Fire Engines may have helped with the attack against Bovril.

† Breaking into a code system such as JN-25 was both an art and a science, requiring intensive labor. A codebreaker first had to determine the meanings of the code numbers. Unless a codebook was stolen or captured, "book building" was a painstaking process that depended on linguistics, familiarity with a sender's habits, and much intuition and luck. The next steps were to determine the contents of the book of additives and what number had been added to (or subtracted from) each code group. This method of "differencing" called for hundreds of calculations on columns of code that codebreakers suspected had been enciphered with the same additives. Such an alignment was called a "depth."

A related method, called stripping, was to try adding likely numbers to the code groups in messages until codes known to occur frequently in Japanese traffic started to emerge. The appearance of high-frequency groups indicated that the codebreaker might have found the right page and starting place of the additives.

manded more manpower than Enigma. For Japanese systems like JN-25, each message presented a separate challenge until Allied code-breakers could reconstruct the current book of additives and identify the keys being used. As Admiral Nimitz prepared for his late 1943 surge into the Pacific islands, the Navy had to ensure that Japanese radio intelligence kept flowing. The pressure was on OP20G.

In October 1943, OP20G's research section was asked to design and build machines that would be many times faster than the best IBM tabulators to help speed up the attack against the Japanese codes. An ex-MIT student, Lawrence Steinhardt, was put in charge of the effort, and it soon became one of OP20G's and Dayton's highest priorities. Navy engineers conferred with the cryptanalysts working on the Japanese problems and began outlining a series of five revolutionary machines, called Copperheads. By November, Desch's team started work on the first Copperhead model—the simplest of the five machines and the only one that seems to have been completed. All five designs were based on the principles of the early Vannevar Bush RAM devices: finely punched and ultrahigh-speed tapes, light-sensing circuits, and electronics.

The first Copperhead was designed to search through the thousands of Japanese messages for "double-hits" of the same enciphered code groups, which indicated that two messages might have been enciphered with the same additives. But the project soon ran into technical troubles: its expensive and complex tape punches proved too slow and unreliable. At best, they could punch only forty messages of average length per hour when hundreds of such messages were needed for a single tape. It took close to one year to work out all the bugs in Copperhead, and it wasn't in operation until November 1944. The other Copperhead plans were shelved.

In addition to using difficult codes, the Japanese Navy showed signs that it might shift more of its most important messages to a machine encryption device. OP20G became aware that the new Jade (JN-157) machine was being used on at least some high-level naval messages in summer 1942, but it had been unable to put a team on the problem until late in the year. Concerned that the use of Jade might become widespread, one of OP20G's brightest was given responsibility. Frank Raven, a 1934 Yale graduate in mathematics and a Phi Beta Kappa scholar, had both cryptanalytic and people skills.

Raven suspected that the Jade device might be a more complex version of the Japanese Purple machine, which had been cracked already and was providing significant information to the Allies. Japan's diplomats continued to use Purple throughout the war, unaware that the Allies were reading their messages. Purple was based on the use of telephone stepping switches, and Raven believed it was a good bet that Jade used them as well.

Raven's group untangled Jade after almost one year's work, then quickly turned to Building 26 to produce a set of analog machines that would both speed decryption and help find settings. Raven also asked for more: a distinct and unique machine to solve Jade keys.

By the end of October 1943, Desch's men were busy constructing the analogs to Jade, called Vipers, while others in Building 26 were designing a new Bombe-like machine for attacking Jade, called Rattler. Delivered to Washington in May 1944, Rattler at last contained an innovation that OP20G had sought in early 1942 for the Enigma problem: electronic rotors. The Rattler and the Vipers were technical triumphs but disappointing in their use—the Japanese sent few messages over Jade, and the encryption device was retired less than three months after Rattler was delivered.

But the experience with Rattler and the Vipers found other vital applications. Raven's team suspected that Jade might be an extension of the latest version of a machine for the Japanese naval attachés' communications, dubbed Coral, that had defied Navy codebreakers since its introduction in late 1939. Agnes Driscoll, who had been successful against earlier Japanese attaché machines, had labored against it for almost a year, without result, until late 1940, when she was ordered to concentrate on the German problems. Driscoll and her small group of experienced civilians were unable to return to the Coral challenge until the last months of 1943.

In early 1944, one member of Raven's group decided to see if he could help with the Coral and its code system, known as JNA-20. By then, Driscoll and her assistants were near giving up, after months of compiling mountains of statistics trying to understand the machine.

They did not object to an outsider's help. With encouragement and help from Bletchley Park, Raven's team soon conquered Coral. By March 1944, OP20G was ordering analogs of the JNA-20 machines, dubbed Pythons in the tradition of naming the Pacific codebreaking devices after deadly snakes. Building 26 produced many of those new Pythons and helped convert the Rattlers to run Coral problems.

By April 1944, the work on JNA-20 was paying off. With Japanese attachés stationed in the major Axis capitals and many neutral nations, Coral provided valuable insights, including information on German technical capabilities and intentions. The messages of the very diligent Japanese attaché in Berlin provided many heads-ups on new German weaponry and technologies and helped the Allies determine whether countertechnologies were needed.

Awed by the Nazis' scientific wizardry, the attaché in Berlin regularly radioed his superiors in Tokyo the entire scope of the German efforts to counter the Allies' antisubmarine strategies. He was especially impressed by the Germans' new radar-search detectors, by their pattern-running torpedoes (*Federapparat*, or FAT), which could loop through a convoy with greater odds of hitting a ship, and by "Aphrodite," a balloon launched by U-boats as a radar decoy. He described in detail the German Navy's emergency training and tactics for counterattacking destroyers, for evading attack from surface ships, and for breaking through convoy-escort screens. Most important, though, he was the first to tip the Allies to the newer and deadlier classes of U-boats envisioned by Dönitz.

The list included the development of the dreaded Walter submarine, which could stay submerged for days at a time, attack at underwater sprint speeds of eighteen knots, and beat a hasty retreat. The submarine was to be powered by a special engine, designed by German scientist Helmut Walter, that used hydrogen peroxide as a source of oxygen for combustion, eliminating the need for a snorkel or to surface. The Allies feared the Walter U-boats might be developed in time to blockade British ports and to launch a mass attack against the D Day invasion fleet. But by that time, the Germans were short on facilities for making either submarines or hydrogen peroxide, thanks to the merciless Allied bombing.

The Japanese attaché also provided helpful information on the new *Schnorchel*-equipped U-boats, with their ability to "breathe" underwater and stay submerged for longer periods of time. However, none of the attaché's scientific advisories can compare to what became one of Ultra's most important contributions to the war: his detailed description of the German fortifications for repelling the D Day invasion.

In 1944, OP20G's codebreakers also discovered a special Enigma that Japan was using, called the T machine. By midyear, work began on a radically new Bombe, named Bulldozer because of the broad statistical nature of its attack, for use against the Japanese device. Although looking much like the double Bombe, the Bulldozer was of a new breed that did not rely on cribs. Instead, it used advanced electronic circuits to see if its many Enigma banks were producing plain language from the cipher text as it plowed through all the possible wheel positions and combinations. Bulldozer was less elegant and less efficient than the Turing menu approach, but it got the job done—taking hours, not minutes, for a single test. Although not in operation until 1945, Bulldozer's application of electronics to statistical methods was a breakthrough for the Americans.*

---

* Although faced with many demanding assignments during the war, OP20G's researchers were never asked to deal with the one German system that might have forced them to explore modern digital electronics: the advanced secret teleprinter the Germans were using to encipher their highest-level military communications, a system known as Fish. In a standard Teletype, each letter is represented by a series of five on/off electrical pulses—what computer types call a five-bit binary code, with zero signaling off and the number 1 signaling on. Those simple on/off pulses or "bits," performed at nearly the speed of light, form the basis of modern computing. A teleprinter might transmit A, for instance, as 11000—meaning two on pulses and three off—and B as 10011. Fish added coding wheels to the teleprinter to automatically encrypt the stream of pulses as they were being transmitted.

If OP20G's bright young researchers and engineers in Building 26 had focused on Fish and its binary approach to coding, they might have come closer to developing an electronic precomputer. Although there were fears that Fish might be used by the German Navy, dealing with the advanced teletype device was left to the British and the U.S. Army's codebreakers.

The British concentrated much of their hard-pressed resources for development in 1943 and 1944 on producing machines for the Fish problem. The nature of the attack led the British into designing machines that worked on bits rather than letters. GCCS built two types of advanced machines to attack Fish, named Robinson and Colossus. The Robinsons were high-speed tape machines somewhat like OP20G's Comparators. The Colossi, first delivered in mid-1944, were more innovative and relied more on electronics—so much so that, although they were special-purpose machines, some view them as the first modern computers.

$$\textbf{13}$$

New Challenges . . .
and Breakdown

February 19, 1944—Washington, D.C., and Dayton, Ohio

EDWARD TRAVIS'S TELEGRAPHED request to Joseph Redman, director of U.S. naval communications, seemed too much to ask in early 1944 even in the context of the close relationship GCCS and OP20G had built over the past three years. As the head of GCCS, Travis explained that the British had learned of German plans to make the four-wheel Enigma a standard for all naval and U-boat systems. With the upcoming Allied invasion perhaps just months away, Travis continued, Bletchley Park might be overwhelmed by a flood of messages and new keys to be solved each day. The British could become locked out of some of their most valuable long-term sources of information at a critical juncture in the war.

On February 19, Travis asked that OP20G build at least fifty more four-wheel Bombes for use in Washington but in service of British codebreakers. Travis may have been unaware that Desch's team had switched to other high-priority work and that the Navy might find it hard to get the funds and workforce to produce more new Bombes, especially so near the planned invasion.

Although with misgivings, the Navy's highest echelons acceded to the British request just two days later. Admiral King ordered OP20G's research team, NCR's management, and Desch to start a new multimillion-dollar Bombe project to build, as quickly as possible, fifty up-dated machines. OP20G's researchers immediately began exploring the logic and mathematics of possible improvements to Desch's original design.

Desch must have been beside himself. He already was pressed by labor shortages and the development of a radically new codebreaking machine, Duenna—one of the few projects during the war that would enable Navy researchers to get ahead of the technological curve in cryptanalysis. Work on Duenna began as early as July 1943, when Engstrom told his mathematicians to think of attacks and machine designs for a much more complex Enigma, based on fears the Germans would change to a fully changeable reflector. That, fortunately, did not happen, and Engstrom's group was shifted to other tasks in 1943. But some important preliminary work on the problem had been done.

The Duenna project was revived in February 1944 when OP20G began to worry that the U-boat Enigma would be refitted by summer with a fully pluggable reflector—that is, a fourth wheel whose internal wiring the operator could change by inserting plugs into different letters. The Allies called the new German device "Uncle Dora," or simply Uncle D, an innocuous label for a device that would add so many more ciphering possibilities that it would shut out the American Bombes completely.

A fast enough attack against Uncle D demanded a powerful new machine using the latest electronics. By early February 1944, the first design for Duenna was ready. For a backup, Engstrom ordered additions to the old Bombes that might help them decipher Uncle D messages once the reflector wiring had been identified. The problem was so worrisome that GCCS and the Army launched their own projects for attacking it as well.

By early March 1944, Engstrom declared Duenna to be of the highest priority, and yet precious resources were now being diverted to the development of fifty more Bombes. By May, Engstrom and Wenger began to protest loudly against the British request—their engineers were swamped with other projects. They also might have believed that the British were not giving their all to their own four-wheel Bombe effort, a result of Britain's failure to communicate how much of their limited manufacturing resources were being strained to produce all types of codebreaking machines. What's more, the British were still worried about the reliability of their own four-wheel Bombes. The development of the new Bombes, they believed, was best left to the Americans.*

Regardless, Engstrom and Wenger asked that the British request be either terminated or scaled back. The ill feelings engendered on both sides of the Atlantic led to a rehashing of some old accusations between the two allies and a bold attempt to rewrite the history of British-American relations.

IN THE MIDST of this new friction, both the British and the American codebreakers began to think ahead to how their superiors and future generations would view their achievements and their collaboration during the war. The British concluded that OP20G would be unlikely to cooperate in writing an objective history of the Battle of the Atlantic after the war. Their instincts were right: Engstrom and Wenger were soon asked by their superiors to write a quick history of their own on the U.S. Bombe project and British-American codebreaking relations. The Navy's motives were political—and perhaps part of a larger negotiation between the two nations' intelligence agencies.

Only Wenger and perhaps Engstrom knew how much information and technical assistance the British had offered the Americans in their 1941–1942 exchanges. Indeed, in a May 13, 1944, memo to his Navy superiors on the history of that period, Wenger had no complaints about the degree of early British cooperation. He stated that GCCS had given OP20G what it had asked for and needed, with the exception of a physical copy of the Enigma, which would not have made a difference anyway. In the same memo, Wenger wrote that Engstrom knew the extent of the British contributions as well.

But less than two weeks later, Wenger, Engstrom, and Meader

---

* Between the summer of 1943 and the war's end, the British increased the number of Bombes in operation from seventy to more than two hundred. They constructed more than sixty four-wheel machines. At the same time, they built ten or more Colossi and a host of other devices for the Fish traffic and for special attacks on difficult Enigma key systems.

wrote an internal history of the U.S. Bombe project that blamed the British for the serious delay in OP20G's ability to understand the workings of the Enigma and create its first Bombe. The history accuses the British of withholding information early in the war and of breaking repeated promises in 1942 to produce a working four-wheel Bombe of their own.

There is no direct evidence to explain OP20G's sudden about-face, but the historical context points to the need for a scapegoat. OP20G's research group was in a difficult political position in May 1944 and needed to defend itself to Admiral King and the American naval hierarchy as to why it was resisting the British request for fifty additional Bombes. The internal history also provided OP20G with a one-sided explanation for why the original NCR Bombes did not appear until autumn 1943 and the agency's anti-Enigma capabilities did not mature until almost the end of that year. The British would have been livid if they had been shown the document.

Tensions between the Allies again ran high, but the success on D Day went a long way toward improving their relations. A few weeks after the Normandy invasion in early June 1944, as Allied bombers and resistance forces cut landlines and forced the Germans to communicate almost exclusively by radio, good cribs for the Army and Air Force codes became plentiful. The two allies realized they would need fewer codebreaking machines and reached a compromise on Britain's Bombe request. As the latest version of the American Bombes were sent from Dayton to Washington in August 1944, it was decided to produce an additional twenty-five rather than fifty for the British. This still must have created workforce and production-planning headaches for NCR, but not so many that the compromise was unworkable.

In less than six months, the twenty-five enhanced Bombes were in operation at the Naval Communications Annex, in service of the British. The new Bombe contract had allowed OP20G and Desch to make the machines more powerful, although they were essentially the same design as the original Bombes. Based on intensive calculations by Navy mathematicians, a "double-input" feature was built into the 1944 machines. In simple terms, that feature allowed the equivalent of two menus to be run simultaneously on the same Enigma problem. It also let the Bombes eliminate more false stops, making them 20 percent more powerful.

Duenna turned out to be a much tougher task for OP20G and Desch—as well as for Bletchley Park and the Army's codebreakers. Although the Army built two exceptional devices, the Autoscritcher and the Superscritcher (the latter being one of the largest electronic machines of the war), both precomputers came too late to help the war effort. GCCS commissioned two less radical machines, the Giant and the Ogre, both variations on the original Bombe's architecture and technology, but they proved far less powerful than the Navy's Duenna.

The completion of Duenna failed to meet the expected August 1944 crisis in the Atlantic by several months. Desch and his team did not deliver the first model until September 1944, and engineers in both Washington, D.C., and Dayton labored feverishly to work the bugs out for a second model. A Duenna machine was not in operation until November.

Despite its late arrival, Duenna was a technological triumph for the Navy: it embodied an innovative and complex version of the no-contradiction tests that were used in the Bombes and could handle menus of eighty letters or more at high speed. Because of the complexity of the tests, Duenna had to be much faster than the Bombes and make more complicated decisions.

Desch and the team in Building 26 had hoped to build Duenna using some three thousand electronic tubes but had to settle for reasons of economy on a combination of traditional relays and three hundred or so electronic tubes, along with a new version of the Bombe's commutator wheels. The machine worked well, but a single test took hours, not minutes. The time to prepare the special menus for a run was formidable, sometimes taking more than a week.

Fortunately for OP20G, Uncle D never appeared on the U-boat networks, and it was used on only a handful of German Air Force and Army systems. The Germans compounded their mistake by sending the same messages on other systems, allowing easier entry into Uncle D once those messages were broken.

Uncle D's pluggable reflector was one more item on a long list of technical and procedural improvements to the Enigma that the Germans squandered through poor planning and piecemeal introduction. "It is not easy to see why the device was not used more effectively," notes American historian Philip Marks.

> Despite the difficulties of distributing [Uncle D] while the Germans were retreating on all fronts, they succeeded in deploying large numbers by August 1944 or even earlier, but then failed to use them on a commensurate scale. No doubt passive resistance from operators was a factor, but unclear instructions on when [the device] should be used also played a part, perhaps leaving too much discretion to field units.

Given the German reluctance to use Uncle D, the expense of constructing a Duenna, and the time needed for a run, OP20G decided to build just three of the machines rather than the ten originally planned. Even so, the Navy and Desch's team could take pride in having been the first with the best.

Designing and building both Duenna and a new Bombe took their toll on Desch in the summer and fall of 1944, and the strain was clearly evident to his colleagues. Desch and his top engineers were now working from 7:30 A.M. to 2:30 A.M. of the following day—a grueling schedule that lasted nearly six weeks, according to Carmelita Bruce, whose husband, Ralph, had been one of the original seven engineers on the NCR research team. "I remember my husband saying at the time, 'Joe Desch is not doing well. We hope we'll get him through before all this is over.' "

June 4, 1944—South Atlantic

TWO DAYS BEFORE D Day, Admiral Dan Gallery's hunter-killer group of antisubmarine vessels was about to end its patrol off the coast of Africa when one of its destroyers thought it had finally located the elusive sub that Gallery had been chasing with the aid of Ultra for several frustrating days: U-505.

Launching planes from his escort carrier, the *Guadalcanal,* Gallery guided his other ships to the location of the submerged U-boat. Depth charges severely damaged the submarine, forcing its wounded skipper, Harold Lange, to surface. Unable to fight off the destroyers, Lange watched as his submarine was boarded by U.S. sailors and its contents seized. Soon, it was towed to an Allied port.

Among the items captured were the keys for the Atlantic and Indian ocean U-boat systems for the first weeks of June. The timing of the seizure was a mixed blessing. With the keys in hand, the Allies might not need to run their Bombes on the two systems for much of June. On the other hand, if Dönitz learned of the capture of *U-505,* then new keys would be issued and, perhaps, extra Enigma security procedures taken that might lock out OP20G and GCCS during the critical days of the Normandy invasion. The British voiced such concerns to the American Navy.

Luck again was with the Allies, however. The German systems were not changed, and, after the captured settings were delivered to the codebreakers, the Allies found they did not have to use the Bombes for Shark or the Indian Ocean U-boat traffic until the last week of June. Hence, during the critical first weeks of the invasion of France, the Bombes were freed for use against the German Army and Air Force systems.

According to an OP20G report, "Almost the entire capacity of OP20G was devoted to Army and Air Force work [in June 1944]. This resulted in a considerable gain in intelligence during a very critical phase of the invasion of France." The German order of battle and critical bombing targets were revealed by Ultra throughout the invasion period. With the increase in cribs from the loss of landlines after D Day, "the volume of decodes was so much greater than previous expectations, that the section charged with their dissemination was virtually swamped," the report concluded.

OP20G gained a greater role in naval Ultra during the invasion period in the summer of 1944 and held on to it through the remainder of the war. A year before, the Navy codebreakers had been working on only two major systems. At the end of 1943, they were participating in breaking a half-dozen naval-related keys. By June 1944, that number had doubled.

OP20G seemed at last to have surmounted Shark as well. With average decrypt times less than sixteen hours by late summer, Wenger and Engstrom thought that they could shift their men to long-term codebreaking solutions. In August 1944, as they laid out new organizational plans for OP20G after the expected victories over Germany and Japan, they asked their young theoreticians to design an all-purpose, electronic "computer" that would advance the Navy's code-breaking research, if not its operational capabilities, well into the future.

But the respite for OP20G did not last long. In September, it began losing its command over Shark, despite the new Bombes and the increased skills of its codebreakers. The Germans were pulling their wolf packs out of harm's way and relying on lone hunters until newer technologies could be introduced to help protect them. The resulting lack of messages and cribs more than doubled the time to find Shark keys. The situation, Wenger reported, was bad and would probably get worse. With fewer U-boats at sea, the Germans were cutting back on weather messages and other "short" signals that had been excellent sources of cribs and locations throughout much of the war. In particular, the Bay of Biscay weather messages, which had proved so vital in breaking the German codes just prior to D Day, would now dry up as the Allies overran France and drove the U-boats from their safe harbor in the bay.

Wenger asked Engstrom and his research group to return to operational problems and focus on finally devising a noncrib, statistical attack on Enigma. Meanwhile, OP20G's operational problems multiplied as the Germans split up more submarine keys and maintained greater radio silence. October's keys took more than forty-five hours to find. November and December took almost as long.

In late 1944, OP20G had to focus on yet another Enigma crisis, one that threatened to wipe out the exceptional power of the Bombe's Diagonal Board. A surprising Nazi innovation to the Enigma, the Uhr box, had been spotted by the British a month after D Day. The Uhr box was an attachment to the Enigma that changed the stecker wiring with just the turn of a knob, allowing a new stecker to appear several times a day. Worse for Allied codebreakers, the new mechanism could make the steckers nonreciprocal, so that A steckered to B would not necessarily mean that B was steckered to A. Eliminating reciprocal steckers would neutralize the effectiveness of the Diagonal Board and reduce the power of both the British and American Bombes by more than half.

But the Germans again made the mistake of introducing the Uhr box in a piecemeal, unplanned fashion—using the attachment on only a few of their networks and transmitting the same messages in many other networks, thus giving the Allies a plentiful supply of cribs for attacking it.

Other Enigma changes, however, proved unconquerable, and only the German reluctance to make a wholesale switch to the new code systems saved Ultra from disaster in the final months of the war. One such challenge, a system known as Sonder, was first noticed by the British in November 1944. It was a limited new submarine network that apparently changed the selection of Enigma wheels and steckers more frequently. The small number of messages on the system compounded the decryption problem.

A February 15, 1945, memo circulated among Navy codebreakers expressed their continuing frustration with the new code. Although the Sonder keys were thought to be of high importance, OP20G had succeeded in breaking only two Sonder messages since its introduction more than three months before, and only because both intercepts had included portions of a message already broken in the Offizier key, the doubly encrypted cipher used exclusively by German naval officers. The memo stated:

> In spite of considerable effort, no other messages have been found to break on these keys or any component part of the keys. From the keys recovered and from the unsuccessful effort applied, it seems probable that each U-boat is equipped with a set of keys having the following properties: a) they are unrelated to daily keys; b) they are unrelated to keys for any other

U-boat; c) they involve a change of wheels or steckers, or both, at least every 10 days. . . . Under the most favorable conditions, the breaking of each Sonder message is equivalent in difficulty to breaking a new month [of keys in another system], and the situation is further complicated by an almost complete absence of cribs.

A few Sonder keys were broken before the end of the war, but only with heroic effort. A March 1945 attack alone took 5,300 Bombe hours. Again, German procedures saved the Allies. Sonder traffic carried important messages, but fortunately it remained a small percentage of all U-boat transmissions. The logistics of introducing the new system to its entire U-boat fleet must have seemed too daunting to the Germans.

OP20G and GCCS also found that a potentially devastating fast-flash radio-transmission system called "Kurier" was not being exploited by the Germans. If they had used it more often and more wisely, its short transmission bursts—usually lasting less than half a second to send a complete message—could have thwarted Allied radio interceptors and even direction-finding equipment.

WHILE ALLIED CODEBREAKERS wrestled with Sonder, the U-boat threat again surfaced in the Atlantic in the late fall of 1944. Sinkings of U-boats dropped from more than 70 percent of operating vessels in August 1944 to 31 percent in September and to less than 25 percent in November: the Germans were again building more boats than they were losing.

After the disruption in operations caused by the D Day invasion, the U-boats were again on the prowl, many of them equipped with the new *Schnorchel* apparatus that allowed them to stay submerged longer. In the winter of 1944–1945, an average of nearly forty U-boats per day menaced the ocean lanes, and the loss of Allied merchant vessels began to rise. December brought a 75 percent increase in tonnage lost, followed by another 20 percent increase in January. The losses remained at more than sixty thousand tons a month until the end of the war. The Kriegsmarine was sinking more merchant ships in the Atlantic and Arctic per month—an average of thirteen each month in 1945 from January through April—than in any month since July 1943. Even so, the shipping losses were far short of the disastrous toll in March 1943.

The Allies were concerned about the Atlantic turnaround, but there are no documents to indicate the kind of panic the British and Americans had felt in 1942–1943. At any rate, the Allies regained the upper hand in March 1945, when U.S. bombers began concentrated attacks against the U-boat pens in Germany and the Baltic. The Kriegsmarine paid dearly for its renewed attacks on Allied shipping. By April 1945, the Germans were sacrificing a U-boat for every four merchant ships sunk—a doubling of their loss ratio from the year before.

But for Joe Desch and his team at NCR, the Atlantic had ceased to be the primary battlefront. They had turned their attention to the even more punishing developments in the Pacific.

November 1944—Dayton, Ohio

SITTING ALONE IN the communications sanctum of Building 26, Joe Desch knew as he hung up the secure phone line to Washington that the information he had just given his superiors at OP20G would mean the deaths of thousands of men. What Desch had told Washington was the solution to a technical problem involving one of the Japanese codebreaking machines, a task that had consumed him non-stop for the past twenty-four hours. For his pains, Desch had been told the purpose and the urgency of his work: it was needed to locate a Japanese convoy laden with troops. Although there are no records to confirm it, the advice OP20G sought may have been related to the decryption of a November 14 intercept in the Philippines, a request for an air escort for two convoys transporting the Japanese 23rd Infantry Division from Manchuria to Luzon. The decrypt gave the precise course and location of the two convoys. Now, U.S. Navy submarines, seeking revenge for the savage kamikaze attacks in the Battle of Leyte Gulf just weeks before, were lying in ambush, ready to send the Japanese troopships and their escorts to the bottom of the Philippine Sea.

Surprise and vengeance in the Pacific had been the name of the game since Pearl Harbor. It seemed to Desch the madness and cruelty—and the constant pressure from the Navy—would never end, "that damned, dirty business of the war," he told his daughter years later.

He snapped. After nearly two years of fourteen-hour days and impossible production deadlines, he walked quietly out of the communications room and out of Building 26, determined never to return. His defiance was the culmination of years of stress, both at home and at work. As he told his daughter not long before his death: "They pushed me and pushed me and pushed me, and told me I had to get all this stuff done because our guys were dying."

But in November 1944, the war was far from over and there was still more work to be done—work that came looking for Desch, no matter how hard he tried to escape.

Tailed by his security shadows, Desch went home that evening and collapsed into bed. Early the next morning, he called up his lifelong friend Mike Moran and asked him a favor. Then he loaded a sledgehammer, spikes, and an ax in the trunk of his car and drove twenty miles east of Dayton to Moran's family farm, not far from Xenia. In the surrounding thickets, he set himself to a simple, thought-numbing series of tasks: clearing out dead trees and splitting wood. When the trunk of his car was filled, he drove home again to the cottage on Greenmount Avenue and burned his day's labor that evening in the fireplace, sitting and talking for hours with Dorothy. It was an intimate scene that even his houseguest and dedicated watchdog, Commander Ralph Meader, dared not intrude upon.

Nearly every day for the next six weeks, Desch went out to the Moran farm and repeated this ritual of oblation—until one day Joe Wenger, the head of OP20G, came from Washington and approached him there. Wenger, who had had his own breakdown, must have understood what Desch was feeling.

Desch and Wenger weren't the only OP20G managers who became victims of their top-secret duties. Howard Engstrom, head of

OP20G's research division, also suffered under the weight of the U.S. Bombe project and from the intense guilt he felt over his role in the aerial assassination of Japanese admiral Isoroku Yamamoto, the naval genius behind the surprise attack on Pearl Harbor. On April 14, 1943, a Japanese message was intercepted and broken revealing that Yamamoto, flying under escort of six Japanese fighter planes, was due to arrive on April 18 for an inspection tour on Ballale, a small island in the Solomons. Sixteen P-38 fighters were dispatched from Henderson Field on Guadalcanal, hastily fitted with long-range fuel tanks for the thousand-mile round-trip journey. Over open ocean and in daylight, with no stars to help them navigate, the pilots relied on dead reckoning and miraculous luck in spotting Yamamoto's airborne entourage. They shot down three Zeros and both Japanese bombers, including the one in which Yamamoto had been flying.

During a self-interview in 1992, Engstrom's daughter, Kristina, broke down several times while recounting her father's wartime experience:

> You know, there were people who were victims of the war that weren't just shot. There were people like [my father]. . . . His secretary [after the war] said, the last time I talked to her, that Daddy used to talk about Admiral Yamamoto and how terrible he felt about his death and that he felt somehow responsible for it because he had been involved in breaking the Japanese code and that's how they knew where Yamamoto was.

Historians appear not to have studied the high frequency of breakdown among codebreakers, and national security officials decline to discuss the issue. But Robert Hogan, a pioneer in personality psychology and a hiring consultant based in Tulsa, Oklahoma, said the long hours of challenging mental work, the emotional strain of war production, and the isolation from families and friends demanded by high-security jobs would have pushed even the most stable personalities to the brink. Added to these external pressures, he said, engineers and research scientists often have a collection of personality traits that make them even more susceptible to stress.

Members of both professions typically score very high on standard personality tests for "prudence conscientiousness," Hogan said. As a result,

> they experience a lot more stress than they should because they're so concerned with meeting deadlines and doing a good job. They really need to learn how to relax, lighten up, back off, but often they can't. This was what Freud was all about: the essence of psychoanalysis was reducing the negative effects of the superego. The superego was all about very strong rules, about getting things done. If you put a person in a high-stress job who also is extremely conscientious, that's just a recipe for a nervous breakdown.

Even before the start of the war, Laurance Safford, then head of OP20G, noted with concern how the strain of codebreaking work was affecting his small staff. In a September 5, 1940, letter of recommendation for a former staffer, Safford said of the man that

> his industry and attention to duty were carried to the extreme that he suffered a nervous breakdown. This may be understood better when I state that my force experienced two other breakdowns and one suicide during the past two years, due to the strain of overwork. [His] physical condition is immeasurably better than when he left the Navy Department and he should be able to handle routine office work without difficulty.

Nor were the university researchers and corporate engineers recruited by the Navy during the war always suited for its military style of management, said Hogan, who served on a destroyer during the Gulf of Tonkin crisis in Vietnam.

> I'm a retired naval officer, and I promise you I know the kind of pressures the Navy can bring to bear. These people are really quite ruthless. It's not about patriotism and a professional military, it's about advancing your career. If you can get the prob-

lem solved, your career looks good. They'll use anything to motivate you. They'll threaten you with prison. They'll threaten
you with execution. They'll use guilt, shame. . . . I promise you
it's part of the [military] culture. They just don't care about
people. People are expendable.

But Wenger cared enough about Desch and the course of the war
effort—and, yes, perhaps his own career—that he traveled to Dayton
in December 1944 to talk with him man to man. Wenger told Desch
that his country desperately needed him: only Desch had the expertise to tackle an engineering problem that had arisen in cracking the
Japanese codes. He had to come back. Desch finally said yes, but on
the condition that his hours be limited and his workload confined to
the Japanese problem. And he insisted that Meader no longer live in
his home. But on that point, the Navy brass wouldn't budge.

While Desch had been gone, his assistant, Bob Mumma, was put
in charge of the German problems and NCR's managerial responsibilities for Building 26. His task was eased by having on his staff talented
Navy engineers such as Ralph Palmer—IBM's leading electronics engineer prior to the war—and by the Germans' continuing inability to
implement widespread code changes.

Even so, the unceasing battle of wits continued to the last days
of the war. In April 1945, the last full month of hostilities with Germany, the Kriegsmarine began using a variable starting position on its
Enigma machines that made codebreaking far more difficult and
time-consuming. The first few days of the new Atlantic keys were
tough to break, but they were broken in time to read the German order
setting up the final wolf pack of the war. Allied forces sank at least
three of the pack's six U-boats.

An American intercept of one of the war's last U-boat messages
also helped calm fears about Japan gaining the Nazis' most advanced
weaponry. Although Germany was near to surrendering, some of its
leaders had planned as a final act of vengeance to provide Japan with
the details of its devastating V-2 rockets and jet-powered fighters, far
faster than anything the Allies could put in the air. On April 15, a
month before the surrender, *U-234* was dispatched from Germany to

Japan. On board were a high-ranking German general, nine other German naval and Air Force officers, two civil engineers, two Japanese, and a "valuable cargo of plans," according to a message report from U.S. naval command to Britain's Admiralty. While the U-boat was en route to the Far East, the Germans officially surrendered and ordered their submarine skippers to give up the fight. *U-234* commander Johann Heinrich Fehler decided to obey the order, but the two Japanese passengers felt they had no other choice: they committed suicide rather than surrender to the Americans. The scientific papers never reached Japan.

After the war, when teams of Allied investigators seized documents and interrogated German codemen, it was discovered that the Nazis, if they had shown better foresight and less confidence in their cipher systems, could have rendered the Bombes useless. They had designs and prototypes for machines such as the "39" version of the Enigma that would have been as secure as America's ECM encrypting machine, which used fifteen rotors as well as irregular rotor movements to baffle its enemies.

The German mistakes allowed Building 26 to concentrate on the pressing Japanese problems.

January 1945—Dayton, Ohio

WHEN DESCH RETURNED to work at NCR, it was clear that Japan would eventually be defeated. The questions were When? and At what cost? The invasion of the Philippines was turning out to be more difficult than expected, and casualty rates soared as war-weary U.S. Marines were forced to root the Japanese from caves and tunnels on island strongholds. All intelligence pointed to Japan's military leaders committing that nation to a suicidal last stand, with hundreds of thousands of Allied casualties the price of invading Japan itself.

OP20G and its centers in the Pacific faced a formidable foe, with an uncanny habit of changing its code systems just before a major strategic move by either side. A significant intelligence blackout hampered the Allies' Marianas campaign in mid-1944 because of such a well-timed Japanese change. OP20G feared a repeat of that experience. It realized as well that, as U.S. forces pressed closer to Japan, its processing capabilities might be overwhelmed by too many intercepts.

Wenger and Engstrom felt a duty to provide advanced technologies for attacking the Japanese codes, especially JN-25, which was the key to Japan's fleet operations, and the daunting weather code, JN-37, which could provide vital information for the U.S. Navy and Army Air Forces groups operating in the region. Britain and the United States had developed efficient methods for attacking JN-25 and at least the fundamentals of an attack on JN-37, but these were tedious and time-consuming. What was needed now was machinery faster and much more powerful than even the special NC tabulators.

The first to get attention was the additive problem of the Japanese codes. In November, OP20G launched its program to build the Selector, an advanced codebusting machine that used electronics and a massive memory. The Selector added numbers to the code groups in a message—the reverse of the subtraction process performed by the Japanese code clerks. Then the Selector instantly searched a huge memory bank holding already known code groups for matches.

Desch and his team again had to admit that a fully electronic device was too costly and unreliable, and they soon turned to a combination of huge banks of telephone relays, IBM card readers, and electronics. The group, led by IBM electronics expert Ralph Palmer, worked quickly and well. By February 1945, the concept began to turn into hardware. In May, the first testing was performed, and a month later the Selector—big enough to fill a grade-school classroom—was making its first contributions. By the end of the war, the device had proved valuable though slow, and a new contract was awarded to NCR to try to build an expanded and more electronic model.

Desch may also have played a role in creating plans for a faster device to break the JN-37 weather code. Despite the use of a high-speed film machine called Hypo, cracking the system took too much time for its information to be of any operational use. OP20G decided in June 1945 to follow a plan suggested by John Howard and build a set of high-speed, film-optic scanning machines, each with the capacity to compare three to five billion code lineups in a single day. Before the million-dollar contract was let to Eastman Kodak, however, the newly conquered Japanese islands, where the Allies were now entrenched, began providing enough weather information in the Pacific that the machine was deferred. The code was no longer worth breaking.

August 14, 1945—Dayton, Ohio

EVELYN VOGEL WILL never forget that evening, how it started raining soon after the news of victory over Japan reached the WAVES at Sugar Camp and how it wouldn't stop raining—and yet the summer torrent was no match for the joy of the occasion. Thousands of revelers headed downtown to drink, dance, and run barefoot through the puddles in the streets. "Commander Meader said we [WAVES] were all free to leave camp and join the celebration, but to remember our manners," Vogel said. "Anyway, we all went downtown, and I had never seen such a scene. Rain all over, but people were shouting and laughing, and, of course, open bottles were being passed around."

Vogel ran into some other WAVES who had made their way downtown, and they decided to head back to the closest thing they knew to their family home: the Desches' cottage on Greenmount Avenue.

It's hard to know how much Joe Desch savored the victory that night and whether he had properly gauged the significance of his own contribution to ending the war. Certainly, he must have been relieved that the violence was at last over. Desch did not discover until years later that he had been part of one of the most brutal and decisive acts of the war. The atom bombs that destroyed Hiroshima and Nagasaki late that summer were developed with the help of a high-speed electronic counter he had designed earlier in the war.

Soon after the war, Desch learned that nearly every member of the Army ordnance unit in which he had been commissioned, the 512th, had been either killed or wounded in action. In his darkest moments, Anderson said, her father used to say, "I would much rather have been with them." Desch had known many of the men in the unit from his twelve years in the Army Reserve Corps. But in October

1940, he had been forced to resign his commission in order to devote himself to his work for the National Defense Research Committee, a duty to which he had been recruited by Vannevar Bush. Desch's letter of resignation to the corps showed his deep ambivalence about leaving the Army for civilian service. In the letter, he spoke of his pride at having served as an officer for twelve years. But despite Desch's feelings of personal loss, he was convinced that the resignation would allow him to perform a more valuable service to his country as a researcher.

At his cottage that rain-soaked summer night in 1945, Desch had stayed in the background while the WAVES and their young friends celebrated the final victory of the war. Vogel said she didn't give much thought that evening to what might have been weighing on Desch's mind. All that mattered to her and to most of the WAVES was that the fighting had finally ended and that they would soon be going home to their loved ones. "We danced on the front lawn in the rain until midnight," she said. "And, yes, we did forget our manners."

After the war, Meader commanded fewer than one hundred WAVES and Navy engineers to carry on what they knew was top secret and vital work at Building 26, all of which is still classified. Finally closing shop and moving to Washington, D.C., in 1946, Meader left his beat-up Nash Rambler in Desch's driveway. Desch had to send several terse letters to naval authorities before they disposed of it.

But the postwar fate of America's frontline anti-Enigma machines—the 120 Bombes built at NCR—is less clear.

Epilogue:
Burying the Past

BY V-J DAY, most of the Bombes in Washington were already being retired and prepared for a secret burial at sea. Whether any Bombes were left at NCR and what happened to them remains a deeper mystery. Most were smashed with sledgehammers and axes. The remaining Bombe parts and the machine tools for making them were removed from Building 26 under cover of night and buried deep below a parking lot, perhaps across West Stewart Street, the busy four-lane road just north of Building 26.

Officials in the National Security Agency, the organizational heir to OP20G and the Army's codebreaking operations, say all but one of the working machines that reached Washington were destroyed. But Phil Bochicchio, the Navy technician who had been in charge of setting up and maintaining the machines in Washington, said he was ordered to ship thirty Bombes to a Navy warehouse in Mechanicsburg, Pennsylvania, soon after the war.

We know that many secret German transmissions were decrypted after the fighting ceased, as shown by dates on messages. That suggests that some machines were held in reserve. The British have let it slip that they kept sixteen of the Bombes they built during the war.

Both Allies had good reason to retain at least some of the Bombes: many European nations, including the Soviet Union and eastern-bloc states, confiscated thousands of Enigma machines from the Nazis after the war and likely put them to use. That raises the question of whether the Soviets had been privy to the Ultra secret during World War II. At least one of the WAVES, Mary Lorraine Johnson, who later became a Utah state legislator, recalled Russian generals being shown the Bombes during a tour of OP20G toward the end of the war. If so, the Soviets may have used America's expertise to spy on its eastern-bloc satellites. However, no Navy officials or government documents have yet corroborated Johnson's story.

NSA officials insist they know of no other existing Bombes except the one now on display behind a glass case at the agency's National Cryptologic Museum at Fort Meade. The machines sent to Mechanicsburg "were probably just excessed and destroyed," said Jack Ingram, curator of the museum. "We don't have any records on it."

Parts of the NCR machines may still be classified. If true, NSA officials won't say why, but it could be that some of the same methods were used against the Soviets or their allies during the cold war. Likewise, NCR's defense role after the war remains unclear. "The Cash" had had its fill of unprofitable military work during the war and, in its aftermath, was faced with hundreds of thousands of back orders from a global clientele impatient to return to peacetime commerce. Even before the end of the war, Wenger and Engstrom had known that NCR and other industrial firms were eager to drop their government work as they geared up to meet the nation's long-suppressed consumer demands. As early as September 1944, NCR management had told the Navy in very direct terms that it wanted no more open-ended demands, no more hard-to-manage military personnel, and no more essentially profitless contracts. Negotiations and calls on patriotism smoothed over the situation, and before the war's end NCR did accept two more large contracts with the Navy. But discontent at NCR remained and, just days after Japan's surrender, executives told the Navy to get its men and women out of NCR's factory.

Even so, NCR continued to be a contractor for the government after the war, although on a much-reduced scale, while Desch retained a seat on the scientific advisory board of the NSA until at least 1961, when his correspondence with the agency came to an end. No

documents have ever been released that confirm NCR's cold-war involvement. Patrick Wheadon, an NSA public-affairs officer, said, "We
can't comment. The closer you get to present day, the less we can discuss."

Rumors abound as to the whereabouts of Adam and Eve and Cain
and Abel, the first four prototype machines, which were never sent to
Washington. Several engineers who worked on the project say the
prototypes were dumped from a railroad overpass into an old canal
bed not far from Building 26, where they remain buried on land now
occupied by the Montgomery County Fairgrounds. Others involved in
the project say the machines lie underneath a parking lot at Building
26, which has undergone numerous expansions and renovations
since the war. Desch himself hinted to his daughter that his war work
was buried deep in the water table below the pavement of Stewart
Street.

There are no known records to support any of these claims.

WHEN THE WAR had at last ended, Joe Desch was ready to bury it,
too, in his past. He had made firm decisions about his future, and it
didn't involve the U.S. Navy. He told Howard Engstrom and Joseph
Wenger that he would not join the new company they wanted to establish to fill the gap left by NCR's withdrawal from top secret codebreaking work—even though the idea had been hatched over
cocktails in Desch's living room in late 1944. He likewise declined an
offer to move to Washington to become the director of research at
OP20G.

In the years after the war, Wenger and the new breed of OP20G
engineers and codebreakers continued to guide Navy communications intelligence and the U.S. military toward a totally electronic era
in cryptanalysis. As early as 1943, they were planning for the day
when they could move beyond the crisis design and engineering that
had dominated and constrained their work to the very last days of the
war. And they vowed to take steps so that America's military would
never again be caught by surprise, as they were so tragically in the
early-morning hours of December 7, 1941. Nor, Wenger vowed,

would OP20G ever find itself desperately behind the technological curve, as it had in its battle against the Enigma. He knew all too well that much had been left unrealized during the war, including the dream, perhaps still unrealized, of codebreaking that relied neither on cribs nor enemy error.

In contrast to Desch, Wenger faced many uncertainties in the summer of 1945. He wanted OP20G to have a permanent research group such as the M section Howard Engstrom had built during the war, and he wanted OP20G to have the engineers and industrial resources that Ralph Meader had commanded in Building 26. He knew that most of his highly valued researchers wanted to return to their universities and corporations and that those who might stay with him would probably be rejected for Navy service because of their age, education, and high-paying rank.

Wenger had nowhere to turn for help. NCR's withdrawal from defense work left OP20G without an industrial partner willing and able to do secret work. No other major corporation or even any other Navy agency, such as the Naval Research Laboratory, seemed willing to concentrate on OP20G's mission. And Wenger feared that his request for higher-paid civilian experts within OP20G would not be approved. In fact, he could not be sure that OP20G itself would exist much longer. The Army, in alliance with the White House, was pushing hard for a unification of all the intelligence services, and "G" might well disappear into a new intelligence group where the Navy played a subordinate role.

If nothing else, Wenger wanted Navy codebreakers to get a share of the diplomatic codebreaking after the war—a role that had traditionally been left to the Army's cryptanalytic staff. Despite the success of its Bombes, OP20G was still chafing under its dependence on the British for analyzing a variety of European radio traffic and was looking ahead to the days when it could focus on Russian codes. The Navy already was intercepting Soviet traffic at the time and had, by 1945, an agreement with Britain to share Soviet intelligence and processing capabilities. It was none too soon: by 1948, America and Britain would discover that the Soviets were far more adept at code warfare than the Germans.

Despite frictions over Britain's colonialist policies in other parts of the world, it was agreed that the Ultra partnership should continue after the end of the war. Liaison groups were established, and sharing of intercepts, methods, and technologies deepened as the transatlantic alliance became permanent. Although postwar Britain was financially bankrupt, it provided America valuable expertise, experience, and facilities.

Finding corporate partners for the Navy's postwar codebreaking ventures would prove far more difficult. By February 1945, the idea of creating a new independent company for OP20G's work had turned into something like a business plan. Knowing that the Navy would be unlikely to keep even the core of the mathematical and engineering groups he had put together during the war, Engstrom envisioned a new company that would hire his researchers and allow them to devote their talents to advanced scientific and secret projects.

The plan was circulated through the Navy hierarchy, and soon it was passed on to some of the nation's most influential bankers and industrialists in hopes that funds would be found for the new company, tentatively titled the National Electronics Laboratory. Engstrom and Meader wrote to banks and investment houses and even approached the nonprofit Rockefeller Foundation. Every response came back no.

But soon after the war, the intertwinings of what would someday be called the military-industrial complex came into play. Through a mutual acquaintance, Ralph Meader was introduced to Nelson Talbott, who was part of Dayton's old aviation elite going back to the Wright brothers and Colonel Deeds. As president of Trans World Airlines and brother to a future secretary of the Air Force, Talbott was a well-connected businessman who had done much planning and contracting for the Army Air Forces during the war and perhaps even lent the family estate for top secret Air Force research. Talbott, in turn, introduced the Meader-Engstrom group to an investor who seemed ideal, John Parker.

Parker was not only a reputable investment banker but a graduate of the U.S. Naval Academy with an interest in computing devices and experience in how to deal with government agencies. During the war, he had built a glider factory and was looking for a way to put his now-idle facilities to use. By the end of 1945 it seemed that the renamed Engineering Research Associates (ERA) might have a future.

In the meantime, Joe Wenger had received some good news. OP20G's postwar budget, though short of his request, was better than he had expected, with authorization to create slots for civilian researchers. With that, Wenger was able to persuade some of the younger men in Engstrom's research and engineering group to remain at OP20G. Among them were men who became the nucleus of the nation's postwar codebreaking efforts: Joe Eachus, Howard Campaigne, Louis Tordella, and James Pendergrass.

Wenger also received a go-ahead for his postwar computer research plans. While the funding was not as great as during the war, it was appreciable. The 1947 budget included $800,000 to acquire new codebreaking equipment and another $1.2 million for machine development, $500,000 of which had been left over from the previous year. Still, all together, those funds could have paid for only one third of the Bombes built at NCR during the war.

DESCH TURNED DOWN nonmilitary opportunities after the war as well, including an offer from Xerox to be its chief engineer. "I was worn out," he said years later in explaining his decision to Carl Rench, his young protégé and confidant who eventually became NCR's vice president for research. Instead, Desch chose to hitch his fate to NCR and his hometown of Dayton.

In his research after the war, Desch returned to the passion that had originally brought him to NCR in 1938: gas-filled tubes. Even though transistors and solid-state technology were to replace the unpredictable and energy-hungry tubes as the basis of modern computing, those developments were still a decade away. In the meantime, Desch reported each day to his own private laboratory in Building 20, climbing a steep, back stairway into a secluded loft. There, under a dense tangle of glass piping and beakers that towered above his workbench almost to the ceiling, Desch was allowed to experiment for the next twenty-five years with what eventually became an outdated technology. His private lab was closed and the room sealed off by bricks in 1973.

Despite his obsession with electronic tubes, Desch did not become a technological throwback. He kept abreast of the more promising developments that were leading to the modern computer and continued to fret over NCR's hesitant entry into that business. By the 1950s, Desch had regained enough of his earlier drive to head the company's advanced research effort into small computer systems, though it was a low priority for the company at the time. By then, his style of management had softened, Rench said. "He perhaps felt that he had had to drive his people too hard during the war and, therefore, he was trying to be more rational in his later life."

Desch soon became head of NCR's military project and research division. Though NCR named him a vice president, much of his advice in the 1950s about the future of computers fell on deaf executive ears. Then–NCR chief Stanley Allyn refused Desch's request to launch a subsidiary of the company devoted to electronic machines and computers. It was a refusal NCR was to regret for years to come.

NCR missed its chance to get a jump on the digital age. By pulling back from its commitment to cutting-edge electronic research and ignoring the rise of data processing and programmable computing, it continued an errant course that some say began as far back as 1914 when one of its forward-thinking young executives, Thomas Watson, left the company after a personal dispute with John H. Patterson. With a then-generous severance pay of fifty thousand dollars from NCR and the moral support of an attractive socialite wife whose introduction he owed to Patterson, Watson started International Business Machines. IBM, already a leader in electromechanics, rose to world dominance in the electronic computer field during the 1960s and 1970s and plagued NCR as one of its chief competitors into the next millennium.

NCR went back to business as usual after the war, still clinging to its heavy-handed centralized organization and its mechanical line of products, even into the early 1970s. Labor strife, high costs, outmoded technology, and a sales force entrenched in pitching the old line of business machines eventually led the company to financial disaster. After posting nearly seventy million dollars in losses in 1972, NCR called home William S. Anderson of its Japan division. As the new president, Anderson began the painful and necessary process of decentralizing and downsizing the company. In the space of two years, NCR's workforce in Dayton declined from 22,000 employees to a mere 5,500, with the bulk of its manufacturing moved overseas and to antiunion states. NCR and Dayton would never be the same.

LIKE DESCH, MANY of the engineers who had been recruited from the major corporations to work on military codebreaking projects during the war became part of a "crypto-reserve" for America's top secret agencies, especially in the ensuing cold-war struggle with the Soviet Union. Joe Eachus, John Howard, Howard Engstrom, and William Norris, a Navy pioneer in radio-direction finding, became prominent figures in the computing industry. Andrew Gleason and other academic mathematicians who became major names in their fields continued to advise OP20G and, later, the NSA. Engstrom even returned to the NSA for a few years in the 1950s to head its research and development program.

Wenger had valued Desch's work during the war and continued to seek his advice throughout the 1950s and 1960s. Wenger had pushed for recognition of Desch's contribution to the war, leading to an honor with an ironic twist. In a secret ceremony at the Navy Department in 1947, Desch was awarded the National Medal of Merit—the highest civilian honor for wartime service—for his work in developing the Bombe. But Desch could tell no one of the nation's gratitude, not even his daughter, Debbie, who for much of her life puzzled over the significance of her father's award and why he had earned it. He seems never to have complained, either, that he had to pay his own way to Washington for the ceremony. The medal hung in the study of his home, without an explanation, until his death in 1987, when it was packed up along with the many other mysterious artifacts of his life and moved into the family basement.

Two years later, Debbie Anderson went searching through her father's things to help her ten-year-old son with an English assignment that he wanted to write about his grandfather. She happened upon two thick transcripts she had retrieved from the piles of papers on her father's desk after his death but had never bothered to read. They were Desch's interviews with Henry Tropp, an historian from the Smithsonian Institution, dated January 17 and 18, 1973.

She began skimming the three-hundred-plus pages of questions and answers, finding mostly technical details about Desch's role in the development of the modern computer. Tropp had been looking for material to add to the Smithsonian's History of Computers project. But beginning on page 111 of the first day's interview and continuing on to page 119, the text had been slashed through forcefully with a fine-point, felt-tipped pen. In the margin was written: "Delete from tape and manuscript." But the felt pen had been no match for the thickness of the bold pica type.

The redacted words spoke of "an electronic cryptanalytic machine," of classified code names, of British scientists, and of top secret equipment dumped and buried in the middle of the night. Anderson devoured the words. Here at last was a glimmer of her father's top secret duties during World War II, the pivotal years in his life he had never shared except in the broadest terms.

As a teenager and young adult, Anderson had felt little curiosity about her father's wartime service. She knew her father had gone on to head the military-research division at NCR during the 1960s, and that's all she cared to know. "I was a true child of the sixties. I was embarrassed that my father was part of the military-industrial complex," she said.

Desch had burned the most crucial NCR war documents but for some reason had left the transcripts atop his heavy Tudor-style desk, "where even his dumb daughter could find them," Anderson said. Now here they were, in Anderson's hands, like a thin ray of light pointing the way to treasure deep inside a cave. For the next decade, Anderson tried to illuminate her father's mystery, often finding herself at odds with national intelligence officials and skeptical historians. But in doing so, she discovered the historic role that her father—as well as NCR—had played in shortening the world's most devastating conflict.

May 4, 1958—Kettering, Ohio

IN THE COLOR home movie, Debbie Desch, then a second-grader at St. Albert the Great, is decked out in her First Communion dress and seated between her mother and father on the living-room sofa. Her father, a proud smile on his face, leafs through her Communion prayer book. A year before, Desch moved his family into the spacious Dutch colonial home in west Kettering, where the First Communion celebration is now taking place.

The same movie shows Desch, his mother, and his two sisters as they gather around the dining-room table. The estrangement of the war years, when Desch had been ordered to limit his family visits for security reasons, was long forgotten. "I remember it was always really hard for Dad's family to relax with us—except for that day," Anderson said. "Everything went right, and everybody was in a good mood."

Anderson learned years later, when she was a parent herself, that it was also the day that her father had received the Blessed Sacrament for the first time since 1943, when, in the midst of his guilt and frustration over not being able to perfect the Bombe, he had quit going to church. Desch had reconciled with his faith just days before Debbie's First Communion, after he had given his confession to Father George Steinkamp, an outspoken priest with a sharp sense of humor who had been his religious mentor at Emmanuel Elementary School. Steinkamp, then in his seventies and in poor health, was the only priest to whom Desch felt close enough to unburden his soul. Desch had phoned Steinkamp personally and asked if he could make special arrangements to have his Confession heard. Steinkamp was so frail he couldn't walk from the rectory to the church, so Desch gathered him in his arms, carried him into the church, and set him in the confessional. "Remember, this was the 1950s," Anderson said. "You had to use a confessional."

Carl Rench said that, by the late 1950s, Desch had found a measure of peace within himself, as well as a deep religious conviction. Often in those days, he and Desch debated each other's interpretations of scripture. "He was a Catholic, and I was a Protestant, and we had a lot of fun doing that," Rench said. "We went through everything Mark, Luke, and John ever wrote. We even compared some of the stories."

Rench said there was no question that Desch was a different man in 1958 from what he was in 1946, when Rench first began to work for him at NCR. "We were both trying to behave the way Jesus would want us to behave," he said. "Joe was very satisfied with his feelings about the church and the Bible. And I got the sense that he was very proud of what he had been able to accomplish, finally, during the war."

Yet none of the men and women who had worked so hard on the NCR Bombe ever sought credit or recognition for their contribution, including the four NCR engineers most intimately involved in its design and production: Joe Desch, Bob Mumma, Lou Sandor, and Vince Gulden. All four received, in secret, certificates of commendation from the Bureau of Ships for their service.

"We worked hard, and we worked long hours, but I wasn't out anywhere where I was being shot at," Sandor said. "Those were the guys really out there doing the tough job."

Age and family responsibilities gave Desch a new perspective on life as well as new burdens, and by the 1960s, Anderson said, her father's heart was no longer in his work. His next quest harked back to his interest in gardening, a hobby that had helped him relax and escape during the war: hunting for mushrooms. Desch was determined to be the first person in the world to cultivate morel mushrooms, a tasty species found in wooded areas. He brought home equipment from his lab at NCR in order to collect and cultivate morel spores. At one point, he inoculated his entire front yard with the tiny spores, but he never succeeded in growing them. He lost interest even in this venture in 1971, when his wife of thirty-six years, Dorothy, died of throat cancer when Desch was sixty-four. "He went into a long depression after that," Anderson said. "He was never the same."

With Debbie away at Ohio State, Desch lived quietly by himself in the family's home in Kettering for the next fourteen years. He was forced to leave the house in 1985 after suffering a series of small strokes and breaking his hip. But in June 1987, following six months in assisted living and nine more months in a nursing home undergoing intensive therapy, he made a remarkable recovery; he insisted on going home.

Anderson recalled the way her father, glancing back at the nursing home on his way to the car, "stuck out his jaw and said, 'Not many people walk out of that place.' He was very proud he'd been able to do that. He really wanted to die at home." He lived his final months there, active and content. Friends and family dropped in frequently, and he spent many hours talking on his ham radio under the call sign of W8ANP and carefully recording his contacts around the world.

On August 3, 1987, when Anderson made her daily phone call to check on her father and got no answer, she knew something was wrong. She and her husband drove the few miles from their Dayton home to her father's. His morning paper was still in the driveway. They found him on the floor beside his bed, partly paralyzed and speechless from a stroke. Anderson and her husband spent the day with her father at Kettering Medical Center, where he died that evening in intensive care. "That's exactly how he wanted to go," she said. "He wanted to be in his own home, and he wanted to go quickly."

But Anderson couldn't help feeling cheated by her father's death. "I know this is selfish and petty, but I can remember thinking once or twice that day, 'Whatever happened during the war, he knows, he still knows, and we're not going to get a thing,'" she said. "I thought, 'Damn it, it's going to be lost.' He never told anybody. He never wrote it down." Just before he died, "I could sense he was trying to speak," Anderson said. But when his time came, he quieted and seemed at peace. "He didn't fight it," she said.

She still doesn't know what kind of peace her father had found. His death, like so much of his life, was cloaked in mystery.

"I don't think at the end he figured it all out. Who does?" she said. "But he had accepted it just the same."

May 10, 1989—Kettering, Ohio

DEBBIE ANDERSON WAS having a late breakfast with her husband, Darrell, chairman of the theater department at the University of Dayton, when a story in the lifestyle section of the *Dayton Daily News* caught her eye. It was about an exhibit at the Smithsonian Institution on the development of the modern computer, called "The Information Age." Part of the exhibit was a decrypting machine built by NCR during the war, on loan from the NSA. NCR archivist Bill West credited Anderson's father, Joe Desch, and Bob Mumma with building the machine. It was the first time Anderson had ever seen anyone publicly give credit to her father for the NCR Bombe.

Anderson decided to travel to Washington, D.C., with her family, including her two sons, ages fourteen and eleven, to see the machine. Her next move was to contact the Smithsonian curator quoted in the newspaper to see if she could find out more. The curator, in turn, told her to phone an historian at the NSA. "I think he was stunned when I called," Anderson said. "I don't think anyone was supposed to give out their names and phone numbers there."

The historian agreed to meet with her, suggesting they do so informally at a coffee shop. But when Anderson told him that she possessed documents of her father's, possibly classified ones, that she hoped to have explained, "there was a pause and he said, 'Oh, you'd better come directly to us.' "

June 23, 1990—Fort Meade, Maryland

THE ANDERSONS' ASTRO van was routed to the rear of the bunkerlike NSA headquarters—a massive concrete structure at Fort Meade, Maryland, twenty miles north of Washington, D.C.—where they were greeted by armed guards and told to remain in their vehicle. Moments later, when the historian who had arranged to meet Anderson arrived at the guard shack, she emerged with her shopping bag filled with documents. But when her sons also started to exit the van, hoping to stretch their legs after the drive from their motel, they were told to stay inside. It was just Anderson the historian wanted to see.

"So Darrell drives off, and here I am surrounded by all these men," she said. "I thought, 'Oh my gosh, what have I gotten myself into?' "

The contents of her bag were emptied and inspected at the guard shack, and Anderson was put through a metal detector before she was permitted to enter the building. Anderson spent the next six hours inside the NSA headquarters, where she did nearly all the talking. "The day was spent looking through the stuff I brought," she said. "People would come and go, and not one time in six hours did they make a comment. They're good at that."

There was one reaction, however. "A younger guy came in, close to my age [forty] at the time, and I don't remember what he was looking at, but all he said was, 'Wow. Can you wait a minute while I show this to somebody?' He went away and came back, but he never said a word about why he was so excited."

When it was time to leave and Anderson started gathering up her father's things, the historian said to her, " 'You realize, of course, I can't let you take these out of the building.' " He said the documents had to be closely examined, to make sure all the material had been declassified. If so, her things would be returned to her by mail. Anderson protested but had no choice. She did, however, insist on an itemized, signed receipt. The material she left behind was returned, by third-class mail, three months later.

Anderson left Fort Meade that day disappointed, but her visit the next morning to the Smithsonian exhibit redeemed the trip. After years of trying to imagine what had consumed her father during the war, Anderson's first look at the NCR Bombe surprised her. "I was amazed at how huge it was," she said. "It was much bigger, much more imposing than what I had expected."

Her next reaction was frustration. The seven-foot-tall, eleven-foot-long, five-thousand-pound electromechanical decoder sat well behind a waist-high partition, with no mention of her father's name in any of the plaques or brochures. "Here I was at the end of a pilgrimage. I felt a connection to this thing, and I wanted to go up and touch it, but I couldn't," she said. "There was a stream of people waiting, and we just had to keep on moving."

The label describing the machine said it was manufactured at

NCR but said nothing about it being designed there or by whom. It was what Anderson had come to dub the "standard, one-line reference" to NCR's role in breaking the German Enigma code. The history books she had read and the few documents that she had thus far been able to obtain from the National Archives gave NCR credit for building the 120 Bombes and nothing more—as if the enormously complex machines had been stamped off an assembly line like so many widgets. "It was so frustrating," she said. "I knew there had to be more to the story, but no one was talking."

On their way back to Ohio, Anderson and her family stopped at the Pennsylvania home of Esther Hottenstein, a member of the WAVES who had operated NCR's secure telephone and telegraph lines to Washington during the war. Hottenstein had worked closely with Desch during her years in Dayton and was very fond of him. She had been present when Desch snapped and walked out of Building 26, vowing never to return. For many years after the war, she had kept in touch with Desch by mail and, after his death, with Anderson.

Anderson was looking forward to at last meeting Hottenstein, and although her visit sealed their friendship ("It was like we had always known each other") it proved useless in her quest to learn more about her father's work. All her questions that day were received with the same polite reticence she had received at the NSA, Anderson said. "It was always, 'Well, gee, I can't tell you about that.' "

September 18, 2002—Dayton, Ohio

ON A CRISP, windswept morning, Building 26 stands empty and quiet at the corner of W. Stewart Street and S. Patterson Boulevard, its future undecided. The first brittle leaves of autumn scuttle across its empty parking lot. The plaque honoring the once secret and vital defense work done inside the building stands separate from it, riveted to a boulder at the corner, signaling perhaps the day when the building will no longer exist. NCR says it has yet to decide what it will do with Building 26. Its fate is one more piece in the company's struggle to downsize, outsource, consolidate, and move ahead into the future—and, like Joe Desch, leave the past behind.

Bibliography

Archives, Libraries, and Other Sources of Primary Data

Charles Babbage Institute, Minneapolis, Minn.
Dartmouth College Library, Hanover, N.H.
Eastman Kodak Company Archive, Rochester, N.Y.
Federal Bureau of Investigation, Washington, D.C.
Hagley Museum and Library, Wilmington, Del.
International Business Machines Archive, White Plains, N.Y.
Library of Congress, Washington, D.C.
Massachusetts Institute of Technology, Cambridge, Mass.
National Cash Register Company Archives, Dayton, Ohio
National Cryptologic Museum, Fort Meade, Md.
National Oceanic and Atmospheric Administration Data Center, Washington, D.C.
National Security Agency, Center for Cryptologic History, Fort Meade, Md.
Naval Cryptologic Veterans Association, Naval Security Group (Wenger) Command Display, Pensacola, Fla.
Naval Historical Center, Biographies Branch, Washington, D.C.
Naval Historical Center, Operational Archives, Washington, D.C.
Naval Security Group Command, Washington, D.C.
Princeton University Alumni Center and Archives, Princeton, N.J.
Public Record Office, Kew, England
Rockefeller Archives, Pocantico Hills, N.Y.
Smithsonian Institution, Washington, D.C.
U.S. Army Record Center, St. Louis, Mo.
U.S. Bureau of Prisons, Washington, D.C.
U.S. Centennial of Flight Commission, Washington, D.C.
U.S. Central Intelligence Agency, Washington, D.C.

U.S. Department of Justice, Washington, D.C.

U.S. National Archives, College Park, Md., Suitland, Md., and Washington, D.C.

U.S. Navy Legal Branch, Washington, D.C.

U.S. Patent Office, Washington, D.C.

U.S. Selective Service Administration, Arlington, Va.

U.S. Social Security Administration, Baltimore, Md.

University of Wyoming, American Heritage Center, Laramie, Wy.

Interviews

Debbie Desch Anderson, by author, January, November, and December 2000; January and November 2001; January, May, June, and August 2002; and June 2003

Phil Bochicchio, by author, January and October 2001

Dorothy Braswell, by author, January 2001

Carmelita Ford Bruce, by author, August 12, 2002

Ralph E. Cook, by author, August 2002

Joan Bert Davis, by author, June 2002

Joseph Desch and Robert Mumma, by Henry Tropp for the Smithsonian Institution, January 17–18, 1973

Harold L. Ditmer, by author, June 8, 2002

Joseph J. Eachus, by author, February 22 and August 9, 2002

Evelyn Urich Einfeldt, by author, January 2001 and July 2002

Kristina Engstrom, self-interview, November 29, 1992, American Heritage Center, University of Wyoming, Laramie, Wy., Clay Blair Papers, Box 168, File 15

Susan Unger Eskey, by author, January 2001 and April 2002

Peg Fiehtner, by author, January 2002 and July 2002

Dorothy Firor, by author, January 2001

Vince Gulden, by Frederik Nebeker for IEEE, September 16, 1995

John R. Hamilton, by author, August 2002

Robert Hogan, by author, April 2002

Lou Holland, by author, 1999–2000

John Hourigan, by author, June 2003

Veronica M. Hulick, by author, October 2001

Mary Lorraine Johnson, by U.S. Naval Cryptologic Veterans Association, 1985

Jack Kern, by Frederik Nebeker for IEEE, September 14, 1995

Alvida Lockwood, by author, July 2002

Don Lowden, by Frederik Nebeker for IEEE, September 17, 1995; by author, January 2002

Alexander C. "Goose" McAuslun, by author, November 2000

Gilman McDonald, by author, July and August 2002

Bruce Meader, by Clay Blair, n.d., American Heritage Center, University of Wyoming, Laramie, Wy., Clay Blair Papers, Box 160

Son of James Montgomery, Jr. (who asked not to be identified), by author, January 1989

Mike Moran, by author, December 2000
Robert Mumma, by Frederik Nebeker for IEEE, September 15, 1995; by author,
    November 2000
Carrell I. Pinnell, by author, September 2002
Catherine Racz, by author, December 2000 and January 2001
Edward P. Rego, by author, February 2002
Carl Rench, by Frederik Nebeker for IEEE, September 16, 1995; by author, No-
    vember 2000
Betty Bemis Robarts, by author, January 2001
George M. Robb, by author, August 2002
Lou Sandor, by author, November 2000
Raymond Torchon, by author, October 2001
Evelyn Vogel, by author, January 2001 and July 2002
James Henry Wakelin, Jr., by Arthur L. Norberg for the Charles Babbage Institute,
    February 27, 1986
Jeffrey Wenger, by author, January 2002

Books and Dissertations

Alsmeyer, Marie Bennett. *The Way of the WAVES: Women in the Navy.* Conway,
    Ark.: HAMBA Press, 1981.
Alvarez, David. *Secret Messages: Codebreaking and American Diplomacy,
    1930–1945.* Lawrence: University of Kansas Press, 2000.
Alvarez, David, ed. *Allied and Axis Signals Intelligence in World War II.* London:
    Frank Cass, 1999.
Bamford, James. *The Puzzle Palace: A Report on America's Most Secret Agency.* New
    York: Penguin, 1983.
Bath, Alan Harris. *Tracking the Axis Enemy: The Triumph of Anglo-American Naval
    Intelligence.* Lawrence: University of Kansas Press, 1998.
Bauer, Friedrich L. *Decrypted Secrets: Methods and Maxims of Cryptology.* 2d ed.
    New York: Springer, 2000.
Benson, Robert Louis. *A History of U.S. Communications Intelligence During
    World War II: Policy and Administration.* United States Cryptologic History,
    Series 4, *World War II*, vol. 8. Fort Meade, Md.: NSA, Center for Cryptologic
    History, 1997.
Benson, Robert Louis, and Michael Warner, eds. *Venona: Soviet Espionage and the
    American Response, 1939–1957.* Washington, D.C.: NSA and CIA, 1996.
Bernstein, Mark. *Grand Eccentrics: Dayton and the Invention of America.* Wilm-
    ington, Ohio: Orange Frazer Press, 1996.
Blair, Clay. *Hitler's U-boat War: The Hunters, 1939–1942.* New York: Random
    House, 1996.
———. *Hitler's U-boat War: The Hunted, 1942–1945.* New York: Random House,
    1998.
Bray, Jeffrey. *Ultra in the Atlantic.* Vol. 1, *Allied Communication Intelligence and
    the Battle of the Atlantic.* Laguna Hills, Calif.: Aegean Park Press, 1994.

———, ed. *Ultra in the Atlantic*. Vol. 2, *U-boat Operations*. Laguna Hills, Calif.: Aegean Park Press, 1994.

———, ed. *Ultra in the Atlantic*. Vol. 3, *German Naval Communication Intelligence*. Laguna Hills, Calif.: Aegean Park Press, 1994.

———, ed. *Ultra in the Atlantic*. Vol. 4, *Technical Intelligence from Allied Communications Intelligence*. Laguna Hills, Calif.: Aegean Park Press, 1994.

Budiansky, Stephen. *Battle of Wits: The Complete Story of Codebreaking in World War II*. New York: Free Press, 2000.

Burke, Colin. *Information and Secrecy: Vannevar Bush, Ultra, and the Other Memex*. Lanham, Md.: Scarecrow Press, 1994.

Bush, Vannevar. *Pieces of the Action*. New York: William Morrow, 1970.

Butler, Elizabeth Allen. *Navy WAVES*. Charlottesville, Va.: Wayside Press, 1988.

Campbell-Kelly, Martin, and William Aspray. *Computer: A History of the Information Machine*. New York: Basic Books, 1996.

Dalton, Curt. *Home Sweet Home Front: Dayton During World War II*. Dayton, Ohio: self-published, 2000.

Deavours, Cipher A., and Louis Kruh. *Machine Cryptography and Modern Cryptanalysis*. Dedham, Mass.: Artech House, 1985.

———. *Cryptology: Yesterday, Today, and Tomorrow*. Boston: Artech House, 1987.

Descriptive Dictionary of Cryptologic Terms, Including Foreign Terms. Laguna Hills, Calif.: Aegean Park Press, 1997.

Dorwart, Jeffery M. *Conflict of Duty: The U.S. Navy's Intelligence Dilemma, 1919–1945*. Annapolis, Md.: Naval Institute Press, 1983.

Drea, Edward J. *MacArthur's ULTRA: Codebreaking and the War Against Japan, 1942–1945*. Lawrence: University of Kansas Press, 1992.

Ebbert, Jean, and Marie-Beth Hall. *Crossed Currents: Navy Women from WWI to Tailhook*. Washington, D.C.: Brassey's, 1993.

Enever, Ted. *Britain's Best Kept Secret: Ultra's Base at Bletchley Park*. Stroud, England: A. Sutton, 1994.

Ensign, Eric S. *Intelligence in the Rum War at Sea, 1920–1933*. Washington, D.C.: Joint Military College, 2001.

Farago, Ladislas. *The Tenth Fleet*. New York: Ivan Obolensky, 1962.

Gallery, Daniel V. *U-505*. New York: Warner Books, 1967.

Gardner, W.J.R. *Decoding History: The Battle of the Atlantic and Ultra*. Annapolis, Md.: Naval Institute Press, 1999.

Hancock, Joy Bright. *Lady in the Navy: A Personal Reminiscence*. Annapolis, Md.: Naval Institute Press, 1972.

Harper, Stephan. *Capturing Enigma: How HMS* Petard *Seized the German Naval Codes*. Stroud, England: A. Sutton, 1999.

Hatch, David, and Robert Louis Benson. *The Korean War: The SIGINT Background*. United States Cryptologic History, Series 5, *The Early Postwar Period, 1945–1952*, vol. 3. Fort Meade, Md.: NSA, Center for Cryptologic History, 2000.

Haynes, John Earl. *Venona: Decoding Soviet Espionage in America*. New Haven: Yale University Press, 1999.

Hinsley F. H., and Alan Stripp, eds. *Codebreakers: The Inside Story of Bletchley Park*. New York: Oxford University Press, 1993.

Hinsley, F. H., et al. *British Intelligence in the Second World War*. Vols. 1–3. London: Her Majesty's Stationery Office, 1979–1984.

Historical Statistics of the United States: Colonial Times to 1951. Washington, D.C.: GPO, 1961.

Hodges, Andrew. *Alan Turing: The Enigma*. New York: Walker and Company, 2000.

Holm, Jeanne. *Women in the Military: An Unfinished Revolution*. Novato, Calif.: Presidio Press, 1982.

Holmes, Wilfred Jay. *Double-Edged Secret: U.S. Naval Operations in the Pacific During World War II*. Annapolis, Md.: Naval Institute Press, 1979.

Holtwick, Jack. *Naval Security Group History to WWII*. Part 1. Washington, D.C.: U.S. Naval Historical Center, Operational Archives.

Intelligence Reports on the War in the Atlantic, 1942–1945. Wilmington, Del.: Michael Glazier, 1979.

Kahn, David. *Seizing the Enigma: The Race to Break the German U-boat Codes, 1939–1943*. Boston: Houghton-Mifflin, 1991.

———. *The Codebreakers: The Story of Secret Writing*. New York: Scribner's, 1996.

Kelley, Stephen J. *Big Machines*. Laguna Hills, Calif.: Aegean Park Press, 2001.

Knepper, George W. *Ohio and Its People*. Kent, Ohio: Kent State University Press, 1989.

Layton, Edwin T. *And I Was There: Pearl Harbor and Midway—Breaking the Secrets*. New York: William Morrow, 1985.

Leslie, Stuart W. *Boss Kettering*. New York: Columbia University Press, 1983.

Lewis, Graydon, ed. *A History of Communications Intelligence in the United States, with Emphasis on the United States Navy*. Eugene, Oreg.: NCVA, 1982.

Listening to the Rumrunners. Fort Meade, Md.: NSA, Center for Cryptologic History, n.d.

Love, Robert W., Jr. *History of the U.S. Navy, 1942–1991*. Harrisburg, Pa.: Stackpole, 1992.

McAfee, Mildred, et al. *The Waves in World War II*. Annapolis, Md.: Naval Institute Press, 1971–1979.

———. *Recollections of Women Officers Who Served in the U.S. Navy and the U.S. Coast Guard in World War II, Including WAVES*. Annapolis, Md.: Naval Institute Press, 1979.

McGinnis, George P., ed. *U.S. Naval Cryptologic Veterans Association*. Paducah, Ky.: Turner Publishing, 1996.

Marcosson, Isaac F. *Colonel Deeds: Industrial Builder*. New York: Dodd Mead, 1947.

Mead, Frank Spencer. *Handbook of Denominations of the United States*. Nashville: Abingdon Press, 1990.

Meigs, Montgomery C. *Slide Rules and Submarines: American Scientists and Subsurface Warfare in World War II*. Washington, D.C.: National Defense University Press, 1990.

Miller, Ray A. *The Cryptographic Mathematics of Enigma*. Fort Meade, Md.: NSA, Center for Cryptologic History, 2001.

Morison, Samuel Eliot. *History of United States Naval Operations in World War II*. Vol. 1, *The Battle of the Atlantic: September 1939–May 1943*. Boston: Little, Brown, 1962.

———. *History of United States Naval Operations in World War II*. Vol. 10, *The Atlantic Battle Won: May 1943–May 1945*. Boston: Little, Brown, 1962.

Mulligan, Timothy. *Neither Sharks nor Wolves: The Men of Nazi Germany's U-boat Arm, 1939–1945*. Annapolis, Md.: Naval Institute Press, 1999.

NSA, Center for Cryptologic History. *Solving the Enigma: History of the Cryptanalytic Bombe*. Fort Meade, Md., ca. 2000.

Obermiller, Philip J., et al. *Appalachian Odyssey: Historical Perspectives on the Great Migration*. Westport, Conn.: Praeger, 2000.

Owens, Larry. "Straight Thinking: Vannevar Bush and the Culture of American Engineering." Ph.D. thesis, Princeton University, 1987.

Parker, Frederick D. *Pearl Harbor Revisited: United States Navy Communications Intelligence, 1924–1941*. United States Cryptologic History, Series 4, World War II, vol. 6. Fort Meade, Md.: NSA, Center for Cryptologic History, 1994.

Parrish, Thomas. *The Ultra Americans: The United States' Role in Breaking the Nazi Codes*. New York: Stein and Day, 1986.

Persico, Joseph E. *Roosevelt's Secret War: FDR and World War II Espionage*. New York: Random House, 2001.

Philby, Kim. *My Silent War*. New York: Grove Press, 1968.

Prados, John. *Combined Fleet Decoded: The Secret History of American Intelligence and the Japanese Navy in WWII*. New York: Random House, 1995.

Rodgers, William. *Think: A Biography of the Watsons and IBM*. New York: Stein and Day, 1969.

Rohwer, Jurgen. *Critical Convoy Battles of March 1943: The Battle for HX229/SC122*. London: Ian Allen, 1977.

Roskill, S. W. *The War at Sea, 1939–1945*. Vol. 1, *The Defensive*. London: Her Majesty's Stationery Office, 1954.

———. *The Navy at War, 1939–1945*. London: Collins, 1960.

Safford, Laurance F., and J. N. Wenger. *U.S. Naval Communications Intelligence Activities*. Laguna Hills, Calif.: Aegean Park Press, 1993.

Sebag-Montefiore, Hugh. *Enigma: The Battle for the Code*. London: Weidenfeld and Nicolson, 2000.

Singh, Simon. *The Code Book: The Science of Secrecy from Ancient Egypt to Quantum Cryptography*. New York: Anchor Books, 1999.

Smith, Bradley F. *The Ultra-Magic Deals: And the Most Secret Relationship, 1940–1946*. Novato, Calif.: Presidio Press, 1993.

———. *Sharing Secrets with Stalin: How the Allies Traded Intelligence, 1941–1945*. Lawrence: University of Kansas Press, 1996.

Smith, Michael. *Station X: Decoding Nazi Secrets*. New York: TV Books, 1999.

———. *The Emperor's Codes: The Breaking of Japan's Secret Ciphers*. New York: Arcade, 2000.

Smith, Michael, and Ralph Erskine, eds. *Action This Day.* New York: Bantam, 2001.

Syrett, David. *The Defeat of the German U-boats: The Battle of the Atlantic.* Columbia: University of South Carolina Press, 1994.

Syrett, David, ed. *The Battle of the Atlantic and Signals Intelligence: U-boat Situations and Trends, 1941–1945.* Ashgate, Hampshire, England: Aldershot, 1998.

Tidman, Keith R. *The Operations Evaluation Group: A History of Naval Operations Analysis.* Annapolis, Md.: Naval Institute Press, 1984.

Tompkins, C. B., et al. *Engineering Research Associates, High Speed Computing Devices.* New York: McGraw-Hill, 1950.

Treadwell, Mattie E. *The Women's Army Corps.* United States Army in World War II, Special Studies. Washington, D.C.: Office of the Chief of Military History, 1954.

West, Nigel. *GCHQ: The Secret Wireless War, 1900–1986.* London: Weidenfeld and Nicolson, 1986.

West, Nigel, and Oleg Tsarev. *The Crown Jewels: The British Secrets at the Heart of the KGB Archives.* New Haven: Yale University Press, 1998.

Whitehead, Don. *The FBI Story: A Report to the People.* New York: Random House, 1956.

Williams, Kathleen Broome. *Secret Weapon: U.S. High-Frequency Direction Finding in the Battle of the Atlantic.* Annapolis, Md.: Naval Institute Press, 1996.

Winton, John. *Ultra at Sea: How Breaking the Nazi Code Affected Allied Naval Strategy During World War II.* New York: William Morrow, 1988.

———. *Ultra in the Pacific: How Breaking Japanese Codes and Cyphers Affected Naval Operations Against Japan, 1941–1945.* London: Leo Cooper, 1993.

Yardley, Herbert O. *The American Black Chamber.* Laguna Hills, Calif.: Aegean Park Press, 1988.

Y'Blood, William T. *Hunter-Killer: U.S. Escort Carriers in the Battle of the Atlantic.* Washington, D.C.: U.S. Naval Institute, 1983.

Zachary, G. Pascal. *Endless Frontier: Vannevar Bush, Engineer of the American Century.* New York: Free Press, 1997.

Published Articles and Web Publications

Alvarez, David. "Beyond Venona: American Signal Intelligence in the Early Cold War." *Intelligence and National Security* 14.2 (summer 1999).

Bowerman, Thomas R., and Agnes Bridger. "The Battle of the Atlantic." WWII U.S. Navy Armed Guard and WW II Merchant Marine website, http://armed-guard.com.

Buckland, Michael. "Emanuel Goldberg, Electronic Document Retrieval, and Vannevar Bush's Memex." *Journal of the American Society for Information Science* 43.4 (May 1992).

Budiansky, Stephen. "The Difficult Beginnings of U.S.-British Codebreaking Cooperation." *Intelligence and National Security* 15.2 (summer 2000).

Burke, Colin. "An Introduction to an Historical Computer Document: The 1946

Pendergrass Report, Cryptanalysis, and the Digital Computer." *Cryptologia* 17.2 (April 1993).

Burke, Colin, and Ralph Erskine. Letters to the editor. *Cryptologia* 15.2 (April 1991).

Chandler, W. W. "The Installation and Maintenance of the Colossus." *Annals of the History of Computing* 5.3 (July 1983).

Coombs, Allen W. M. "The Making of Colossus." *Annals of the History of Computing* 5.3 (July 1983).

Crawford, David J. "The Autoscritcher and the Superscritcher." *Annals of the History of Computing* 14.3 (July 1992).

Currier, Prescott. "My 'Purple' Trip to England in 1941." *Cryptologia* 20.3 (July 1996).

Davies, Donald W. " 'The Bombe': A Remarkable Logic Machine." *Cryptologia* 23.2 (April 1999).

———. "Effectiveness of the Diagonal Board." *Cryptologia* 23.3 (July 1999).

Deavours, Cipher A. "The Black Chamber: La Methods des Batons." *Cryptologia* 4.4 (October 1980).

———. "The Autoscritcher." *Cryptologia* 19.3 (April 1995).

Deavours, Cipher A., and Louis Kruh. "The Turing Bombe: Was It Enough?" *Cryptologia* 14.4 (October 1990).

DeBrosse, Jim. "NCR and WWII: The Untold Story." *Dayton Daily News,* an eight-part series, February 25–March 4, 2001.

Drea, Edward J. "Were the Japanese Army Codes Secure?" *Cryptologia* 19.2 (April 1995).

Erskine, Ralph. "Ultra and Some U.S. Navy Carrier Operations." *Cryptologia* 19.1 (January 1995).

———. "Naval Enigma: An Astonishing Blunder." *Intelligence and National Security* 11.3 (fall 1996).

———. "The First Naval Enigma Decrypts of World War II." *Cryptologia* 21.1 (January 1997).

———. "Kriegsmarine Short Signal Systems and How Bletchley Park Exploited Them." *Cryptologia* 23.1 (January 1999).

———. "The Holden Agreement on Naval Sigint: The First BRUSA?" *Intelligence and National Security* 14.2 (summer 1999).

———. "What Did the Sinkov Mission Receive from Bletchley Park?" *Cryptologia* 24.2 (April 2000).

———. "Enigma: Allied Breaking of Naval Enigma." Http://www.uboat.net/technical/enigma_breaking.htm, August 6, 2001.

Erskine, Ralph, and Gilbert Bloch. "Enigma: The Dropping of the Double Encipherment." *Cryptologia* 10.3 (July 1986).

Ferris, John. "The Road to Bletchley Park: The British Experience with Signals Intelligence, 1892–1945." *Intelligence and National Security* 16.1 (spring 2001)

Flowers, Thomas H. "The Design of Colossus." *Annals of the History of Computing* 5.3 (July 1983).

Gladwin, Lee A. "Cautious Collaborators: The Struggle for Anglo-American Cryptanalytic Cooperation, 1940–1943." In Alvarez, *Allied and Axis Signals Intelligence in World War II*.

Gladwin, Lee A. "Visit to National Cash Register Corporation of Dayton, Ohio" (by Alan M. Turing). *Cryptologia* 30.1 (January 2001).

Godson, Susan H. "The Waves in World War II." *Proceedings* (December 1981).

Hamer, David H. "Enigma: Actions Involved in the 'Double Stepping' of the Middle Rotor." *Cryptologia* 21.1 (January 1997).

Hamer, David H., et al. " 'Enigma Variations': An Extended Family of Machines." *Cryptologia* 22.3 (July 1998).

Hanyok, Robert. "Still Desperately Seeking 'Miss Agnes': A Pioneer Cryptologist's Life Remains an Enigma." *NCVA Cryptolog* (fall 1997).

"In Memoriam: Solomon Kullback, April 3, 1907–August 5, 1994." *Cryptologia* 19.2 (April 1995).

"John E. Parker." *IEEE Annals of the History of Computing* 14.4 (1992).

Kahn, David. "Britain Reveals Its Bombe to America: From the Archives." *Cryptologia* 26.2 (April 2002).

Kruh, Louis. "Why Was Safford Pessimistic About Breaking the German ENIGMA Cipher Machine?" *Cryptologia* 14.3 (July 1990).

Lewis, Graydon A. "Setting the Record Straight on Midway." *Cryptologia* 22.2 (April 1998).

Lujan, Susan M. "Agnes Meyer Driscoll." *Cryptologia* 15.1 (January 1991).

Marks, Philip. "Umkehrwalze D: Enigma's Reworkable Reflector, Part I." *Cryptologia* 25.2 (April 2001).

———. "Umkehrwalze D: Enigma's Reworkable Reflector, Part II." *Cryptologia* 25.3 (July 2001).

———. "Umkehrwalze D: Enigma's Reworkable Reflector, Part III." *Cryptologia* 25.4 (October 2001).

Michie, Donald. "Colossus and the Breaking of the Wartime 'Fish' Codes." *Cryptologia* 26.1 (January 2002).

Mulligan, Timothy. "The German Navy Evaluates Its Cryptographic Security." *Military Affairs* 49.2 (April 1985).

Parker, Frederick D. "How OP-20-G Got Rid of Joe Rochefort." *Cryptologia* 24.3 (July 2000).

Phillips, Cecil. "The American Solution of a German One-Time-Pad, Cryptographic System (G-OTP)." *Cryptologia* 24.4 (October 2000).

Ratcliff, R. A. "Searching for Security: The German Investigations into Enigma's Security." In Alvarez, *Allied and Axis Signals Intelligence in World War II*.

Rohwer, Jurgen, and Patrick Beesley, et al. "Ultra and the Battle of the Atlantic." *Cryptologic Spectrum* 8.1 (winter 1978).

Sale, Tony. "Enigma and the Bombe: Lecture by Tony Sale." Http://codesand ciphers.org.uk/lectures/enigbnbt.html, February 9 and 16, 2002.

———. "Bigrams, Trigrams and Naval Enigma." Http://www.codesandciphers.org. uk/lectures/naval1.htm, n.d.

Scott, Norman. "Solving Japanese Naval Ciphers 1943–1945." *Cryptologia* 21.2 (April 1997).

Snyder, Samuel S. "The Influence of U.S. Cryptologic Organizations on the Digital Computer Industry." *Journal of Systems and Software* 1 (1979).

Syrett, David. "The Infrastructure of Communications Intelligence: The Allied D/F Network and the Battle of the Atlantic." *Intelligence and National Security* 17.3 (autumn 2002).

Tucker, Dundas P. "Rhapsody in Purple." *Cryptologia* 6.3 (July 1981).

U.S. Maritime Service Veterans. "The Merchant Marine in World War II." Http://www.usmm.org.

U.S. Senate Committee on Naval Affairs. *A Bill to Expedite the War Effort . . . : Hearings on S. 5257,* 77th Cong., 2d sess., May 19 and June 23, 1942.

Whitehead, David. "The U-boat Ciphers and the 4-Wheel Bombes." In "CSOS Cheadle 1938–1995, *OPEN DAY,* 6th August 1994."

———. "Cobra and Other Bombes." *Cryptologia* 20.4 (October 1996).

Young, Evan A. "Lone Star Justice." Wikipedia website, www.wikipedia.org/wiki/ Tom+C.+Clark.

Notes

Abbreviations

ACC	accession
ASW	Anti-Submarine Warfare
Crane	Naval Security Group Detachment (Crane, Ind.)
CNO	Chief of Naval Operations
CNSG	Commander Naval Security Group
DOJ	U.S. Department of Justice
ERA	Engineering Research Associates
FBI	Federal Bureau of Investigation
FOIA	Freedom of Information Act (documents obtained via)
GCCS	Government Code and Cypher School
HCC	Historic Cryptologic Collection
HW	records created and inherited by GCHQ (GCCS)
IEEE	Institute of Electrical and Electronics Engineers
MIT	Massachusetts Institute of Technology
NARA	National Archives and Records Administration
NC	Navy Change Machines
NCML	Naval Computing Machine Laboratory
NCR	National Cash Register Company
NCVA	Naval Cryptologic Veterans Association
NDRC	National Defense Research Committee
NOAA	National Oceanic and Atmospheric Administration
NSA	National Security Agency
NSA FOIA	Records obtained via FOIA requests to the NSA
NSGC	Naval Security Group Command
ONI	Office of Naval Intelligence

OP20G	Communications Division of Office of the CNO
OSRD	Office of Scientific Research and Development
PRO	Public Record Office
RAM	Rapid Analytical Machines
RAM File	documents on OP20G's machine projects provided by the NSA via FOIA requests
RG	Record Group
RG 38	records of the Office of the CNO
RG 457	records of the NSA
RIP	Registered Intelligence Publication
SIS	Signal Intelligence Service, U.S. Army
SRH	Special Research Histories
SRMN	Special Research Materials Navy, Discrete Records of Historical Import: U.S. Navy
SSA	Signal Security Agency, U.S. Army
USDJ	U.S. Department of Justice
USDJ/FBI FOIA	documents provided by DOJ and FBI via FOIA requests

Double quotation marks indicate formal titles for documents. Single quotation marks are for content indicators created by the authors.

Prologue

xviii **He was also cold** Edward P. Rego interview.
By midnight, a wolf pack Winton, *Ultra at Sea,* p. 120.
Just before midnight Edward P. Rego interview; Blair, *Hitler's U-boat War: The Hunted, 1942–1945,* p. 255; Bowerman and Bridger, "The Battle of the Atlantic."

xix **In all, fifty-one** http://armed-guard.com.
And so it went Morison, *Battle of the Atlantic,* p. 412.
In ten days Parrish, *Ultra Americans,* p. 159.

xx **"If a submarine sinks** Morison, *Battle of the Atlantic,* pp. 127–28.
But unknown to the Allies NARA RG 457, Box 112, SRH 368, "Evaluation of the Role of Decryption Intelligence in the Operational Phase of the Battle of the Atlantic"; NARA RG 457, NR1695, as in the Clay Blair Papers, American Heritage Center, University of Wyoming, Box 166, File 11, "German Naval Communications Intelligence."

xxi **Theoretically, at least** Miller, *Cryptographic Mathematics of Enigma.*
xxiii **With twenty letters** Ibid.
xxiv **Going by the list** Sale, "Bigrams, Trigrams and Naval Enigma"; NARA RG 457, HCC, Box 621, ACC7465 CBKJ18, "German Cipher Key Logs."
xxvi **The hurdle was too much** Rohwer and Beesley et al., "Ultra and the Battle of the Atlantic"; Rohwer, *Critical Convoy Battles of March 1943,* p. 240; Hodges, *Alan Turing,* p. 224.

No wonder that Kahn, *Seizing the Enigma,* p. 217.

xxvii **To grapple with Shark** PRO HW 3/93 'Bombe Story,' and PRO HW 3/93, 'Wynn-Williams Assigned.'

Progress was slow NARA RG 38, RIP, Box 169, RIP 403, April 21, 1942, 'Following for Tiltman from Travis'; NARA RG 38, RIP, Box 169, RIP 403, 'Special British Reports on German Cryptography.'

After a misguided start NARA RG 38, Crane, CNSG Library, Box 183, 5750/441, "Bombe Correspondence Reel 141394, Correspondence on IC Machines," memorandum to John H. Howard by Robert B. Ely, April 25, 1942, 'Future IC machine and planned U.S. Bombe'; NSA FOIA, RAM File, Ralph Meader, Report to J. N. Wenger, Part 2, "Resume of the Dayton, Ohio, Activity During World War II."

The obvious choice Burke, *Information and Secrecy,* esp. chap. 2.

xxviii **Although the official** NARA RG 457, Box 43, SRH 142, Commander Jerry C. Russell, USN, "Ultra and the Campaign Against the U-boats in World War II." The estimates of the role of decryptions are compiled from: NARA RG 38 (Crane-Orange Intercepts), Translations of Intercepted Enemy Radio Traffic and Misc. World War II Documents, 1940–1946. Lists of U-boats sunk came from Roskill, *The War at Sea, 1939–1945*; NARA RG 457, Box 43, SRH 142, Commander Jerry C. Russell, USN, "Ultra and the Campaign Against the U-boats in World War II"; and Bray, *Ultra in the Atlantic,* vols. 1 and 2.

xxix **The eight hundred U.S. Navy** Peg Fiehtner interview.

1. Building the Perfect Machine

3 **"No more excuses!** Jack Kern interview; Carl Rench interview, September 1995; Debbie Desch Anderson interviews, January 2000.

What Desch couldn't tell NSA FOIA, RAM File, Ralph Meader, Report to J. N. Wenger, Part 2, "Resume of the Dayton, Ohio, Activity During World War II." On the promised delivery date: NSA FOIA and NARA RG 38, Crane, CNSG Library, Box 183, 5750/441, OP20G, "Cryptanalysis of the German Cipher Machine," September 3, 1942; NARA RG 38, Crane, CNSG Library, Box 11, 3200/54, October 23, 1942, 'Desch to Meader: Maintenance Crew for Bombes.'

4 **Behind the building** Jack Kern interview.

As late as August NARA RG 38, RIP, Box 171, RIP 607, A. Clifford, "The American Hot Point Method."

A big part of NARA RG 38, Crane, CNSG Library, Box 183, 5750/441, Joseph Desch, "Memo of Present Plan for an Electromechanical Analytical Machine, September 14, 1942"; NSA FOIA, RAM File, July 7, 1942, 'For Travis from OP-20-G, re Ely and Eachus visit,' and July 11, 1942, from GCCS, 'Ely and Eachus have arrived'; NARA RG 38, Crane, CNSG Library, Box 183, 5750/441, Bombe Correspondence, 'From London, July 27, 1942,' CXG 550, Following from TRAVIS, 'Drawings on way' and 'Travis from Tiltman,' etc.; NSA FOIA, RAM File, Ralph Meader, "Report to J. N. Wenger," Part 2, "Resume of the Dayton, Ohio, Activity During World War II."

5 **Though not gravely injured** Debbie Desch Anderson interviews, November 2001.

He could be brash Debbie Desch Anderson interviews, January 2001.

6 **"a damned, dirty** Debbie Desch Anderson interviews, June 2002.

"He loved taking Ibid.

The deciding factor Mike Moran interview.

7 **"was desperately eager** Bernstein, *Grand Eccentrics,* p. 3.

8 **But Desch lost** Desch résumé provided by Debbie Desch Anderson; Debbie Desch Anderson interviews, November 2001.

9 **"It can now** Letter from Bush to Desch, November 26, 1942, provided by Debbie Desch Anderson.

In the late 1930s Debbie Desch Anderson interviews, January 2002.

10 **"He and I** Jack Kern interview, September 14, 1998.

2. Guesswork, Moxie, and Just Plain Luck

12 **In fact, when the Americans** NARA RG 38, Crane, CNSG Library, Box 183, 5750/441, Bombe Correspondence, 'From London, July 27, 1942,' CXG 550, Following from TRAVIS, 'Drawings on way' and 'Travis from Tiltman,' etc.

The first Cobra Whitehead, "Cobra and Other Bombes," pp. 289ff.; PRO HW 3/164 7989, "Squadron Leader Jones' Section"; Budiansky, *Battle of Wits,* p. 235; NARA RG 38, Crane, CNSG Library, Box 183, 5750/441, Bombe Correspondence, August 6, September 18, and October 29, 1942, 'GCCS and Eachus report problems with British High Speed Bombe.'

13 **These contained a kind of** Erskine, "Kriegsmarine Short Signal Systems," pp. 65ff.; NARA RG 38, Crane, CNSG Library, Box 183, 5750/441, Bombe Correspondence, June 3, 1943, 'GCCS informs OP20G of critical need for four wheel Bombes due short signal problem.'

OP20G's request for Kruh, "Why Was Safford Pessimistic About Breaking the German ENIGMA Cipher Machine?" pp. 253ff.; Burke and Erskine, letters to the editor, pp. 154ff.; NARA RG 38, Crane, CNSG Library, Box 183, 5750/441, OP20G, "Cryptanalysis of the German Cipher Machine," September 3, 1942; NARA RG 457, HCC, Box 159, RIP 403, 'Travis to Tiltman, April 21, 1942'; NARA RG 38, Crane, CNSG Library, Box 110, RI Operations 5750/155, L. F. Safford, for OP-20, "Security of Information Obtained from Enemy Communications," March 18, 1942.

The Allies got Ratcliff, "Searching for Security," pp. 146ff.; NSA FOIA, as supplied by Ralph Erskine, "Report of Interrogation of Lt. Frowein of OKM/4 SKL III, on His Work on the Security of German Naval Four Wheel Enigma," June 21, 1945.

14 **Before the war, codebreakers** Deavours, "The Black Chamber," pp. 263ff.;

Sale, "Enigma and the Bombe"; NARA RG 457, HCC, Box 1009, NR3175 ACC11289 CBNM78, "Cryptanalysis of the Yellow Machine."

The breakthrough PRO HW 25/1, Hugh Alexander, "Cryptographic History of Work on the German Naval Enigma"; Sale, "Bigrams, Trigrams and Naval Enigma."

15 **One of his methods** Kahn, *Codebreakers,* p. 384.

16 **As soon as they had** PRO HW 25/1, Hugh Alexander, "Cryptographic History of Work on the German Naval Enigma"; NARA RG 38, Crane, CNSG Library, Box 66, 5750/772, "German Cipher Problem: II Attempted Solution by Analytical Mathematical Methods"; Bauer, *Decrypted Secrets,* p. 319.

Turing had predicted Davies, " 'The Bombe,' " pp. 108ff.; Sebag-Montefiore, *Enigma,* appendix 2.

18 **Keen, BTMC's** Burke, *Information and Secrecy,* p. 266; PRO HW 3/164 7989, "Squadron Leader Jones' Section"; PRO HW 3/93, "History of the Bombe as Taken from Mr. Fletcher's Files."

19 **The Keen Bombe** Davies, " 'The Bombe,' " pp. 108ff.

Those stubborn relays PRO HW 3/93, "Bombe Story"; PRO HW 3/93, December 1941, 'Re Wynne [*sic*] Williams.'

21 **If the Bombe operator** NARA RG 38, RIP, Box 171, RIP 607, Clifford, "The American Hot Point Method"; NARA RG 38, RIP, Box 171, RIPs 605–8.

22 **Keen thus increased** Bauer, *Decrypted Secrets,* section 19.

For that, Keen needed Davies, "Effectiveness of the Diagonal Board," pp. 229ff.; NARA RG 457, HCC, Box 705, 35701 CBLH17, Bombe History Folder, 'OP20G Communications re Bombe,' and March 24, 1944, 'Bombes—History of.'

In early 1942 Hodges, *Alan Turing,* p. 252.

Even at that NARA RG 457, SRMN 037; Kahn, *Seizing the Enigma,* p. 225.

23 **In light of** NARA RG 38, Crane, CNSG Library, Box 183, 5750/441, Bombe Correspondence, 'From London, July 27, 1942,' CXG 550, Following from TRAVIS, 'Drawings on way' and 'Travis from Tiltman'; NARA RG 38, Crane, CNSG Library, Box 113, 5750/177, "Cold Spot Method, Short Row Test, New Bombe"; NARA RG 38, Crane, CNSG Library, Box 117, 5720/205, "Easy Research to Date," July 24, 1942.

Desch had much NARA RG 38, Crane, CNSG Library, Box 183, 5750/441, Joseph Desch, "Memo of Present Plan for an Electromechanical Analytical Machine," September 14, 1942.

3. Miss Aggie's Big Blunder

24 **From the moment** PRO 14/45, August 18, 1941, Denniston, "Interrupted Conference with Commander Safford," and 'List of Driscoll questions to GCCS re E and its solution.'

24 **After months of** Budiansky, "Difficult Beginnings of U.S.-British Code-breaking Cooperation," pp. 49ff.; Gladwin, "Cautious Collaborators," pp. 119ff.

25 **As a result, the leg** George M. Robb and John R. Hamilton interviews.
Despite their differences Hanyok, "Still Desperately Seeking 'Miss Agnes'"; Lujan, "Agnes Meyer Driscoll"; Kahn, *Seizing the Enigma*, pp. 188ff.; Dr. Diana M. Henderson, University of Edinburgh, e-mail correspondence with author, and "Scots and the British Secret Service," www-saw.arts.ed.ac.uk/secret/secretservice.html.

26 **Both he and Driscoll** Burke, *Information and Secrecy*, chap. 3.

27 **She was born** Lujan, "Agnes Meyer Driscoll"; Hanyok, "Still Desperately Seeking 'Miss Agnes'"; John R. Hamilton interview.

28 **Even the Navy** Lujan, "Agnes Meyer Driscoll," pp. 48ff.
But given her skills Kahn, *Codebreakers*, p. 370.
Meyer so impressed Fabyan Hanyok, "Still Desperately Seeking 'Miss Agnes.'"

29 **Driscoll began her** NARA RG 457, Box 108/9, SRH 355, "Naval Security Group History to World War II," p. 82 and passim. Also in U.S. Naval Historical Center Operational Archives.
A good example Budiansky, *Battle of Wits*, pp. 5, 77.

30 **The results shocked** Lujan, "Agnes Meyer Driscoll," p. 52.

31 **"Miss Aggie," as she** NARA RG 457, Box 108/9, SRH 355, "Naval Security Group History to World War II," part 1, p. 79; Burke, *Information and Secrecy*, chap. 3.
"paid for our peacetime Layton, *And I Was There*, p. 58.
In the mid-1930s NARA RG 457, Box 108/9, SRH 355, "Naval Security Group History to World War II," part 1, p. 161.

32 **"was sensitive to** Layton, *And I Was There*, p. 58.
Driscoll may have been Lujan, "Agnes Meyer Driscoll," pp. 56ff.

33 **When she finally returned** NARA RG 457, Box 108/9, SRH 355, "Naval Security Group History to World War II," part 1, p. 160; Pioneers in U.S. Cryptology, Part II, "The NSA Family 35 Year Celebration."
As the team labored Budiansky, *Battle of Wits*, p. 8.
OP20G had begun intercepting Bray, *Ultra in the Atlantic*, vol. 4, p. 62.

34 **Driscoll decided to attack** NARA RG 38, Crane, CNSG Library, Box 66, 5750/772, "German Cipher Problem: Attempted Solution by Analytical Mathematical Methods."
Safford, who may have Tucker, "Rhapsody in Purple," pp. 221ff.; NARA RG 38, Crane, CNSG Library, Box 110, 5750/147, "April 15, 1947, Administrative History of World War II: Cryptographic Research Section."

35 **Certainly, as bombs rained** PRO HW 14/8, 'letter to England November 4, 1940'; HW 14/45, memorandum of November 22, 1940; NARA RG 457, HCC, NR2738, Box 940, "Chronology of Correspondence Between SSA and the London Office of GCCS"; NARA RG 457, HCC, NR4565, Box 1413,

"Sinkov Papers"; NARA RG 457, HCC, Box 1127, Robert L. Benson, "The Origins of U.S.-British Communications Intelligence Cooperation."

Roosevelt and his advisers NSA FOIA, George Howe, *U.S. Cryptologic History: American Signals Intelligence in Northwest Africa and Western Europe,* Ft. Meade, NSA, n.d.; Bradley Smith, *The Ultra-Magic Deals: And the Most Secret Special Relationship, 1940–1946,* Novato, Calif. Presidio Press, 1995, pp. 50–51; Stephen Budiansky, "The Difficult Beginnings of U.S.-British Codebreaking Cooperation," *Intelligence and National Security* 14 (summer 2000), pp. 49ff.

"Sometimes I think Budiansky, *Battle of Wits,* p. 296.

36 **"Don't you Yanks** Joseph Eachus interview, August 2002.

Friedman's Army group NARA RG 457, HCC, NR2738, Box 940, "Chronology of Correspondence"; PRO HW 14/8, "To Hopkinson," November 4, 1940.

37 **"We are entitled** PRO HW 14/8, November 15, 1940, 'The Director (Personal)'; Yardley, *American Black Chamber.*

Thus, the British PRO HW 14/45, November 22, 1940, 'from Major-General F. G. Beaumont-Nesbit.'

"steps will be taken" Ibid.

By mid-December Currier, "My 'Purple' Trip to England in 1941," pp. 193ff.; U.S. Navy Historical Center Operational Archives, "Naval Security Group History to World War II," part 1; PRO HW 14/9, December 20 and 22, 1940, 'F.O.C. 3 B.'

38 **Lieutenant Weeks, from** NARA RG 38, Crane, CNSG Library, Box 66, 5750/772, "German Cipher Problem: II Attempted Solution by Analytical Mathematical Methods."

Originally, Robert B. Ely Currier, "My 'Purple' Trip to England in 1941," pp. 193ff.

Likewise, William Friedman PRO HW 14/45, January 1, 1941, 'to Denniston'; Kahn, *Codebreakers,* p. 23.

39 **"So at twelve o'clock** Smith, *Station X,* p. 165.

Two large cars PRO HW 14/49, 'Arrangements were made for you to be billeted'; Currier, "My 'Purple' Trip to England in 1941," pp. 193ff.

Their working quarters Enever, *Britain's Best Kept Secret,* p. 60.

The four American codebreakers PRO HW 1/2, 'To Director'; NARA RG 457, HCC, NR2738, Box 940, "Chronology"; NARA RG 457, HCC, Box 1127, Robert L. Benson, "The Origins of U.S.-British Cooperation"; NARA RG 457, HCC, NR3813, Box 1296, 'Sinkov Report.'

The double copies were Irwin G. Newman, "Did the British Renege?" U.S. Naval Cryptological Veterans Association official history, Turner Publishing Company, Paducah, Ky., p. 35.

40 **Permission to show** PRO HW 14/9, February 24, 1941; PRO HW 14/12, February 24, 1941; PRO HW 3/93, February 26–27, 1941, ' "C" to Churchill and return'; PRO HW 14/45, March 3, 1941, 'Weeks to Commander Denniston.'

40   **Although critics later complained** Ralph Erskine; PRO HW 14/45, March 19, 1941, 'Partial list of items given to Weeks by GCCS, including items from Turing.'
The first electromechanical Bombe PRO HW 3/164 7989, "Squadron Leader Jones' Section"; NARA RG 457, HCC, NR 3175, Box 1009, "Cryptanalysis of the Yellow Machine."

41   **But such captures** Kahn, *Seizing the Enigma*, p. 137; NARA RG 38, Crane, CNSG Library, Box 117, 5750/205, "American Cryptanalysis of the German Naval Enigma," July 7, 1944.
The Navy's team did not PRO HW 14/45 March 19, 1941, 'Partial list of items given to Weeks by GCCS, including items from Turing'; PRO HW 14/45 69629, December 18, 1940, 'For Mr Hopkinson, arrange Friedman Rosen visit to England,' and March 3, 1941, 'our American colleagues informed of "E," and other related memos.'

41n **Soon after, the British** Davies, "Effectiveness of the Diagonal Board," pp. 229ff.
The new Standard Bombe PRO HW 3/164, 'BP Bombes.'

42   **they had learned of Britain's** NARA RG 457, HCC Box 1413, 'General Marshall's Letter to Field Marshal of 23/12/42.'
Currier concluded Currier, "My 'Purple' Trip to England in 1941," 193ff; NARA RG 38, 'Wenger Memorandum for OP20G,' May 13, 1944, as supplied by Erskine; PRO HW 14/45 (69629) March 3, 1941, 'our American colleagues informed of E.'
The knowledge was never PRO HW 14/45, March 3, 1941, 'Weeks to Commander Denniston.'
Rosen, the technological PRO HW 14/46, Denniston Memorandum, 'U.S. Agencies, 1942.'

43   **"complete cooperation"** PRO HW 1/2, March 3, 1941, 'To Director.'
But trouble came PRO 14/13, March 10, 1941, 'The officer who talked.'
GCCS received a letter PRO 14/45, August 5, 1941, 're British-U.S. cryptologic relations.'
It sent a list NARA RG 38, Crane, CNSG Library, Box 183, 5750/441, Bombe Correspondence, "Washington and E Traffic"; PRO HW 14/45, 'list of items requested.'

43n **The American visitors** PRO HW 14/45, May 9, 1941, 'Denniston Report'; PRO HW 3/93, November 30, 1941, 'Memorandum on U.S.'
"stopped by a roadblock Smith, *Station X*, p. 166.

44   **"C" wrote to Churchill** PRO HW 1/6, June 24, 1941, ' "C" to Churchill.'
In mid-1941, Agnes Driscoll PRO 14/45, August 18, 1941, 'List of Driscoll questions to GCCS re E and its solution'; PRO 14/45, Denniston, "Interrupted Conference with Commander Safford," August 18, 1941.
Catalog attacks were PRO HW 25/3, 'Turing History of the Attack on Enigma.'

44n **Driscoll's anti-Enigma** PRO HW 14/129, 'Catalog Room,' June 2, 1945; NSA FOIA, RIP 425, OP-20-G, "American Attack on German Naval Ciphers"; Sale, "Enigma and the Bombe"; NARA RG 38, Crane, CNSG Library, Box 104, ca. October 1941, 'Turing Critique of Driscoll Methods'; NARA RG 38, RIP, Box 170, RIP 603, "Recovery of the Grundstellen."

45 **Driscoll launched** NARA RG 457, HCC, NR 1737, Box 705, 'Enigma Conferences—Swiss Enigma.'
And there are few NARA RG 38, Crane, RIP, Box 168, RIP 401, "The Catalog and Its Uses."

46 **In a last-gasp tactic** PRO HW 14/45, August 5, 1941, 'Denniston re future American visit.'
But he was surprised PRO HW 14/45, September 5, 1941, 'Denniston Report.'
Denniston concluded PRO HW 14/45, memorandum of August 5, 1941; HW 14/45, October 9, 1941, 'Dear Eddie.'
"Believe me, no one loses Parrish, *Ultra Americans,* p. 95.
Denniston agreed PRO HW 14/45, 'Notes on Conference Held August 14/15, 1941.'

47 **But a few days later** PRO HW 14/15, "Interrupted Conference with Commander Safford," August 18, 1941.
Driscoll declared Ibid.
She believed that PRO HW 14/45, December 12, 1941, 'Hastings / Denniston.'

48 **But when he invited** PRO HW 14/45–46, August 18, 1941, 'Denniston Report.'

48n **At the very least** PRO HW 25/3, 'Turing History of the Attack on Enigma'; NARA RG 457, HCC, Box 705, NR173, 'Bombe History' folder.

49 **Yet she did not suggest** Ibid.
The list was very specific PRO HW 14/45, 'List of Questions' following 'Denniston Report of August 18, 1941' meeting.
In late 1941, he approved NARA RG 38, Crane, CNSG Library, Box 2, "List of Personnel Assignments, OP20GY, 1941."
In mid-December 1941, Driscoll PRO HW 14/45, "CXG 129," December 13, 1941.
And as Turing pointed out NARA RG 38, Crane, CNSG Library, Box 104, 'Turing Critique of Driscoll Methods.'

50 **Given Driscoll's obstinacy** NARA RG 38, "Washington and 'E' Traffic," supplied by Stephen Budiansky; PRO HW 14/45, "CXG 130, Copy to Commander Denniston," December 12, 1941.
Denniston's early October PRO HW 14/45, October 9, 1941, 'Dear Eddie.'
Noyes didn't mince PRO HW 14/45, Hastings to GCCS, December 2, 1941; HW 14/45, "CXG 115-117," December 2, 1941.
"I still cannot understand PRO 14/45, 'From Denniston,' December 5, 1941.

50n **Denniston and his colleagues** PRO HW 14/45, November 27, 1941, 'Washington to GCCS.'

50n **"There is grave** PRO HW 14/45, 'Washington to GCCS,' November 27, 1941.

51 **Then, belying later** NARA RG 38, Crane, CNSG Library, Box 183, 5750/441, Bombe Correspondence, "Washington and E Traffic."
"Luke Chapter 15, v 9" PRO HW 14/45, December 13, 1941, 'Navy Department to unknown.'

52 **Denniston left Washington** PRO HW 14/45, September 4, 1941, 'Denniston Report.'

4. Toward an American Bletchley Park

53 **The meeting at OP20G** NSA FOIA, RAM File, November 5, 1941, Memorandum for OP-20-A, "Report of Conference," re 'Professor Howard'; NSA FOIA, RAM File, OP-20-G, 'Meeting with Howard 11-3-41'; NARA RG 457, Box 108/9, SRH 355, "Naval Security Group History to World War II," also copy in U.S. Naval Historical Center Operational Archives.

54 **The only hope** Ibid., pp. 279–82.
The three MIT students NARA RG 457, Box 77, SRH 197, "U.S. Navy Communications Intelligence Organization 1941–5."

55 **They had scoured** Burke, *Information and Secrecy,* p. 224.
Engstrom had the perfect Engstrom self-interview; NARA RG 457, Box 108/9, SRH 355, "Naval Security Group History to World War II."

56 **He had returned to Yale** NARA RG 457, Box 108/9, SRH 355, "Naval Security Group History to World War II," p. 330.
Another of the more senior Ely biographical data from Princeton University Alumni Center and Archives, Princeton, N.J.
Not present at Information on Wenger's background, career, and health was gained from "Rear Admiral Joseph N. Wenger, United States Navy Retired, Navy Biographies Branch," Naval Historical Center, Washington, D.C.; interviews and discussions with Joseph Eachus, George M. Robb, and Jeffery Wenger.
He and Stanford Burke, *Information and Secrecy,* p. 10.

57 **He became the driving** Ibid., p. 61.
Even at Annapolis Naval Security Group Command Display.
"He was all business George M. Robb interview, August 2002.
"made everybody he Joe Eachus interview, August 9, 2002.

58 **Bush was not only** Zachary, *Endless Frontier;* Burke, *Information and Secrecy,* chap. 2.

59 **In 1935, as Hooper** Burke, *Information and Secrecy,* p. 68.

60 **At the 1925 International** Buckland, "Emanuel Goldberg, Electronic Document Retrieval, and Vannevar Bush's Memex," pp. 284ff.

61 **The friendship between** Burke, *Information and Secrecy,* chap. 4.

62 **By the end of** Knepper, *Ohio and Its People,* p. 286.
Deeds and Kettering were familiar U.S. Centennial of Flight Commission website, www.centennialofflight.gov/essay/Aerospace/WWi/Aero5.htm.

As a member of Leslie, *Boss Kettering*; Marcosson, *Colonel Deeds*.
In a classic Bush, *Pieces of the Action*, p. 30.

63 **His experience included** Burke, *Information and Secrecy*, p. 96.

64 **He hoped** Ibid., p. 153.

65 **By this time, Driscoll** NARA RG 38, Crane, CNSG Library, Boxes 104, 130, OP20G War Diaries, October 1941 and January 1942.
Some two weeks after NSA FOIA, RAM File, November 5, 1941, Memorandum for OP-20-A, "Report of Conference," re 'Professor Howard'; NSA FOIA, RAM File, OP-20-G, 'Meeting with Howard 11-3-41,' and OP20G 'to Howard,' November 14, 1941. The late 1941 critique of Driscoll's method by Alan Turing may have played a significant role: NARA RG 38, Crane, CNSG Library, Box 104; also Box 117, 5720/205, 'Turing Critique of Driscoll Methods.'

65n **Three separate attempts** Ibid., chap. 7.

66 **Wenger's belief** Burke, *Information and Secrecy*, p. 220.
In early 1942 NSA FOIA, RAM File, "Establishment of OP-20-G GM research section"; NARA RG 457, Box 77, SRH 197, "U.S. Navy Communications Intelligence Organization 1941–5"; NSA FOIA, RIP 425, OP-20-G, "American Attack on German Naval Ciphers," provided by Ralph Erskine; NARA RG 457, HCC, Box 169, RIP 403, April 24, 1942, 'Questions Handed to Colonel Tiltman.'

67 **Wenger asked Engstrom's** Ibid.
On top of the U-boat Burke, *Information and Secrecy*, p. 275; NSA FOIA, RAM File, 'To the President March 17, 1943'; NARA RG 457, Box 110, SRH 361, "History of the Signal Security Agency," vol. 2, p. 260; NARA RG 38, Crane, CNSG Library, Box 183, Bombe Correspondence, 'April 1942, Tiltman to Travis.'
Britain again rushed PRO HW 14/46, 'Tiltman Report'; PRO 14/16, February 5, 1942, 'Denniston on U.S. and Enigma'; NARA RG 38, Crane, CNSG Library, Box 110, 5750/147, "Administrative History of World War II: Cryptologic Research Section," April 15, 1947.

68 **And while the American** NARA RG 457, SRH391, Box 114, 'U.S. Cryptologic History, American Signals Intelligence in Northwest Africa and Western Europe'; NSA FOIA (George Howe) 'U.S. Cryptologic History, American Signals Intelligence in Northwest Africa and Western Europe,' Ft. Meade, n.d.
In a memo to NARA RG 38, Crane, CNSG Library, Box 183, 5750/441, "Bombe Correspondence Reel 141394, Correspondence on IC Machines," memorandum to John H. Howard by Robert B. Ely, April 25, 1942, 'Future IC machine and planned U.S. Bombe'; NSA FOIA, RAM File, August 5, 1942, 'Wenger to Ely.'
Starting in April NARA RG 38, RIP, Box 169, RIP 403, "Special British Reports on German Cryptography."
OP20G wouldn't even realize Joseph Eachus interview and correspondence; RG 457, HCC, Box 705, NR4384 and NR5484, April 24, 1944, "History of the Bombe Project."

69   **Even as late as mid-1942**   NARA RG 38, Crane, CNSG Library, Box 183, Bombe Correspondence; NSA FOIA, RAM File, September 4, 1942, Wenger to Eachus, 'Electronics infeasible will pattern our Bombe on British'; NARA RG 38, Crane, CNSG Library, Box 117, 5750/205, July 12, 1942, to OP— "Easy Research to Date."

   OP20G informed the British   NSA FOIA, RAM File, Wenger to GCCS, August 5, 1942.

70   **In the midst of**   Debbie Desch Anderson interviews, January 2002; Jack Kern interview.

   Then, in early July   NSA FOIA, RAM File, Ralph Meader, Report to J. N. Wenger, Part 2, "Resume of the Dayton, Ohio, Activity During World War II."

   But it was a "mustang"   Parker, "How OP-20-G Got Rid of Joe Rochefort," pp. 212ff.; Kahn, *Codebreakers,* p. 569.

5. A Giant Leap . . . and a Step Backward

72   **a totally electronic**   NARA RG 38, RIP, Box 171, RIP 607, A. Clifford, "The American Hot Point Method."

   "you had to light   Jack Kern interview.

73   **Desch's tubes had been**   Final OSRD Report, Div. 17, Beggs and Youst, "Development and Application of Electronic Counting Circuits, 1946," esp. chap. 6, Hagley Museum and Library, Wilmington, Del., ACC 1825, *Honeywell v. Sperry Rand,* Trial Records, Desch deposition.

   Wright and Desch were   Debbie Desch Anderson interviews, January 2002.

   Wenger, Engstrom, and   NSA FOIA, RAM File, Wenger to Eachus, September 4, 1942, 'Electronics infeasible will pattern our Bombe on British.'

74   **How Desch felt**   Debbie Desch Anderson interviews, November 2000.

   After graduating   Parrish, *Ultra Americans,* p. 155.

   "As a matter of fact   Joseph Eachus interview, February 2002.

   One of the first vital   NARA RG 38, Crane, CNSG Library, Box 113, 5750/177, "Cold Spot Method, Short Row Test, New Bombe"; NSA FOIA, RIP 425, "The American Attack on the German Naval Ciphers," CNO, October 1944; NSA FOIA, RAM File, Ely-Eachus to OP20G, July 16, 1942.

75   **Blueprints for the four-wheel**   NARA RG 38, Crane, CNSG Library, Box 183, 5750/441, Bombe Correspondence, GCCS to Engstrom September 23, 1942; NARA RG 38, Crane, CNSG Library, Box 183, 5750/441, Bombe Correspondence, 'From London, July 27, 1942,' CXG 550, Following from TRAVIS, 'Drawings on way,' and August 2, 1942, Eachus/Ely, 'full wiring diagram on way.'

76   **By mid-September, Desch**   NARA RG 38, Box 183, 5750/441, Bombe Correspondence, Joseph Desch, "Memo of Present Plan for an Electromechanical Analytical Machine, September 14, 1942."

   But such a Bombe   NARA RG 38, Crane, CNSG Library, Box 183,

5750/441, OP20G, "Cryptanalysis of the German Cipher Machine, September 3, 1942"; NARA RG 38, Crane, CNSG Library, Box 11, 3200/54, file 2 of 3, October 1942, Desch to Meader, 'Maintenance Crew for Bombes.'

77 **OP20G was desperate**   NSA FOIA, RAM File, Ralph Meader, Report to J. N. Wenger, Part 2, "Resume of the Dayton, Ohio, Activity During World War II"; NSA FOIA, RAM File, Director of Naval Communications to Vice Chief of Naval Operations, March 17, 1943, 'Navy Contract Nxs7892.'

78 **He granted it**   NSA FOIA, RAM File, March 17, 1943, 'in from the President, give Nxs 7892 highest possible preference rating,' also in NARA RG 38, Crane, CNSG Library, Box 183, 5750/441, Bombe Correspondence.
At times, OP20G had   Burke, *Information and Secrecy,* p. 290.
Only if your name   Jack Kern interview.

79 **"Hey, do you have**   Carmelita Bruce interview.
The end result   NSA FOIA, RAM File, Report of R. I. Meader, Captain USNR to J. N. Wenger, Captain USN, "14 Days Training Duty, Report of," January 21, 1949, parts 1–3.
In mid-1942, when Deeds   Ibid.; NSA FOIA, RAM File, Admiral Newton to Deeds, ca. December 28, 1942, 'NXS7892 Needs Highest Priority at NCR.'
Although over forty   Bruce Meader interview; Tompkins, *Engineering Research Associates,* biographical sections.

80 **She kept her show-business**   Bruce Meader interview.

81 **"The sailors were**   Jack Kern interview.
Once NCML and Meader   NSA FOIA, RAM File, Horn to Robinson, December 11, 1942, and CNO to Deeds, December 28, 1942.
Meader, to his credit   NSA FOIA, RAM File, R. I. Meader, Captain USNR to J. N. Wenger, Captain USN, "14 Days Training Duty, Report of," January 21, 1949, parts 1–3.

82 **That approach soon ended**   NSA FOIA, RAM File, Deeds to Admiral Newton, January 7, 1943, 'NCR Giving Highest Priority to NXS 7892', R. I. Meader, Captain USNR to J. N. Wenger, Captain USN, "14 Days Training Duty, Report of," January 21, 1949; NSA FOIA, RAM File, Admiral Newton to Deeds, ca. December 28, 1942, 'NXS7892 Needs Highest Priority at NCR'; NARA RG 38, Crane, CNSG Library, Box 109, 5750/116, various on relations with NCR and OP20G and funds to NCR.

83 **"I had a habit**   Lou Sandor interviews.
One NCR engineer   Carmelita Bruce interview.
"not to disclose   "Pledge of Secrecy," signed by Joseph R. Desch, March 31, 1941, supplied by Debbie Desch Anderson.

84 **In May 1942, he spent**   Debbie Desch Anderson interviews, November 2000.
"You could see   Jack Kern interview.
Desch's mother, Augusta   Debbie Desch Anderson interviews, November 2000; Desch family records.

85 **Unable to explain**   Debbie Desch Anderson interviews, November 2000.

85   Meader "practically slept   Debbie Desch Anderson interviews, November 2000; Robert Mumma interview, November 2000.
86   "We were losing   Robert Mumma interview, November 2000.
87   The design for the pilot   NSA FOIA, RAM File, From OP20G to Meader, January 20, 1943, 'Desch's newer Bombes should have one size wheel.'

6. The Turing Memo

88   When Alan Turing   NARA RG 38, Crane, CNSG Library, Box 183, 5750/441, Bombe Correspondence, 'Visit to National Cash Register Corporation of Dayton, Ohio,' December 1942, by Alan Turing.
     The thirty-year-old mastermind   Hodges, *Alan Turing,* pp. 35, 96, 116, 108.
89   He had already   NARA RG 38, Crane, CNSG Library, Box 117, 5720/205, July 7, 1944, "Op-20-GY-A, American Cryptanalysis of German Naval Systems."
     In November 1942   NARA RG 38, Crane, CNSG Library, Box 183, 5740/441, Bombe Correspondence, 'GCCS to OP20G, November 6, 1942.'
     The British had already   Erskine, "What Did the Sinkov Mission Receive from Bletchley Park?" pp. 97ff.; Joseph Eachus interviews.
     GCCS, in fact, asked   NSA FOIA, RAM File, from London, December 28, 1942, 'Following for Wenger from Travis, "Drunken Drive," etc.'
90   Two months before Turing's   Erskine, "Holden Agreement on Naval Sigint," pp. 187ff.
     Joan Clarke, Turing's fiancée   Debbie Desch Anderson interview, June 2003.
     The memo began   NARA RG 38, Crane, CNSG, Box 183, 5750/441, Bombe Correspondence, 'Visit to National Cash Register Corporation of Dayton, Ohio,' December 1942, by Alan Turing.
     The four OP20G   Joseph Eachus interview, August 2002.
91   Desch shared Turing's interests   Debbie Desch Anderson interviews, January 2002.
     "These Americans have   Hodges, *Alan Turing,* p. 123.
     There's no evidence   Robert Mumma interview, November 2000.
     "complained of Alan   Hodges, *Alan Turing,* p. 249.
92   " 'You know at Cambridge   Ibid.
     In 1952, the same   Ibid., pp. 471, 474.
     By 1943, the war   Dalton, *Home Sweet Home Front,* pp. 32–43, 84.
94   Eachus said he   Joseph Eachus interview, August 2002.
     Phil Bochicchio, a Navy mechanic   Phil Bochicchio interview, January 2001.
     Although Desch left no   Joseph Desch and Robert Mumma interview, 1973.
95   Turing provided valuable   NSA FOIA, RAM File, from London, December 28, 1942, 'Following for Wenger from Travis'; NSA FOIA, RAM File, Eng-

strom to Meader, January 5, 1943, 're Turing visit and report and need to keep Bombe design flexible.'

The British, in fact NARA RG 38, Crane, CNSG Library, Box 117, 5750/205, July 12, 1942, to OP—"Easy Research to Date"; PRO, HW 14/45, Welchman to Travis, September 12, 1941, 'on new Bombes.'

We were given NARA RG38, Crane, CNSG, Box 183, 5750/441, Bombe Correspondence, 'Visit to National Cash Register Corporation of Dayton, Ohio,' December 1942, by Alan Turing.

96 **Engstrom originally had** NSA FOIA, RAM File, Engstrom to Desch, September 23, 1942, 'Your plan for Bombe approved'; NSA FOIA, RAM File, Engstrom to Meader, January 5, 1943, 're Turing visit and report and need to keep Bombe design flexible'; NSA FOIA, RAM File, From OP20G to Meader, January 20, 1943, 'Desch's newer Bombes should have one size wheel.'

"smile inwardly NARA RG38, Crane, CNSG, Box 183, 5750/441, Bombe Correspondence, 'Visit to National Cash Register Corporation of Dayton, Ohio,' December 1942, by Alan Turing.

Providing the eleven thousand NSA FOIA, RIP 425, OP-20-G, "American Attack on German Naval Ciphers," provided by Ralph Erskine.

97 **"advise Mr. Desch** FOIA, RAM File, to Meader, January 20, 1943, 'Desch's newer Bombes should have one size wheel.'

Engstrom passed NSA FOIA, RAM File, Engstrom to Meader, January 5, 1943, 're Turing visit and report and need to keep Bombe design flexible.'

"in order to permit NSA FOIA, RAM File, January 5, 1943, Engstrom to Meader, 're Turing visit and report and need to keep Bombe design flexible.'

98 **"After the war** Joseph Desch and Robert Mumma interview, 1973.

Desch and his team PRO HW 3/164 7989, "Squadron Leader Jones' Section."

7. Troubles with Adam and Eve

100 **As one of the first** Phil Bochicchio interview, January 2001.

101 **In March 1943, Engstrom** NARA RG 457, HCC, Box 1414, NR4584, Zema 34, 2479a, "History of the Bombe Project, 30 May, 1944"; NSA FOIA, RAM File, to Meader, January 20, 1943, 'Desch's newer Bombes should have one size wheel.'

OP20G's September 1942 memo NARA RG 38, Crane, CNSG Library, Box 183, 5750/441, OP20G, "Cryptanalysis of the German Cipher Machine," September 3, 1942. See also NARA RG 38, Crane, CNSG Library, Box 11, 3200/54, Desch to Meader, October 23, 1942, 'Maintenance Crew for Bombes.'

102 **More than twice as many** Morison, *Battle of the Atlantic*, p. 410; NARA RG 457, HCC, Box 621, ACC7465 CBKJ18, "German Cipher Key Logs."

The destruction might Burke, *Information and Secrecy*, p. 292.

The codebooks, plus Erskine, "Enigma," p. 4.

103 **During tests in April** Whitehead, "Cobra and Other Bombes," pp. 289ff.; PRO HW 14/84, August 12, 1943, 'Friedman's Report on GCCS.'
They instructed him NSA FOIA, RAM File, from OP20G to DNC, March 17, 1943, 'Navy Contract Nxs 7892'; NARA RG 38, Crane, CNSG Library, Box 183, 5750/441, Bombe Correspondence, June 3, 1942, 'GCCS Informs OP20G short signal problem means critical need for four wheel Bombes.'
Only one other company National Cash Register publications, Dayton, Ohio, 1943–1945.

104 **Thousands of different** NSA FOIA, RAM File, Ralph Meader, Report to J. N. Wenger, Part 2, "Resume of the Dayton, Ohio, Activity During World War II"; Lou Sandor interview.
"From an engineering Lou Sandor interview.
Even when the secrecy NARA RG 38, Box 183, 5750/441, Joseph Desch, "Memo of Present Plan for an Electro mechanical Analytical Machine," September 14, 1942; Author's communication on British and American Bombe speeds with Ralph Erskine, 2002.
The technical hurdles NARA RG 38, Crane, CNSG Library, Box 39, 3228/2, Watch Officers Logs; NSA FOIA, RAM File, Enciphered Telegraph Link (incoming/outgoing), Washington-Dayton, Desch and Meader to OP20G, July 26 and 29, 1943, 'Bombe Won't Work' and 'Fast wheel is the problem.'

105 **"just got worse** Bob Mumma interview, November 2000.
Vince Gulden, another Vince Gulden interview.
The idea was Dalton, *Home Sweet Home Front,* p. 35.
"The boys in the foxholes Ibid.

106 **On a business trip** Letters from Joe Desch to Dorothy, July 11, 1938, supplied by Debbie Desch Anderson.
"Mom said more Debbie Desch Anderson interviews, November 2000.
So had demands NARA RG 457, Box 81, SRH 208, COMINCH to Admiralty, "U.S. Navy Submarine Warfare Message Reports," April 30, 1943.
The M section NARA RG 457, HCC, Box 621, ACC7465 CBKJ18, "German Cipher Key Logs"; NARA RG 457, Box 117, SRH 403, "Selections from the Cryptologic Papers Collection of Rear Admiral J. N. Wenger, USN"; Burke, *Information and Secrecy,* p. 295.

107 **Message clerks started** Kahn, *Codebreakers,* p. 440.
With IBM already Interview and correspondence with Lou Holland; NARA RG 38, Crane, CNSG Library, Boxes 138–39, 5750/325, "Japanese Weather Systems," chap. 22, "Application of Rapid Analytical Machinery to the Cryptanalysis of Japanese Weather Systems."

108 **Admiral Joseph Redman** NSA FOIA, RAM File, Enciphered Telegraph Link (incoming/outgoing), Washington-Dayton, May 20, 1943, 'Wenger, Redman coming to Dayton'; NARA RG 38, Crane, CNSG Library, Box 111, OP20G War Diaries.
Not long after lunch Phil Bochicchio interviews.

108n **While IBM could deliver** Lou Holland correspondence, 1999–2000.

109 **"We concluded that** Phil Bochicchio interview, October 2001.

110 **That first hit** NARA RG 457, HCC, Box 621, ACC7465 CBKJ18, "German Cipher Key Logs"; NARA RG 38, Crane, CNSG Library, Boxes 111–13, OP-20-GM-1-c-3, War Diaries, May–June 1943, 'June 22, 1943 first results from Bombe.'

As Dayton entered NSA FOIA, RAM File, Enciphered Telegraph Link (incoming/outgoing), Washington-Dayton, Desch and Meader to OP20G, July 26 and 29, 1943, 'Bombe Won't Work' and 'Fast wheel is the problem.'

8. U-boats on the Run

111 **It was a choice** NARA RG 38, WWII Action Reports; NARA RG 38, Tenth Fleet, ASW; Erskine, "Ultra and Some U.S. Navy Carrier Operations," pp. 81ff.; Alexander C. "Goose" McAuslun interview; Y'Blood, *Hunter-Killer*, p. 53.

112 **U-217 was the first Nazi** Ralph Erskine; NARA RG 457, Box 43, SRH 142, Commander Jerry C. Russell, USN, "Ultra and the Campaign Against the U-boats in World War II."

They had evolved Kahn, *Seizing the Enigma*, p. 242; NARA RG 38, WWII Operational Records, Tenth Fleet.

The Allies sank forty-one NARA RG 38, Crane Library, Box 95, "GCCS Naval History," vol. 8, p. 443.

By May 24, Dönitz Morison, *Atlantic Battle Won*, p. 83.

Of the 42 sunken subs NARA RG 457, Box 112, SRH 368, "World War II OP20G Final Report Series on the Battle of the Atlantic, Evaluation of the Role of Decryption Intelligence in the Operational Phase of the Battle of the Atlantic," Annex 4.3, Table I, Decryptions on Individual U-Boats; NARA RG 457, Box 43, SRH 142, Commander Jerry C. Russell, USN, "Ultra and the Campaign Against the U-boats in World War II."

113 **Although Desch's prototype** NARA RG 457, HCC, Box 621, ACC7465 CBKJ18, "German Cipher Key Logs"; Clay Blair Papers, American Heritage Center, University of Wyoming, Box 177, "Op-20-GM-GM1, Synopsis of War Diary, 1943"; NARA RG 38, Crane, CNSG Library, Box 4, Folder 2000, "OP-20-G, Index of Outgoing Messages." (The solution was for May 31, 1943.)

At a Führer Conference Morison, *Atlantic Battle Won*, p. 59.

114 **As Samuel Eliot Morison wrote** Ibid., p. 11.

The two-year, nearly unbroken Kahn, *Seizing the Enigma*, p. 263; NARA RG 38, Crane, CNSG Library, Box 110, 5750/147, "Administrative History of World War II: Cryptologic Research Section," April 15, 1947; NARA RG 457, Box 117, SRH 403, "Selections from the Cryptologic Papers Collection of Rear Admiral L. N. Wenger, USN." (The Germans were able to penetrate other convoy-related codes during the remainder of 1943, however.)

115 **From that June** Morison, *Atlantic Battle Won*, p. 365.

115 **Allied technical developments** Meigs, *Slide Rules and Submarines*, p. 57 and passim.

116 **Their contact fuses** Ibid., p. 57.
In May 1943, the U.S. Navy Farago, *Tenth Fleet*; Morison, *Atlantic Battle Won*, pp. 22–25.
Under the command Morison, *Atlantic Battle Won*, pp. 90, 245.

117 **By staying on the surface** Meigs, *Slide Rules and Submarines*, p. 146.
The single most significant Morison, *Atlantic Battle Won*, p. 53.

118 **Admiral Low planned** Meigs, *Slide Rules and Submarines*, p. 118.
With the promised help Ibid., p. 11.
"While I am equally NARA RG 457, Box 81, SRH 208, "U.S. Navy Submarine Warfare Message Reports."
"that will enable you Meigs, *Slide Rules and Submarines*, p. 147.
OP20G's own history NSA FOIA, RIP 425, OP-20-G, "American Attack on German Naval Ciphers," p. 60.
But log sheets NARA RG 457, HCC, Box 621, ACC7465 CBKJ18, "German Cipher Key Logs"; NARA RG 38, Crane, CNSG Library, Boxes 111–13, OP-20-GM-1-c-3 War Diaries, May–June 1943; Clay Blair Papers, American Heritage Center, University of Wyoming, Box 177, "Op-20-GM-GM1, Synopsis of War Diary, 1943."

119 **Bletchley solved** Burke, *Information and Secrecy*, pp. 294–95; NARA RG 38, Crane, CNSG Library, Boxes 30–31, OP-20-GM Watch Officer Logs; NARA RG 38, Crane, CNSG Library, Box 4, Folder 2000, "OP-20-G, Index of Outgoing Messages."
In July, the Germans Clay Blair Papers, American Heritage Center, University of Wyoming, Box 177, "OP-20-GM-GM1, Synopsis of War Diary, 1943"; NARA RG 38, Crane, CNSG Library, Boxes 111–13, OP-20-GM-1-c-3 War Diaries.
In June, the British NARA RG 457, HCC, Box 621, ACC7465 CBKJ18, "German Cipher Key Logs."
The June 18 order NSA FOIA, RAM File, Enciphered Telegraph Link (incoming/outgoing), Washington-Dayton, OP20G to NCML, June 18, 1943.

120 **He dashed off** Ibid., Meader and Engstrom messages, June 18, 1943.
"We were plagued" Gilman McDonald, letter to Debbie Desch Anderson, August 13, 2002, supplied by Anderson; McDonald interview, July 2002.
"were completely mystified" NSA FOIA, RAM File, Enciphered Telegraph Link (incoming/outgoing), Washington-Dayton, Meader to OP20G, July 26, 1943; NARA RG 38, Crane, CNSG Library, Box 39, 3238/2, Watch Officer's Log.
But Desch relied McDonald interview; NSA FOIA, RAM File, Enciphered Telegraph Link (incoming/outgoing), Washington-Dayton, Desch to OP20G, July 28, 1943.
The tiny copper slivers Gilman McDonald, letter to Debbie Desch Anderson, August 13, 2002.

121 **The maintenance crew** Phil Bochicchio interview, October 2001.

Desch requested   Gilman McDonald interview, August 2002.

After nearly fourteen   Morison, *Atlantic Battle Won*, p. 122.

They had been alerted   NARA RG 457, Box 43, SRH 142, Commander Jerry C. Russell, USN, "Ultra and the Campaign Against the U-boats in World War II," and "The Sinking of U-117."

Wildcat pilot Arne   Blair, *Hitler's U-boat War: The Hunted, 1942–1945*, p. 383.

122   **Both subs let**   Morison, *Atlantic Battle Won*, p. 123.

But the only U-tanker   Blair, *Hitler's U-boat War: The Hunted, 1942–1945*, p. 384.

As planned, the Allies   Ibid., p. 356.

Shark decrypts played   NARA RG 457, Box 112, SRH 368, "Evaluation of the Role of Decryption Intelligence in the Operational Phase of the Battle of the Atlantic," p. 109, table 2.

Dönitz ordered   Meigs, *Slide Rules and Submarines*, pp. 149–50.

123   **Despite their successes**   Blair, *Hitler's U-boat War: The Hunted, 1942–1945*, p. 415.

Enigma decrypts would   Ibid.

"a new U-boat war   NARA RG 457, COMINCH file, October 1944, 'Translation of Intercept from Doenitz to U-boat Fleet,' p. 209.

By August, the machines   NARA RG 457, HCC, Box 621, ACC7465 CBKJ18, "German Cipher Key Logs."

British codebreakers decrypted   NARA RG 457, HCC, Box 192, NR908, August 13, 1943, 'On August 10 the following message came from KO Switzerland.'

124   **But the list**   *United States Government Manual*, 1943–1945.

Standing guard on   Raymond Torchon interview.

125   **Perhaps least certain**   NARA RG 38, Crane, CNSG Library, Box 117, 5720/205, "Op-20-GY-A, American Cryptanalysis of German Naval Systems," July 7, 1944; also Jeffrey Wenger interview.

Wenger was still in   NARA RG 457, Box 117, SRH 403, "Selections from the Cryptologic Papers of Rear Admiral J. N. Wenger, USN."

By December, the average   NSA FOIA, RIP 425, OP-20-G, "American Attack on German Naval Ciphers."

9. The WAVES Come Aboard

127   **"It rained**   Catherine Racz interview, December 2000.

128   **One of them was**   Evelyn Vogel interview, January 2001.

The WAVES organization   Holm, *Women in the Military*, p. 26; U.S. Senate, *A Bill to Expedite the War Effort . . . : Hearings on S.2527*.

But once Congress   McAfee, *Recollections*, p. 43; Alsmeyer, *Way of the Waves*, p. 3; Hancock, *Lady in the Navy*; U.S. Public Laws, 1942, Title V, "Women's Reserve," p. 730.

Donating his work   Butler, *Navy Waves*, p. 10.

129   **The WAVES leaders**   Treadwell, *Women's Army Corps,* p. 513.
      One of the WAC leaders   Holm, *Women in the Military,* pp. 28, 46–55;
      Treadwell, *Women's Army Corps,* p. 156.

130   **"Oh my goodness**   Joan Bert Davis interview, June 2002.
      "It felt like   Dalton, *Home Sweet Home Front,* p. 46; Jimmie Lee Long, let-
      ter to Debbie Desch Anderson, July 29, 1995.
      "We had been cooped   Jimmie Lee Long, letter to Debbie Desch Ander-
      son, July 29, 1995.
      Those who married   Butler, *Navy Waves,* p. 71.

131   **"We were marched**   Catherine Racz interview, December 2000.
      "I'm afraid   Robert Shade, letter to Debbie Desch Anderson, July 24, 1995,
      supplied by Anderson.
      "We never talked   Dalton, *Home Sweet Home Front,* p. 47.

132   **"I would stand**   Ibid., p. 48.
      "The loveliest thing   Ibid.
      Those who failed   Phil Bochicchio interview, January 2001.

133   **One tired WAVES**   NSA FOIA, RAM File, Enciphered Telegraphic Link
      (incoming/outgoing), Washington-Dayton, Dayton to Washington, August
      14, 1943, 'WAVE too nervous'; Dayton to Washington, August 31, 1943,
      'WAVE Breaks Security'; Dayton to Washington, September 14, 1943,
      'WAVE cracks doing short runs.'
      A more delicate   NSA FOIA, RAM File, Enciphered Telegraphic Link (in-
      coming/outgoing), Washington-Dayton, Dayton to Washington, September
      28, 1943.
      "Wherever we were   Evelyn Vogel interview, January 2001.
      Firor recalled   Dorothy Firor interview, January 2001.

134   **"People must have thought**   Evelyn Urich Einfeldt interview, January
      2001.
      "even the people in   Dorothy Braswell interview.
      Betty Bemis Robarts   Betty Bemis Robarts interview.

135   **"He liked the ladies**   Alvida Lockwood interview, July 2002.
      "He wasn't what   Evelyn Vogel interview, July 2002.
      "He wasn't the kind   Alvida Lockwood interview, July 2002.
      "There were a lot   Evelyn Urich Einfeldt interview, July 2002.
      "We didn't join   Ibid., January 2001.
      "I must have cried   Betty Bemis Robarts interview.

136   **"There was no record**   Catherine Racz interview, January 2001.
      "if pertinent files   Rear Admiral G. P. March, letter to Mrs. Ray L. Hulick,
      March 24, 1978, supplied by Veronica Hulick.
      Even before production   NARA RG 38, Crane, CNSG Library, Box 183,
      Bombe Correspondence, J. N. Wenger, memorandum for OP-20, Establish-
      ment of Op-20-G activities at Dayton, Ohio, October 1942.

137   **The site in Miami Township**   "The Era of Chautauqua Over," *The Middle-
      town Journal,* November 7, 1987.
      In his memo   NARA RG 38, Crane, CNSG Library, Box 183, Bombe Cor-

respondence, J. N. Wenger, memorandum for OP-20, Establishment of Op-20-G activities at Dayton, Ohio, October 1942.

"whose main objection NARA RG38, Crane, CNSG Library, Box 183, Bombe Correspondence, memorandum for OP-20, Establishment of Op-20-G activities at Dayton, Ohio, by J. N. Wenger, October 1942.

138 **In November 1942** Naval Security Group Command, Washington, D.C., historical brochure, n.d.

At the end of its Butler, *Navy Waves*, p. 44.

10. A Well-Oiled Machine

139 **"The noise factor"** Mary Lorraine Johnson interview.

140 **On some of those "Hoppity"** NSA FOIA, RIP 425, OP-20-G, "American Attack on German Naval Ciphers."

Recreational activities Butler, *Navy Waves*, p. 59.

141 **"For some time it** NARA RG 38, Crane, CNSG Library, Box 1, 1040/4, General Personnel, 'Examples of WAVE letters, permissions and complaints by Washington D.C. residents.'

American and British field Ibid.

142 **Once its network** NSA FOIA, RIP 425; NARA RG 38, Crane, CNSG Library, Box 83, 5400/13, OP-20-G, 'Organization 1941–1944.'

The Communications Group NSA FOIA, RIP 425, OP-20-G, "American Attack on German Naval Ciphers."

143 **Following the spring 1942** NARA RG 38, Crane, CNSG Library, Box 113, 5750/176, OP20GY A1, War Diaries; NARA RG 457, Box 808, NR2336, "British Communications Intelligence," p. 2; NARA RG 457, HCC, Box 1424, NR4685, ZemaA4, 43785A, A. P. Mahon, "The History of Hut 8 1939–1945"; *Descriptive Dictionary of Cryptologic Terms, Including Foreign Terms.*

Throughout the war NARA RG 38, Crane, CNSG Library, Boxes 102–4, 111–13, War Diaries.

144 **Once the menus** NSA FOIA, RIP 425, p. 134.

Veronica Hulick "Unlocking Enigma's Secrets," Smithsonian News Service, May 1990.

144n **The British explored** NARA RG 38, Crane, CNSG Library, 5750/177, Box 113, GYA War Diaries Summary, "Analysis of Wheels, Wheel Orders, Ringstellungs, Grundstellunge, and Initial Settings Used from February 1941 to January 1942," October 10, 1942.

145 **"If you were good-looking** Veronica Hulick interview.

"It was one Peg Fiehtner interview, July 2002.

11. An Enemy Within?

146 **But he was hardworking** Montgomery work records supplied by NCR and Social Security Administration contributions/work records.

147 **As he rooted around**   NSA FOIA, RAM File, Enciphered Telegraphic Link (incoming/outgoing), Washington-Dayton Meader to Stone, November 1943, also in NARA RG 38, Crane, CNSG Library, Box 180, 3222/160.

149 **Montgomery completed**   Information provided by local school district, local directories, and Montgomery's Social Security records; interviews with Montgomery's son.
She had been seriously   Mary Ellen Blanton death certificate and newspaper obituaries, August 1926; Martha Trent death certificate and obituaries, May 1931.

150 **He wrote to**   USDJ/FBI FOIA, investigation reports by USDJ and FBI, November–December 1943.
Despite his uncle's   Social Security records and interview with Montgomery's son.
His registration card   U.S. Selective Service–supplied materials on family members.
Perhaps his frustration   NSA FOIA RAM File, Enciphered Telegraphic Link (incoming/outgoing), Washington-Dayton, Meader to Stone, November 1943; USDJ/FBI FOIA reports, ca. November 30, 1943.

151 **"always kept to**   Interview with Montgomery's son.
"He hated those   Ibid.
Lillian decided   NCR work records; Dayton area directories.

152 **The Navy investigators**   NSA FOIA, RAM File, Enciphered Telegraph Link (incoming/outgoing), Washington-Dayton, Meader to Stone, November 9, 1943, and USDJ/FBI FOIA reports, November 1943.
"I remember they   Don Lowden interview, 2002.

152n **By the time**   "Getting Along as a Member of the NCR Family," NCR in-house publication, Dayton, Ohio, 1944.

153 **The WAVES working**   Evelyn Urich Einfelt interview, January 2001.
"Certainly, at the time   Evelyn Urich Einfeldt interview.
Meader later informed   NSA FOIA, RAM File, Enciphered Telegraph Link (incoming/outgoing), Washington-Dayton, Meader to Stone, November 9, 1943; USDJ/FBI FOIA, FBI memorandum, November 18, 1943.

154 **Further heightening the tension**   PRO HW 14/91, Alexander to Travis, November 4, 1943.
Hoover had wanted   NARA RG 457, Box 78, SRH 200, and Box 92, SRH 270; NARA RG 38, Crane, CNSG Library, Box 115, 5750/193, "Summary of Coast Guard Intercepts and Distribution" and "History of OP-20-GU."

155 **"of such nature**   Bruce Meader interview, n.d.
They instructed   USDJ/FBI FOIA, FBI report, November 1943.
Meader wrote   NSA FOIA, RAM File, Enciphered Telegraph Link (incoming/outgoing), Washington-Dayton, Meader to Stone, November 9, 1943.

156 **As for the electronic**   USDJ/FBI FOIA, Belmont report to Washington, November 1 and 13, 1943.
"very scared   USDJ/FBI FOIA, FBI reports, November 1943.

Crawford very publicly "Reappointment Blocked by Cox, Crawford Says," Dayton *Journal Herald,* April 25, 1944.

At age forty-four, Clark Young, "Lone Star Justice"; Wikipedia website, www.wikipedia.org/wiki/Tom+C.+Clark.

157 **Clark, Crawford, and** USDJ/FBI FOIA, Crawford/McInerney to Dept. of Justice, November 18, 1943.

158 **Belmont must also** USDJ/FBI FOIA, FBI Headquarters to Belmont, November 11, 1943.

"take the matter USDJ/FBI FOIA, ONI to FBI, November 13, 1943.

if the Navy Ibid.

In the midst of USDJ/FBI FOIA, Crawford to Clark, November 18, 1943.

They persuaded him USDJ/FBI FOIA, FBI reports to Washington, November 13–26, 1943.

Meanwhile, with the grand jury USDJ/FBI FOIA, FBI memorandum, November 19, 1943.

He remained incommunicado USDJ/FBI FOIA, FBI to Justice Department, November 18, 1943.

159 **Montgomery's oral request** Ibid.

"I trust this USDJ/FBI FOIA Crawford to Clark/McInerney, November 18, 1943.

"had already received Ibid.

160 **"Montgomery's arrest** "Pleads Guilty to Federal Charge," Franklin *Chronicle,* December 2, 1943.

An FBI check USDJ/FBI FOIA, FBI to Belmont (Department of Justice), November 19 and 26, 1943.

To help strike USDJ/FBI FOIA, McInerney (Department of Justice) to Crawford, November 26, 1943.

Crawford and the FBI USDJ/FBI FOIA, FBI reports, November 18–26, 1943.

161 **Sitting secretively** USDJ/FBI FOIA, Crawford to Clark and McInerney, November 27, 1943.

Instead, prison officials USDJ/FBI FOIA, Crawford to McInerney, December 6, 1943; Tamm of FBI re Bennett conversations, December 12, 1943.

Bennett, in turn USDJ/FBI FOIA, report of Crawford call to Bennett, December 20, 1943; McInerney report, January 4, 1944.

162 **Tamm informed Bennett** USDJ/FBI FOIA, Tamm memorandum re Bennett discussion, December 12, 1943; Tamm memorandum re visit by Schurlman, Chief ONI, November 11, 1943.

In a December 18 letter USDJ/FBI FOIA, Crawford to Clark, December 18, 1943.

On December 29, Montgomery U.S. Bureau of Prisons, Washington, D.C., Montgomery file.

"[McInerney] stated USDOJ/FBI FOIA Tamm memorandum re McInerney conversations, January 4, 1944.

163 **Hoover didn't declare**   USDJ/FBI FOIA, Hoover to Cincinnati FBI office, February 17, 1944; FBI memorandum, 'Walters,' February 2, 1944.
Montgomery, it seems   USDJ/FBI FOIA, Donald Anderson to McInerney, March 8 and 9, 1944.

164 **Another compromise**   USDJ/FBI FOIA, Stone's office to Dept. of Justice, March 26 and May 24, 1944.
Certainly, Montgomery was   Selective Service records for Montgomery; Dayton newspaper articles; and U.S. Army records.
Montgomery was released   U.S. Bureau of Prisons records, Arlington, Va.

165 **It wasn't until 1953**   Social Security records and Dayton directories.
In 1967, they   County Court records, Montgomery County, Ohio, August 2, 1967.
He died in   Death certificate and probate records.

12. Triumph!

166 **On February 6**   NARA RG 38, Box 183, 5510, Tenth Fleet, AS VI Action Reports; NARA RG 38, Box 107, "Orange Transmissions"; Carrell Pinnell interview; Morison, *Atlantic Battle Won*, p. 293.

167 **"was so close**   Carrell Pinnell interview.

168 **Despite their late**   NSA FOIA, RIP 425, OP-20-G, "American Attack on German Naval Ciphers."
The new average   NARA RG 457, Box 117, SRH 403, "Selections from the Cryptologic Papers Collection of Rear Admiral J. N. Wenger, USN"; NARA RG 38, Crane, CNSG Library, Box 117, 5570/205, "Brief Resume of Op-20-G and British Activities vis-a-vis Compilation and Solution of U-boat Keys, Britain and U.S. 1943–44"; and data in NARA, RG 457, HCC, Box 621, ACC7465 CBKJ18, "German Cipher Key Logs."
By March 1944   NARA RG 38, Crane, CNSG Library, Boxes 111–13, 5750/176, War Diaries.
Admiral Dönitz had decided   Morison, *Atlantic Battle Won*, pp. 152, 248.
Even so, the Americans   RG 457, HCC, Box 621, ACC7465 CBKJ18, "German Cipher Key Logs"; NARA RG 457, Box 621, Transmissions re various U-boats, and October 2, 1944, 'Key Situation.'

169 **With the faster**   The estimates of the role of decryptions compiled from NARA RG 38 (Crane-Orange Intercepts), Translations of Intercepted Enemy Radio Traffic and Misc. World War II Documents, 1940–1946. Lists of U-boats sunk are from Roskill, *The War at Sea, 1939–1945*; NARA RG 457, Box 43, SRH 142, Commander Jerry C. Russell, USN, "Ultra and the Campaign Against the U-boats in World War II"; and Bray, *Ultra in the Atlantic*, vols. 1 and 2.
Over the next three months   Morison, *Atlantic Battle Won*, p. 366.
More important   Ibid., p. 365; Bray, *Ultra in the Atlantic*, vols. 1 and 2.
According to a jubilant   NARA RG 38, Crane, CNSG Library, Box 117, "OP-20-GYA Brief Rescue of OP-20-G and British Activities vis-a-vis Ger-

man Cipher Machines, July 15, 1944"; see also NARA RG 457, Box 117, 5570/205, SRH 403, "Selections from the Cryptologic Papers Collection of Rear Admiral J. N. Wenger, USN," p. 71.

170 **Wenger, Engstrom, Desch** "Report on Interrogation of Lt. Frowein," June 21, 1945, supplied by Ralph Erskine; Davies, " 'The Bombe,' " pp. 108ff.
While the Germans Ratcliff, "Searching for Security," pp. 146ff.
With the British decoding NARA RG 457, HCC, Box 1283, 29871, "Project 68003" (Madame X); Crawford, "Autoscritcher and the Superscritcher," pp. 9ff.; NARA RG 457, HCC, Box 705, NR1736/7 35701, CBLH17 35701, Enigma Conferences, Bombe History Folder, "U.S. Navy and U.S. Army Bombe Equipment," February 16, 1945.

171 **The machine's balance** NSA FOIA, RAM File, CNO, Communications Intelligence Technical Paper -TS-5, "Comparison of the N1530 to N5300 Bombe," Washington, D.C., n.d.; NARA RG 38, Crane, CNSG Library, Box 39 3238/2–, Watch Officers' Log 1943–; NSA FOIA, RAM File, "History of OP20G-4e."
The American Bombes were Calculated from data supplied by Ralph Erskine and Philip Marks.

171n **Some of the limitations** NSA FOIA, RIP 425, OP-20-G, "American Attack on German Naval Ciphers"; NARA RG 38, RIP, RIP 603.

172 **During the last two years** NARA RG 38, Crane, CNSG Library, Box 117, 5570/205, "Brief Resume of OP-20-G and British Activities vis-a-vis German Cipher Machines," July 15, 1944; NARA RG 38, Crane, CNSG Library, Box 66, 5750/774, "Summary of Attack on Enigma"; NARA RG 38, Crane, CNSG Library, Boxes 111–13, OP-20-G, War Diaries, "Op-20-Gy-A-1, Synopsis of War Diaries."
Too embarrassed to NARA RG 38, Crane, CNSG Library, Boxes 102–4, 111–13, OP-20-G War Diaries, passim; NSA FOIA, RIP 425, OP-20-G, "American Attack on German Naval Ciphers"; NSA FOIA, RAM File, CNO, Communications Intelligence Technical Paper, "N-800 Bombe."

172n **OP20G had been working** NARA RG 457, Box 98, SRH 306, 'Exploits and Commendations, Memoranda to and from GCCS, etc.'; NSA FOIA, RIP 425, OP-20-G, "American Attack on German Naval Ciphers."

173 **Although the British** National Cryptologic Museum, Ft. Meade, Md., Museum Library Vertical File 34-3, "GCCS Naval SIGINT vol. XIV, W/T Intelligence."
The Navy's Pacific NARA RG 38, Crane, CNSG Library, Boxes 138–39, 5750/325, "Japanese Weather Systems," chap. 22, "Application of Rapid Analytical Machinery to the Cryptanalysis of Japanese Weather Systems."

173n **Much more limited** NSA FOIA, RAM File, CNO, Communications Intelligence Technical Paper -TS-14, "The Inverted Bombe," Washington, D.C., n.d.; NARA RG 38, Crane, CNSG Library, Box 111, OP-20-G, War Diaries, "Op-20-Gy-A-1, Synopsis of War Diaries August 1–31, 1944"; NARA RG 38, Crane, RIP, Box 169, RIP 601, "Statistical Bombe."
A related method Budiansky, *Battle of Wits,* p. 243; NSA FOIA, CNO,

Communications Technical Paper, T2-24, Copperhead II, Final Report, Washington D.C., n.d.; NARA RG 38 Crane, CNSG Library, Box 138, 5750/325, Japanese Weather Systems (NC 6).

174 **An ex-MIT student** "Steinhardt, Lawrence S.," Hagley Museum and Library, Wilmington, Del., ACC2015, ERA collection; Steinhardt vita, Vannevar Bush Papers, Library of Congress.

All five designs NSA FOIA, RAM File, CNO, Communications Intelligence Technical Paper-TS-42, "Copperhead I Theory and Equipment," Washington, D.C., June 1945; NSA FOIA, CNO, Communications Intelligence Technical Paper TS-24, "Copperhead II, Final Report, Washington," n.d.

175 **Raven suspected** Deavours and Kruh, *Machine Cryptography and Modern Cryptanalysis,* p. 249; NARA RG 457, HCC, Box 1368, "History of JNA20-Coral"; *Descriptive Dictionary of Cryptologic Terms, Including Foreign Terms.*

By the end of October NSA FOIA, RAM File, "N 950 Drawing List, Python, Mamba, Viper, Ricky and Class Numbers Used on Navy Projects"; NSA FOIA, RAM File, CNO, Communications Intelligence Technical Paper -TS-33, "Final Report on Rattler #2, N-2200," Washington, D.C., March 1945; NSA FOIA, RAM File, CNO, Communications Intelligence Technical Paper -TS-23, "Rattler Modification," Washington, D.C., n.d.; NSA FOIA, July 12, 1983, 'Compilation of Information on Rattler Considered Top Secret.'

176 **With Japanese attachés** NARA RG 457, HCC, Box 1368, 'Coral'; Prados, *Combined Fleet Decoded,* p. 438.

Awed by the Nazis' Meigs, *Slide Rules and Submarines;* NARA RG 38, Crane, CNSG Library, Box 20, 3222/77, 'JNA20, Japanese Naval Attache in Berlin, reports'; NARA RG 457, Box 10, SRMN 032, "COMINCH File of Memoranda Concerning U-Boat Tracking Room Operations, 2 January 1943–6 June 1945"; NARA RG 457, Box 18, SRMN 040, "COMINCH File: Assessment of U-boat Fleet at the End of World War II, June–October 1945."

177 **In 1944, OP20G's** NARA RG 38, Crane, CNSG Library, Box 113, "GY-a1A War Diaries Summaries"; NSA FOIA, RAM File, CNO, Communications Intelligence Technical Paper -TS-20, "Bulldozer Operating Manual," Washington, D.C., July 1945; NARA RG 38, Crane, RIP, Box 169, RIP 601, "Statistical Bombe"; NSA FOIA, RAM File, OP20G, September 9, 1944, 'Need for Statistical Bombe'; NARA RG 457, HCC, Box 600, NR4815 ZEMA57, "The Bulldozer," March 26, 1945.

177n **Although faced with** Coombs, "Making of Colossus," pp. 253ff.; Flowers, "Design of Colossus," pp. 239ff.

13. New Challenges . . . and Breakdown

178 **Edward Travis's telegraphed** NARA RG 38, Crane, CNSG Library, Box 117, 5750/205, various on history of Bombe project and British-OP20G relations.

179 **OP20G's researchers** NSA FOIA, RAM File, CNO, Communications Intelligence Technical Paper -TS-5, "Comparison of the N1530 to N5300 Bombe," Washington, D.C., n.d.; NARA RG 38, Crane, CNSG Library, Box 111, "OP-20-G, War Diaries, Op-20-Gy-A-1, Synopsis of War Diaries August 1–31, 1944"; NSA FOIA, RIP 425, OP-20-G, "American Attack on German Naval Ciphers."

Work on Duenna Marks, "Umkehrwalze D," part 1, pp. 101ff.; NARA RG 457, HCC, Box 705, NR1736, Enigma Conferences, Bombe History Folder.

For a backup NSA FOIA, RAM File, Enciphered Telegraphic Link (incoming/outgoing), Washington-Dayton, OP20G to NCML, 'More Complex Machine Needed,' July 5, 1944.

The problem was so NARA RG 457, HCC, Box 1126, NR3620, various items concerning U.S. SSA and GCCS including Freidman Report; PRO HW 3/164 7989, "Squadron Leader Jones' Section"; Crawford, "Autoscritcher and the Superscritcher," pp. 9ff.

By early March 1944 NSA FOIA, RAM File, Enciphered Telegraphic Link (incoming/outgoing), Washington-Dayton, Engstrom to NCML, 'Duenna Needed,' March 4, 1944.

By May, Engstrom NARA RG 457, HCC, Box 705, NR4384 and NR5484, April 24, 1944, "History of the Bombe Project"; NARA RG 457, Box 1124, NR1736 CBTD76, ACC17640, OP20G, "History of the Bombe Project," May 30, 1944.

180 **The British concluded** PRO HW 14/125, April 19, 1944, 'politics in America make it unlikely U.S. will cooperate on history.'

Indeed, in a May 13 J. N. Wenger, memorandum for OP-20-G, May 13, 1944, 'British had supplied us with needed information on Enigma in 1941,' provided by Ralph Erskine.

But less than two weeks NARA RG 457, Box 1124, NR1736 CBTD76, ACC17640, OP20G, "History of the Bombe Project," May 30, 1944; NARA RG 457, HCC, Box 1414, ACC2479 CBIB16, OP20G, "History of the Bombe Project," May 30, 1944.

180n **At the same time, they** PRO HW 3/93, "History of the Bombe as Taken from Mr. Fletcher's Files."

181 **As the latest version** NARA RG 38, Crane, CNSG Library, Box 117, 5750/205, various on history of Bombe project and British-OP20G relations, including September 7, 1944, 'limit to 25 new Bombes.'

The new Bombe contract NSA FOIA, RAM File, CNO, Communications Intelligence Technical Paper -TS-5, "Comparison of the N1530 to N5300 Bombe," Washington, D.C., n.d.; NARA RG 38, RIP, Box 171, RIP 607 #7, "Double Input Bombes."

182 **GCCS commissioned** PRO HW 3/64, "Squadron Leader Jones' Section."

A Duenna machine Marks, "Umkehrwalze D," part 1, pp. 101ff.

183 **"It is not easy** Ibid., part 3, pp. 307ff.

Designing and building Carmelita Bruce interview.

"I remember my Carmelita Bruce interview.

184 **Launching planes** Gallery, *U-505*; NARA RG 457, Box 43, SRH 142, Commander Jerry C. Russell, USN, "Ultra and the Campaign Against the U-boats in World War II"; NSA FOIA, RIP 425, OP-20-G, "American Attack on German Naval Ciphers."
The German systems NARA RG 457, HCC, Box 621, ACC7465 CBKJ18, "German Cipher Key Logs."
According to an OP20G report NARA RG 38, Crane, CNSG Library, Box 117, 5570/205, "Brief Resume of OP-20-G and British Activities vis-a-vis German Cipher Machines," p. 4.

185 **In August 1944** RG 457, HCC, Box 1004, NR 3126, "OP20G, Memoranda on future research and policies, circa 1944–1947," Howard Engstrom, "Electronic Research Computer, August 7, 1944"; NARA RG 457, HCC, Box 1008, Lieutenant J. V. Connorton, "The Status of U.S. Naval Communication Intelligence After World War II," December 17, 1943; see also Box 1008, NR3169 CBNM77 11241A, 'Connorton History of OP20G and Policies for the Future of U.S. Codebreaking'; NARA RG 38, Crane, CNSG Library, Boxes 102–4, 111–13, "OP-20-G, War Diaries, August 1945, 'Serpent.' "
Wenger asked Engstrom NSA FOIA, RAM File, OP20G Memorandum, September 4, 1944, 'Statistical Bombes needed'; NARA RG 457, HCC, Box 600, NR4815 ZEMA57, "The Bulldozer," March 26, 1945.
October's keys NARA RG 38, Crane, CNSG Library, Box 66, 5750/774–, "Summaries of the Attacks on Enigma Traffic"; NSA FOIA, RIP 425, "American Attack on German Naval Ciphers."

186 **Eliminating reciprocal** PRO HW 14/108, July 17, 1944, 'Uhr introduced'; Davies, " 'The Bombe,' " pp. 108ff.
It was a limited NARA RG 38, Crane, CNSG Library, Box 64, 5750/760, February 15, 1945, "Sonder, Position Report on."
"In spite of NARA RG 38, Crane, CNSG Library, Box 64, 5750/760, February 15, 1945, "Sonder, Position Report on."

187 **A few Sonder keys** NARA RG 38, Crane, CNSG Library, Box 111, OP20G War Diaries, April 4, 1945.
If they had used Erskine, "Kriegsmarine Short Signal Systems," pp. 65ff.
While Allied codebreakers Morison, *Atlantic Battle Won,* p. 366.

188 **The Kriegsmarine was** Ibid., p. 365.
Sitting alone Debbie Desch Anderson interviews, August 2002.
The decrypt gave Winton, *Ultra in the Pacific,* p. 186.

189 **"that damned, dirty** Debbie Desch Anderson interviews, June 2002.
Howard Engstrom, head Kristina Engstrom self-interview.

190 **On April 14, 1943** Budiansky, *Battle of Wits,* p. 319.
During a self-interview Kristina Engstrom self-interview.
Added to these Robert Hogan interview.

191 **Even before the start** NARA RG 38, Crane, CNSG Library, Box 175, 1200/2, "Civilian Personnel," 'To Granat, Safford recommends ex-employee,' September 5, 1940.

192 **Wenger told Desch** Debbie Desch Anderson interviews, January 2001.
     In April 1945 NSA FOIA, RIP 425, "American Attack on German Naval Ciphers."
     Allied forces sank Ibid., p. 181.
     On April 15, a month NARA RG 457, Box 81, SRH 208, "U.S. Navy Submarine Warfare Message Reports, COMINCH to Admiralty."

193 **They had designs** NSA FOIA, "European Axis Signals Intelligence in World War II as Revealed by 'Ticom' Investigations, Other Prisoner of War Interrogations and Captured Material, Principally German, in Nine Volumes; Notes on German High Level Cryptography and Cryptanalysis," Chief Army Security Agency, May 1, 1946.
     A significant intelligence NARA RG 457, HCC, Box 117, SRH 403, "Selections from the Cryptologic Papers Collection of Rear Admiral J. N. Wenger, USN."

194 **Britain and the United States** NARA RG 38, Crane, CNSG Library, Boxes 138–39, 5750/325, "Japanese Weather Systems," chap. 22, "Application of Rapid Analytical Machinery to the Cryptanalysis of Japanese Weather Systems"; National Cryptologic Museum, Ft. Meade, Md., Museum Library Vertical File 34-3, "GCCS Naval SIGINT vol. XIV, W/T Intelligence."
     In November, OP20G NSA FOIA, RAM File, "Full Selector," and Enciphered Telegraphic Link (incoming/outgoing), Washington-Dayton, OP20G to NCML, October 14, 1943, 'Additive Machine,' and Washington-Dayton, OP20G to NCML, May 12, 1945, 'Test Full Selector.'

195 **Before the million-dollar** NARA RG 38, Crane, CNSG Library, Box 138, 5750/325, "History of Japanese Weather Decryption."
     "Commander Meader said Evelyn Vogel interview, January 2001.

196 **In the letter,** Joseph Desch, letter to Officer in Charge, October 14, 1940; supplied by Debbie Desch Anderson.
     Meader left his Desch to Navy, January 13, 1947, 'Please have Meader car removed,' letter supplied by Debbie Desch Anderson.

Epilogue: Burying the Past

197 **But Phil Bochicchio** Phil Bochicchio interview, January 2001.
     The British have let PRO HW 3/164 7989, "Squadron Leader Jones' Section."

198 **At least one** Mary Lorraine Johnson interview; conversations and correspondence with F. T. Johnson, her widower, 2002–2003.
     If so, the Soviets West and Tsarev, *Crown Jewels,* p. 217.
     Parts of the NCR Alvarez, "Beyond Venona," pp. 178ff.
     "The Cash" had Harold Ditmer interview.
     As early as September 1944 NARA RG 38 Crane, CNSG Library, Box 114, 5750/220, Memoranda on Various Subjects, for OP-20-G, typed June 15, 1945, "Recent Developments in Communications Intelligence Research—U.S. Naval Computing Machine Laboratory."

198 **Negotiations and calls** NSA FOIA, RAM File, Ralph Meader, Report to J. N. Wenger, Part 2, "Resume of the Dayton, Ohio, Activity During World War II."

Even so, NCR continued NSA FOIA, RAM File, Ralph Meader, Report to J. N. Wenger, Part 2, "Resume of the Dayton, Ohio, Activity During World War II"; Joseph Desch papers, from Debbie Desch Anderson.

199 **He told Howard** Debbie Desch Anderson interviews, June 2003; NARA RG 457, Box 92, SRH 267, "History of Engineering [Research] Associates."

He likewise declined Joseph Desch papers, from Debbie Desch Anderson; Carl Rench interview, September 1995.

As early as 1943 NARA RG 457, HCC, Box 1008, Lieutenant J. V. Connorton, "The Status of U.S. Naval Communication Intelligence After World War II," December 17, 1943; see also Box 1008, NR3169 CBNM77 11241A, 'Connorton History of OP20G and Policies for the Future of U.S. Codebreaking'; and Box 1004, NR3126 CBNM72 10101A, OP20G, memoranda on future research and policies, ca. 1944–1947.

200 **He knew that most** NSA FOIA, RAM File, "The Continuation and Development of Communication Intelligence," August 21, 1945.

The Army, in alliance NSA FOIA, RAM File, "The Continuation and Development of Communication Intelligence," August 21, 1945; NARA RG 38, Crane, CNSG Library, Box 83, 5400/27, memorandum to Wenger, October 20, 1945, 'Organization Function, Status'; and memorandum for General Marshall and Admiral King, August 22, 1945, 'Signals Intelligence.'

Despite the success NARA RG 38, Crane, CNSG Library, Box 114, 5750/220, OP-20-G, "Diplomatic Ultra Intelligence, Priority of Countries to Intercept," December 18, 1945; and "Memorandum for the President, Collaboration with the British Foreign Office"; and "Memorandum for the Secretary of War and the Secretary of the Navy, 25 August 1945, Cryptanalytic Effort"; and June 15, 1945, 'Rattan, all of Gy-A GI-A assigned to it.'

201 **Despite frictions** NARA, RG 457, HCC, Zema 173, Box 1364, NR4244 ACC17542 Loc CBTD12, "U.S. Communications Intelligence Board."

By February 1945 NARA RG 457, HCC, Box 1004, NR3126 CBNM72 10101A, SSA Policies, 'OP20G, Memoranda on future research and policies, circa 1944–1947.'

The plan was circulated NARA RG 457, Box 92, SRH 267, "History of Engineering [Research] Associates."

Engstrom and Meader wrote James Henry Wakelin, Jr., interview.

Through a mutual acquaintance Hagley Museum and Library, Wilmington, Del., ACC2015, ERA Minute Books, January 1946; and ERA, Engstrom to Norris, 'Projects, November 11, 1946.'

As president of Debbie Desch Anderson interviews, June 2002; "John E. Parker," pp. 67ff.

202 **Among them were men** NSA FOIA, RAM File, to CNO, "Allocation of Funds for Fiscal Year 1947," August 7, 1946; and "OP20G Research and Development Projects and Funding"; NARA RG 38, Crane, CNSG Library, Box

197, 5750/622, SRMN 084, "The Evolution of the Navy's Cryptologic Organization."

203 **He kept abreast** Campbell-Kelly and Aspray, *Computer,* p. 129.
By pulling back William Rodgers, *Think.*
NCR went back NCR corporate histories, NCR Archive, Dayton, Ohio, ca. 1984.

204 **Engstrom even returned** Bamford, *Puzzle Palace,* p. 428.205
Wenger had valued Joseph Desch papers, from Debbie Desch Anderson, 'Letters re awards and commendations.'

205 **Two years later** Debbie Desch Anderson interviews, December 2000.

206 **In the color home movie** Debbie Desch Anderson interviews, May 2002.

207 **Often in those days** Carl Rench interview, November 2000.
"We worked hard Lou Sandor interview.
"He went into Debbie Desch Anderson interview, May 2002.

208 **"I could sense** Ibid., November 2000.

209 **Debbie Anderson was** Ibid.
The Andersons' Astro van Ibid.

211 **Hottenstein had worked** NSA FOIA, RAM File, Enciphered Telegraph Link (incoming/outgoing), Washington-Dayton, 'Biographical sketches, re Executive Officer Hottenstein,' ca. 1943.
NCR says John Hourigan interview.

Index

ABOUT THE AUTHORS

JIM DEBROSSE grew up in Dayton and graduated from Harvard and Columbia. He has worked as a reporter for a number of newspapers and is currently a features writer for the *Dayton Daily News*. He's the author of three mystery novels published by St. Martin's Press and has won numerous journalism awards, including the National Press Club Award.

COLIN BURKE graduated from San Francisco State College. After almost two decades as a professional musician, he obtained a Ph.D. from Washington University in St. Louis. He taught at University of Maryland Baltimore County, and researched, wrote, and lectured in several fields. Among his published works are *Information and Secrecy* and *American Collegiate Populations*. He has received grants from the National Science Foundation, the National Endowment for the Humanities, and major private foundations. He has recently been a Research Fellow at Yale University's Program on Nonprofit Organizations and also the Eugene Garfield Fellow at the Chemical Heritage Foundation.

ABOUT THE TYPE

This book was set in Fairfield, the first typeface from the hand of the distinguished American artist and engraver Rudolph Ruzicka (1883–1978). In its structure, Fairfield displays the sober and sane qualities of the master craftsman whose talent has long been dedicated to clarity. It is this trait that accounts for the trim grace and vigor, the spirited design, and sensitive balance of this original typeface.

Rudolph Ruzicka was born in Bohemia and came to America in 1894. He set up his own shop, devoted to wood engraving and printing, in New York in 1913, after a varied career working as a wood engraver, in photo-engraving and banknote-printing plants, and as an art director and freelance artist. He designed and illustrated many books, and was the creator of a considerable list of individual prints—wood engravings, line engravings on copper, and aquatints.